Mobility & Politics

Series Editors
Martin Geiger
Carleton University
Ottawa, Canada

Nicola Piper
School of Law
Queen Mary University of London
London, UK

Parvati Raghuram
Open University
Milton Keynes, UK

Editorial Board Members
Tendayi Bloom
University of Birmingham
Birmingham, UK

Michael Collyer
University of Sussex
Brighton, UK

Charles Heller
Graduate Institute
Geneva, Switzerland

Elaine Ho
National University of Singapore
Singapore, Singapore

Shadia Husseini de Araújo
University of Brasília
Brasília, Brazil

Alison Mountz
Wilfrid Laurier University
Waterloo, Canada

Linda Oucho
African Migration and Development Policy Centre
Nairobi, Kenya

Marta Pachocka
SGH Warsaw School of Economics
Warsaw, Poland

Antoine Pécoud
Université Sorbonne Paris Nord
Villetaneuse, France

Shahamak Rezaei
University of Roskilde
Roskilde, Denmark

Sergey Ryazantsev
Russian Academy of Sciences
Moscow, Russia

Carlos Sandoval García
University of Costa Rica
San José, Costa Rica

Everita Silina
The New School
New York, NY, USA

Rachel Simon-Kumar
University of Auckland
Auckland, New Zealand

William Walters
Carleton University
Ottawa, Canada

Mobility & Politics

Series Editors:
Martin Geiger, Carleton University, Ottawa, Canada
Nicola Piper, Queen Mary University of London, UK
Parvati Raghuram, Open University, Milton Keynes, UK

Global Advisory Board:
Tendayi Bloom, University of Birmingham, UK
Michael Collyer, Sussex University, UK
Charles Heller, Geneva Graduate Institute, Switzerland
Elaine Ho, National University of Singapore
Shadia Husseini de Araújo, University of Brasília, Brazil
Alison Mountz, Wilfrid Laurier University, Waterloo, Canada
Linda Oucho, African Migration and Development Policy Centre, Nairobi, Kenya
Marta Pachocka, SGH Warsaw School of Economics, Poland
Antoine Pécoud, Sorbonne University Paris Nord, France
Shahamak Rezaei, University of Roskilde, Denmark
Sergey Ryazantsev, Russian Academy of Sciences, Moscow, Russia
Carlos Sandoval García, University of Costa Rica
Everita Silina, The New School, New York, USA
Rachel Simon-Kumar, University of Auckland, New Zealand
William Walters, Carleton University, Ottawa, Canada

Human mobility, whatever its scale, is often controversial. Hence it carries with it the potential for politics. A core feature of mobility politics is the tension between the desire to maximise the social and economic benefits of migration and pressures to restrict movement. Transnational communities, global instability, advances in transportation and communication, and concepts of 'smart borders' and 'migration management' are just a few of the phenomena transforming the landscape of migration today. The tension between openness and restriction raises important questions about how different types of policy and politics come to life and influence mobility.

Mobility & Politics invites original, theoretically and empirically informed studies for academic and policy-oriented debates. Authors examine issues such as refugees and displacement, migration and citizenship, security and cross-border movements, (post-)colonialism and mobility, and transnational movements and cosmopolitics.

This series is indexed in Scopus.

Veysi Dag

Voices of the Disenfranchized

Knowledge Production by Kurdish-Yezidi Refugees from Below

Veysi Dag
Hebrew University of Jerusalem
Jerusalem, Israel

ISSN 2731-3867 ISSN 2731-3875 (electronic)
Mobility & Politics
ISBN 978-3-031-46808-7 ISBN 978-3-031-46809-4 (eBook)
https://doi.org/10.1007/978-3-031-46809-4

© The Editor(s) (if applicable) and The Author(s), under exclusive licence to Springer Nature Switzerland AG 2024
This work is subject to copyright. All rights are solely and exclusively licensed by the Publisher, whether the whole or part of the material is concerned, specifically the rights of translation, reprinting, reuse of illustrations, recitation, broadcasting, reproduction on microfilms or in any other physical way, and transmission or information storage and retrieval, electronic adaptation, computer software, or by similar or dissimilar methodology now known or hereafter developed.
The use of general descriptive names, registered names, trademarks, service marks, etc. in this publication does not imply, even in the absence of a specific statement, that such names are exempt from the relevant protective laws and regulations and therefore free for general use.
The publisher, the authors, and the editors are safe to assume that the advice and information in this book are believed to be true and accurate at the date of publication. Neither the publisher nor the authors or the editors give a warranty, expressed or implied, with respect to the material contained herein or for any errors or omissions that may have been made. The publisher remains neutral with regard to jurisdictional claims in published maps and institutional affiliations.

This Palgrave Macmillan imprint is published by the registered company Springer Nature Switzerland AG.
The registered company address is: Gewerbestrasse 11, 6330 Cham, Switzerland

Paper in this product is recyclable.

Foreword

In recent years, my work has taken me to various locations across Australia and New Zealand. I've had the privilege of visiting both urban and rural areas, including small towns and communities in Western and Central Australia as well as the northernmost part of New Zealand. What consistently struck me was the presence of Kurds from different generations in the audiences wherever I went. It left me wondering why Kurds seemed to be present everywhere I traveled. This pattern continued as I journeyed through Europe. I would invariably meet Kurds hailing from different parts of Kurdistan, each eager to share their thoughts and stories. As a fellow Kurd, I found it difficult to see them solely as individuals; they embodied the history of a nation that had endured colonization and displacement across the globe. They weren't just recounting personal experiences; they were carrying with them the collective history of Kurdistan, marked by warfare, genocide, discrimination, and persecution. This history has forced people to leave their homelands and seek refuge in distant corners of the world.

I believe this book, *Voices of the Disenfranchized: Knowledge Production by Kurdish-Yezidi Refugees from Below*, adeptly weaves together these stories, serving as a genuine reflection of this facet of Kurdish history that resonates globally. While I recognize its significance as a valuable resource for anthropologists, sociologists, and policymakers involved in migration studies, I, as a Kurd, primarily view it as a connection to our shared memories, collective traumas, and, most importantly, the wisdom that has emerged from Kurdistan's resistance.

viii   FOREWORD

Kurdish literary and cultural traditions have long drawn from oral and folk wisdom, encompassing poetry, melodies, myths, and epic tales, which have enriched our modern literature. Many of these cultural elements have been transcribed or recorded through various mediums. This profound folk heritage now finds new expression on a contemporary platform. Similar to this tradition, the book employs an approach rooted in oral testimonies and narratives. This distinctive characteristic underscores its vital role within the context of Kurdish studies. Additionally, considering that these narratives are conveyed by ordinary refugees who have personally experienced colonization, a broader perspective comes into focus. It's crucial that we delve into the enduring colonial system that has cast a shadow over Kurdistan for decades, we also acknowledge that this mechanism of colonization does not cease for those who have departed their homeland and sought refuge in the West. They continue to grapple with the multiple layers of this colonial mindset. First and foremost, their identity is not fully recognized by the system, particularly in relation to their nationality and Kurdish heritage. This circumstance perpetuates ongoing domination and oppression, even on foreign soil, prompting a meticulous examination of their identity. The most profound layer of colonialism emerges through the lens of being refugees. The very concept, imagery, and label of being a refugee can overshadow their individual identity. The term "refugee" encapsulates an extensive process of dehumanization that erodes people's sense of self and targets their dignity.

Voices of the Disenfranchized Knowledge Production by Kurdish-Yezidi Refugees from Below endeavors to uncover these colonial mindsets and intricate colonial mentalities. Essentially, the book paves the way for empowering individuals who have been marginalized and, in this instance, colonized twice—first due to their Kurdish lineage and subsequently due to their refugee status. Empowerment remains elusive unless individuals seize control of the discourse that inherently belongs to them. True empowerment materializes when we recognize people's agency, and this book effectively accomplishes that.

Wellington, New Zealand   Behrouz Boochani
August 2023

Fig. 1 A self-built shack in an Italian forest. (Source: The image was taken by the author, 2019)

Fig. 2 A refugee is standing before a makeshift shack in an Italian forest. (Source: The image was taken by the author, 2019)

Fig. 3 Several Kurdish Yezidis share a room and their meals in Italy. (Source: The image was taken by the author, 2019)

Fig. 4 Kurdish-Yezidi refugees inhabited an abandoned building in Italy. (Source: Image was taken by the author, 2019)

FOREWORD xi

Fig. 5 Inside a Kurdish association in France. (Source: The image was taken by the author, 2019)

Fig. 6 Kurdish-Yezidi refugees and their German friends watch a Kurdish film screened during the Kurdish Film Festival in Germany. (Source: The image was taken by the author, 2019)

Fig. 7 In Sweden, Kurdish-Yezidi refugees protest against the repressive policy of the Turkish government in their homeland! (Source: The image was taken by the author, 2019)

Fig. 8 Kurdish-Yezidi refugees in Germany are on hunger strike to support their compatriots' struggle in Turkey. (Source: The image was taken by the author, 2019)

Acknowledgments

Prior to my academic engagement, I chose to conceal my refugee background since refugees frequently come under scrutiny in the general public as "suspicious," "pitiful," "criminal," and "dangerous" individuals whose social prejudice has become routine. These stereotyped perceptions were also a part of my own lived experiences of persecution, discrimination, and criminalization in Turkey on account of my Kurdish identity. Consequently, my Kurdish origin in Turkey and my refugee status in Europe have been the primary causes of my persistent discrimination, prejudices, and humiliation. Therefore, I adopted a desperate stance to avoid disclosing my refugee background to protect myself from ongoing negative implications for my living experiences. Yet, I reflected on this approach and realized that concealing a part of my own reality leads to the erasure of my life's trajectories, which are filled with traumatic events, emotions, and tragedies. My reflective engagement in the academic environment resulted in a change in my skepticism toward my refugee identity in Europe. Reflecting on my refugee reality, I encourage refugees to talk about their experiences in their own voices.

To this end, I embark on an epistemic journey with the goal of creating an autonomous space for disenfranchised and marginalized Kurdish-Yezidi refugees to share similar stories and reflect on their life narratives. However, I was not alone on my journey. First, Kurdish-Yezidi refugee participants accompanied me on this journey and provided me with direct and profound insights into their daily lives in Germany, Sweden, Denmark, Austria, France, and Italy. They shared with me first-hand accounts of

xiv   ACKNOWLEDGMENTS

their lived experiences of violence, persecution, torture, and mistreatment in their countries of origin, as well as their struggles for survival in transit countries and for "integration" and settlement in new countries. They performed as both objects and subjects of their narratives, which serve as the bedrock of refugee-centric knowledge from below. Each of them has my deepest gratitude.

At the outset of this journey, Professor Fiona B. Adamson played a crucial role. She assisted me in finding a place in academia and engaging in cooperative data collection and interpretation processes. I cannot thank her enough for her valuable guidance and support, without which I would not have accomplished this project. I will be eternally grateful for her unwavering encouragement, academic interaction, thoughtful advice, and friendship.

I would like to express my sincere thanks to every member of the MAGYC (Migration Governance and Asylum Crises) project team for their cooperation, especially our SOAS team member, Dr. Catherine Craven. She accompanied me to conduct interviews in Berlin and shared with me her insightful feedback. I would also like to thank the ISRF (Independent Social Research Foundation) and the DFG (Deutsche Forschungsgemeinschaft) for providing funding that enabled me to transcribe and translate hundreds of interviews over the course of thousands of hours and structure these tales. I also acknowledge the funding provided by the Horizon 2020 Research and Innovation Programme of the European Commission under Grant Number 822806.

Lastly, I am grateful to two anonymous reviewers and the Palgrave Macmillan editorial team for their substantial feedback and insightful comments that contributed to the book's improvement.

Last but not least, I would like to thank my family and friends for their support and positive energy. I am grateful to each one of them.

This work is dedicated to the deceased Kurdish youngster Alan Kurdi!

Jerusalem   Veysi Dag
August 2023

Contents

1 Introduction — 1
Context of the Kurdish-Yezidi Population — 5
Emergence of Kurdish-Yezidi Refugee Movement — 12
Knowledge Production and Kurdish-Yezidi Refugees — 15
Refugee-Centric Episteme and Kurdish-Yezidi Self-Representation — 23
Process of Interviews and Data Collection — 27
My Positionality as a Refugee Researcher in the Process of Knowledge Production — 30
Structure of the Book — 34
References — 37

2 Homeland Conditions: "Speaking Kurdish Was Equal to a Crime" — 43
The Roots of Discrimination — 47
Constant Persecution — 55
Language of Emotions — 59
Statelessness — 64
References — 66

3 Escape: "I Had Seen the Deaths of My Children with My Own Eyes" — 69
Smuggler Networks — 71
Country Search — 78
Survival — 82
Solidarity — 86

xv

xvi CONTENTS

4 Asylum Processes and Challenges: "We Neither Die nor Live but Receive Some Breath" 93
Refugee Camp 95
Abandonment and Discrimination 99
Exploitation 110
Liminality 115

5 Toward Integration: "We Cannot Achieve Integration Without Struggle" 125
Negligence 128
Bureaucratic Burden 134
Unsettledness 137
Social Isolation 142
Struggle for Integration 145
Criminalization 154

6 Self-Governance from Below: "Self-Help Services Are Necessary to Mitigate Our Suffering" 165
Identity Re-construction 167
Community Creation 170
Self-Governance 175
Intra-community Affairs 184
Critical Expressions 191
Reference 203

7 Exile: "I Have Not Dreamed of Being Here Since I Still Live There" 205
Uprootedness 208
Being Lost 210
Homeland Connection 213
Committed Mobilization 220
Reference 225

8 Conclusion 227
Refugee Production 229
Europe in Refugees' Viewpoint 232
Refugees' Constraints and Agency in the Integration Process 233

CONTENTS   xvii

Contradiction of Exile 238
Homeland Dilemma 240
Final Words 242
References 243

Appendix A: Interview Questions 245

List of Interviewed Participants 251

References 259

Index 267

List of Abbreviations

AKP	Adalet ve Kalkınma Partisi (The Justice and Development Party)
AME	Aide Médicale de l'État (Government Medical Aid)
DBP	Demokratik Bölgeler Partisi (Democratic Regions Party)
DFG	Deutsche Forschungsgemeinschaft (German Research Foundation)
EU	European Union
HDP	Halkların Demokratik Partisi (People`s Democratic Party)
IS	Islamic State of Iraq and Syria
ISA	The International Studies Association
ISRF	Independent Social Research Foundation
KCK	Koma Civakên Kurdistan (Group of Communities in Kurdistan)
KOMALAH	Jiyanaway Kurdistan (Society for the Revival of Kurdistan)
KRG	Kurdish Regional Government
KRI	Kurdistan Region of Iraq
MAGYC	Migration Governance and Asylum Crises
MESA	Middle Eastern Studies Association
MHP	Milliyetçi Hareket Partisi (The Nationalist Movement Party)
MIT	Millî İstihbarat Teşkilatı (National Intelligence Organization)
NATO	The North Atlantic Treaty Organization
OFPRA	Office Français de Protection des Réfugiés et Apatrides (French Office for the Protection of Refugees and Stateless Persons)
PDK-Iran	Partiya Demokrat a Kurdistan Iran ê (Kurdistan Democratic Party in Iran)
PDK-Iraq	Partiya Demokrat a Kurdistan Irak ê (The Kurdistan Democratic Party in Iraq)
PDK-Syria	Partiya Demokrat a Kurdistan Syri ê (Kurdistan Democratic Party in Syria)

xx   LIST OF ABBREVIATIONS

PJAK   Partiya Jiyana Azad a Kurdistanê (Party of Free Life of Kurdistan)
PKDW   Parlemanê Kurdistan li derveyî Welat (Kurdistan Parliament in Exile)
PKK   Partiya Karkerên Kurdistan (Kurdistan Workers' Party)
PMF   Quwwāt al-Ḥashd ash-Shaʿbī (Popular Mobilization Forces)
PUK   Yekîtiya Nîştimanî ya Kurdistan (Patriotic Union of Kurdistan)
TOKI   Toplu Konut İdaresi Başkanlığı (the Mass Housing Development
        Administration)
UAR   United Arab Republic
UN   United Nations

CHAPTER 1

Introduction

This book aims to create an autonomous space for Kurdish-Yezidi[1] refugees from Iraq, Syria, and Turkey to express and analyze their uninterpreted narratives about their respective experiences of oppression, displacement, and escape from persecution in their home countries in the form of oral history in their own languages and voices. It also makes it possible for refugees to speak about the bureaucratic and structural challenges in their reception and integration processes, their engagement in cultural and political practices for homeland affairs, and the re-construction of their diasporic identities in receiving societies in the North, South, and West of Europe. The narratives of Kurdish-Yezidi refugees reveal their historical and social contexts, intra-community relationships, conflicts, emotional and traumatic experiences, traditional way of life, and how they use their agency to develop coping strategies to survive their precarious journeys to escape and overcome structural barriers in receiving states. By addressing all of these obstacles, this book presents ground-breaking

[1] The "Kurdish-Yezidi" term refers to the shared experiences of the Kurdish-Yezidi population in terms of statelessness, oppression, marginalization, displacement, and refugee status, as well as their shared geographical and cultural identities, languages, and oral traditions. Although Yezidis adhere to a distinct belief system, they are typically classified as Kurdish-speaking people. Nevertheless, they have frequently been subjected to severe repression on account of their Yezidi faith. Therefore, I use Kurdish-Yezidi refugees as an inclusive term, referring to distinct and collective experiences of both communities as an indivisible entity without comparing the severity of their sufferings.

© The Author(s), under exclusive license to Springer Nature Switzerland AG 2024
V. Dag, *Voices of the Disenfranchized*, Mobility & Politics, https://doi.org/10.1007/978-3-031-46809-4_1

1

insights on refugees' lived experiences before migration as well as throughout the reception, settlement, and integration phases. The book is centered on the development of refugee-centric knowledge by, and with, refugees, who are the objects and subjects of their narratives. There are no hierarchical, structural, or unequal relations of power between academics and refugees in this book. This book's objective is to break this linear correlation between objects and subjects. It enables the ordinary refugees in question to assess their experiences from multiple perspectives in a collaborative process, recognizing that they are a part of the collective historical, political, and social processes and lived experiences of their respective homelands or populations. They do not merely have a history in the homeland and a present in the countries in which they currently reside; rather, they embody both spatiotemporal contexts simultaneously, combining the sentiments and experiences of fellow compatriots who are both in the homeland and in exile at the same time. In this context, while the objectification of the Kurdish-Yezidi refugees is rejected, they are also not only the subjects of their narratives about their lived experiences, conditions, and views as experimental data up for description and uninformed interpretation, but they are even co-authors who narrate, describe, interpret, and analyze their own stories that are intimately intertwined with the events, policies, and politics in both their home countries and the countries in which they are now living. While stressing refugee-centric knowledge, this book transcends neoliberal humanitarian, state-centric, and colonial hegemonic approaches and epistemes that limit refugees' epistemic capabilities and viewpoints to data sources.

The influx of Kurdish-Yezidi refugees is a continual movement as a result of politically adverse and tragic circumstances and violent conflicts in their countries of origin, notably Turkey, Iraq, and Syria. Their repressive policies continue to produce displacement and flight among Kurdish-Yezidis in various ways. Kurdish-Yezidi refugee waves from their traditional homeland have been especially intense since the early 2010s, as a result of violent conflicts caused by the IS in 2011, the rise and onslaughts of the IS in 2014, the failure of the so-called peace process between the PKK and the Turkish state, which resulted in the re-escalation of violent clashes with Turkish armed forces since 2015, and constant Turkish military operations in Turkey's Kurdish region and invasions in Syria and Iraq since 2016. These incidents resulted in significant political disasters for the stateless, oppressed, and minoritized Kurdish-Yezidi population. A significant number of Kurdish-Yezidi people embarked on perilous journeys to escape these atrocities and seek shelter and secure environments, using the services of smugglers to cross the national borders of multiple government entities. Many asylum seekers, however, were often unable to reach their desired countries of destination due to human traffickers, who frequently abandoned these asylum seekers as commodities to be abused. Border guards imprisoned and deported hundreds of these traumatized and vulnerable subjects who had been duped by smugglers; some of them had perished from abuse, starvation, and torture. Despite these formidable challenges, a significant number of Kurdish-Yezidi asylum seekers were able to reach their final destinations. They have, however, had to deal with further structural obstacles encountered during their asylum, integration, and settlement processes in new social environments, such as challenges with a lack of legal status, bureaucratic quagmires, institutional racism, discrimination, stereotypes, and a general lack of understanding among national citizens of receiving states. Moreover, despite their sincere efforts to persuade authorities that they deserve refugee status, which at least guarantees legal status in the country, these refugees frequently struggle to express themselves due to language, cultural, and social hurdles. Even if they were granted refugee status, they were frequently required to acquire the language skills of their host societies, meet housing and employment requirements, and navigate the numerous institutional constraints imposed upon them by different authorities, often with little assistance. They must also overcome social isolation and negative feelings of detachment from their previous social environments.

The narratives of these Kurdish-Yezidi refugees have been the subject of several anthropological, cultural, and sociological studies, which certainly merit our recognition. Nonetheless, these studies typically have treated refugees as experimental subjects, excluding them from the power of interpretation and acknowledging little of their epistemological agency in the process of knowledge production. Instead, the narratives of refugees' complex and traumatic experiences are subject to the interpretive power of researchers with subjective positionalities, distinct historical, political, and social contexts, educational privileges, and unobstructed access to institutional venues. Consequently, we understand the contexts, identities, and obstacles of refugees through their viewpoints. How does this knowledge production about refugees' experiences reflect their political and social reality? Indeed, the politically unbiased stance of researchers and the politically impartial representation of Kurdish refugees cannot always be justified. During ethnographic fieldwork, the inability to speak the languages of the examined refugee populations may impede a nuanced understanding, interpretation, and analysis of refugee narratives. Several studies have provided a significant amount of knowledge but have contributed to an inadequate level of understanding of the self-perspective of Kurdish-Yezidi refugees on themes that prompted their flight from their homeland and affected their lives in new environments. Kurdish-Yezidi refugees have limited authority to interpret their own narratives, grounded in their lived experiences of persecution in their home countries and political and structural constraints in their receiving countries. To put it another way, the presentation and interpretation of refugees' selfhood and experiences are often filtered through the lenses of uncritical, unreflective, and state-centric scholarship. Deliberately or unintentionally, such studies undermine the first-hand experiences and perspectives of refugees by preventing them from speaking for, about, and with themselves, and their narratives are exploited as dull and experimental data, which frequently results in the depoliticization of their cases. This scholarship precludes them from addressing their cultural, political, and social realities by suppressing their self-identification and voices, thereby stifling the dynamic agency that prompted them to flee to other countries. This book unpacks various forms of scholarship in relation to Western-centric, state-centric, and colonial frameworks. This type of knowledge predominates in our reading and comprehension of refugee experiences. I'll go into more detail about it below.

The accounts of Kurdish-Yezidi refugees in this book disrupt the hierarchical knowledge production from above that permeates the institutional spaces and the medium and provide a window into the lives of refugees on the ground. As an autonomous space, this project empowers refugees to convey their voices, narratives, and self-interpretations of their experiences and, most importantly, to choose how their own realities are articulated and presented. It aspires to produce organic knowledge from below, knowledge created by and in collaboration with Kurdish-Yezidi refugees, in the radical tradition of Gramsci (Mouffe 1979; Fontana 1993). In other words, the power to create knowledge is transmitted and delegated to refugees, resulting in a zone devoid of dominance and power hierarchies. Consequently, this book affords an unfettered power to share the Kurdish-Yezidi refugees' voices, perceptions, sentiments, and experiences, all of which I captured and immortalized on paper. As the culmination of hundreds of stories and thousands of hours of transcription, the collective action of speaking, writing, and reading the narratives of this book empowers its primary narrators, the Kurdish-Yezidi refugees, to reject their objectification and the knowledge created about them. The refugees themselves demonstrate their ontological truths, which are a component of their collective history of statelessness, lack of protection, and tyranny in the Middle East. In this respect, the book is equally concerned with the voices and spaces of Kurdish-Yezidi refugees.

Based on 129 interviews with 109 male and 21 female Kurdish-Yezidi refugees, asylum seekers, diaspora leaders, activists, and naturalized citizens in urban and rural areas of Germany, France, Sweden, Austria, Denmark, and Italy in 2019, the interviewees share their first-hand accounts of hardship and persecution, the social and violent conflicts they encountered, and the economic and social challenges they endured in their countries of origin that pushed them to leave. They recount their journeys and encounters with smugglers and border patrol officers. They outline the troubles they encounter while submitting their requests for asylum, going through the integration process, and navigating structural, social, and cultural barriers in their new environments. They further articulate a desire to return to their homeland, discuss the conditions of their exile, talk about their political activities, critique the political attitudes of their actors, and offer insight into the nature of their peer interpersonal relationships. The self-presentation derived from the original narratives of Kurdish-Yezidi refugees is an integral component of their organic knowledge. We will be significantly less able to completely comprehend the lived experiences and accounts of these Kurdish-Yezidi refugees if we fail to incorporate their descriptive and analytical organic narratives and storytelling in their own languages.

CONTEXT OF THE KURDISH-YEZIDI POPULATION

Historically, the Kurds and Yezidis—a Kurdish-speaking segment with a distinct non-Islamic religion system—have been minoritized and marginalized communities in the Middle East. They have been reported in several studies in connection to violent conflicts, turmoil, statelessness, and discrimination in the Middle East, as well as denial of their identities, the experience of forced migration, and political engagement in European nations. They are dispersed throughout European states as a result of these tragic political events with roots in their native countries. They also embody the past and present predicaments, as well as the uncertain future, of their compatriots. The Kurdish reality with its own name, language(s), culture, history, customs, and rituals continues to be contested by each nation-state that governs the traditional Kurdish-Yezidi homeland and treats the Kurdish-Yezidi population as "second-class," "subhuman," "uncivilized," or "subversive" people (Yeğen 2006). Its various social components, with their distinctive dialects, religions, and tribes, are regarded as a stateless nation with no legal right to exert cultural and political sovereignty over the territories they inhabit (Eliassi 2021). They are thought to be the world's second-largest stateless group of people, after Tamils (Minahan 2016) but have been excluded from both their ancient homeland and the official map of the area, which is split geographically between Turkey, Iran, Iraq, and Syria. They share a common destiny of statelessness in the four states above, where they have endured decades of political and social discrimination and persecution without obtaining political or cultural recognition of their identities and cultural rights. The ruling regimes view them as a security and domestic threat to their nationalistic political and social agendas. Consequently, they are confronted with cultural extinction as a result of forced and physical assimilation schemes and draconian measures implemented by the governing Turkish, Iranian, and Syrian regimes, as well as the Iraqi regime, until the early 2000s. These repressive approaches have influenced the fate of the Kurdish-Yezidi people by depriving them of their cultural and political autonomy, resulting in the flight, refugeehood, and exile of their politicians, intellectuals, leaders, and activists.

Kurdish segments with Yezidi, Alevi, and Jewish beliefs are one of the indigenous populations of Mesopotamia, with their historical connections to territories known as Kurdistan (McDowall 2005). They are historically descended from the Medes, an ancient Gutis people who spoke a Persian-like language (Nisan 2002: 33). They speak Kurmancî, Sorani, Palewani, Dimili/Zaza, and Hewrami/Goran, all of which belong to the Kurdish subset of Indo-European languages (Izady 1992; McDowall 2005: 8–9). They have always inhabited the territories now split among the four states mentioned above. Therefore, rather than being considered latecomers, as is usually assumed, Kurds are regarded as native inhabitants of Mesopotamia and the Middle East (Edmonds 1971).

Kurdish-Yezidi population and their traditional homeland were first divided by Turkish and Iranian forefathers in the sixteenth century, when the Ottoman and Safavid rulers agreed to recognize Kurdistan as a "buffer zone" between themselves. Kurdistan as a territory was separated into two regions in the 1639 Zuhab Treaty (Treaty of Qasr-e Shirin) between the

Turkish Ottoman Empire and the Iran's Safavid Empire (Entessar 1992: 3; Hassanpour 1992: 53). This division of Kurdistan in the seventeenth century led to the development of a political consciousness among the Kurds based on their cultural, linguistic, and tribal differentiation from Turkish, Persian, and Arab realities (Vali 2003: 79). For instance, the Kurdish poet and writer, Ehmedî Xanî encouraged the Kurdish chieftains to unify around common political agendas for Kurdish nationalism in his love story *Mem û Zîn* in 1693–1694. He pointed out that the Kurdish chieftains need to agree on a king who would protect them and promote Kurdish language and literature (Hassanpour 1992: 55–56). The rise of Turkish nationalism at the hands of the Young Turks in 1908 and its progression in 1923 coincided with the rise of Iranian nationalism following the military coup of the Pahlavi regime in 1921, with both factors having reactionary implications for the growth of modern Kurdish nationalism in the Middle East (Hassanpour 1992: 58, 1994; Halliday 2006: 6; McDowall 2005: 2–3). However, the Turkish and Iranian nationalists have been implementing forced assimilation strategies against the Kurds to eliminate the national Kurdish-Yezidi ambition with violence. After Iraq and Syria gained their independence in 1932 and 1946, respectively, Arab nationalists joined the anti-Kurdish coalition.

Woodrow Wilson the 28th president of the United Nations announced 14 principles for world peace in 1918 and offered the Kurds and Armenians outstanding chances to form their own independent states. Wilson's Fourteen Points allowed Kurds and Armenians, as well as other non-Turks and non-Muslims, the possibility to constitute their independent self-governance, which ultimately gave rise to the Treaty of Sévr (McDowall 2005: 115). Articles 62 and 64 of the Treaty of Sévr, according to McDowall, guaranteed the establishment of an autonomous territory that would have been granted the authority to vote for full independence within one year after the existence of the self-governed region, in the event that the League of Nations came to terms with its capability for achieving that independence (ibid., 137). The Treaty of Sévr, however, was never implemented for two reasons: first, the Kurdish tribal representatives were fragmented, untrustworthy, and squandered chances to rule. Even while the urban Kurdish intellectuals and diplomats created a political scheme of a self-governing Kurdistan, they were nonetheless hampered by tribal mentalities and their impact on the Kurdish people (Dag 2017). Secondly, the British interest in the oilfields in Kerkuk and Mosul, the cautious behaviors of British and French conquerors, and Ataturk's betrayal and devious cooperation with some Kurdish chieftains in wars for Turkish independence against Christian presence in association with Armenians, Greeks, and Russians led to abandoning the Treaty of Sévr (Meho 1997: 9; McDowall 2005: 171).

The Treaty of Sévr was then superseded by the Treaty of Lausanne, which had been signed and ratified on July 23, 1923, in Lausanne, Switzerland, by the Turkish envoy and those from Great Britain, France, Japan, Italy, Romania, Greece, and the Serbian, Croatian, and Slovenian kingdoms. The new treaty abandoned any basic rights to any ethnic populations, but Articles 38 and 39 stressed the freedom of religious and non-Muslim minorities (McDowall 2005: 142–143; Izady 1992: 61). During the Lausanne negotiations, the Turkish delegates denied the existence of the Kurds as an ethnic "minority" and claimed that the Kurds fought alongside their Turkish counterparts in the Turkish War of Independence. Consequently, they did not require the identical rights accorded to non-Muslim communities (Kartal 2002: 13; McDowall 2005: 210). Not only did the Turkish representatives deny the Kurdish right to self-determination, but they also aimed to assimilate the Kurds as a distinct cultural, ethnic, and linguistic group. Subsequently, the Turks designated the Kurds as "mountain Turks" at official levels, despite the fact that the Kurds in no way resembled cultural, linguistic, or historical Turkish reality (Entessar 1992: 13). Since the Lausanne Treaty was ratified, the Turkish government has consistently refuted the existence of the Kurds and sought their forced and violent assimilation in an effort to exterminate them (Dag 2017).

The Treaty of Lausanne led to the establishment of the Turkish Republic, while Iraq was placed under the supervision of a British mandate and Syria fell under the jurisdiction of a French mandate. The Iranian portion of the Kurdish homeland had already been divided by the Treaty of Zuhab (Treaty of Qasr-e Shirin) in 1639 between the Turkish Ottoman and Persian Safavid empires. The Treaty of Lausanne compelled Kurdistan to undergo a second round of grave separation among Turkey, Iran, Iraq, and Syria. In each of the four nations, the Kurdish population appeared destined to share a common fate, having no control over their own fate or future (Wimmer 2002: 116–118). They promptly transformed into objects of absorption and oppression because they were incapable of embracing any chance presented to them to fill the power vacuum created by the collapse of Ottoman control (Dag 2017). While each of the four states suppressed the Kurds and prevented them from experiencing their Kurdish-Yezidi culture and autonomy, they violently forced the Kurds to surrender to severe assimilation, resulting in collective sufferings, victim-hood, and martyrdom. Kurdish history since the Lausanne Treaty has mostly been a series of disasters. Thus, the regimes that have ruled Kurdistan since the end of World War I have not even acknowledged the Kurdish-Yezidi population as "cultural minorities." These governing regimes are rather naturally aligned against the common "separatist" Kurdish-Yezidi insurgents (Romano and Gurses 2014). While Iran has acknowledged the existence of the Kurdish language despite prohibiting its official use, the Syrian regime denies its existence. Kurdish-Yezidi popu-lations in Iraq have gained some cultural, linguistic, and political recogni-tion since the beginning of the twenty-first century; however, the Kurdish authorities are not allowed to claim de-jura sovereignty over any territory or natural resources. The Turkish government not only denies Kurdish reality but also feels compelled to undermine any Kurdish achievements in the Middle East and beyond, as Kurds have long been portrayed as an existential threat to the Turkish state and its assimilationist and expansion-ist policies (Dag 2017). Despite the overwhelming evidence that the Kurdish-Yezidi population is a distinct people with a shared history, cul-ture, mythology, and linguistic identity, the aforementioned four govern-ing states have denied their aspirations to be recognized as a nation and enjoy its cultural identity and traditional way of living (Edmonds 1971; Izady 1992; McDowall 2005; Romano 2006).

The Kurdish political and social theorist Abbas Vali grasped the concept of Kurdish nationalism to identify the Kurds as a "common national ori-gin... a political community with a uniform identity given to history, and a political project involving state formation" (2003: 58). This concept, in my view, could be defined as the political form and power-seeking ambi-tions of Kurdish elites who tap into nationalism. Moving away from the political idea of Kurdish elites, the Kurds can be classified as a hybrid soci-ety because of their diverse belief systems, linguistic groups, social classes, geographical regions (plain and mountainous landscapes), and, most importantly, the tribes that form the basis of their social structures. These objective characteristics establish a sense of belonging and collective iden-tities among distinct Kurdish-Yezidi segments, but they all unite around shared territories, cultures, and ways of life. These components, including common persecution and displacement experiences, are driving factors among them to sustain and nurture their cohesiveness, belonging, and shared identities. To put it another way, the political and social conscious-ness, which underpins their collective mobilization, is based on culturally objective factors as well as a tragic shared experience brought on by violent conflicts, persecution by governments in control of their traditional homeland, and subsequent resistance, all of which result in shared narratives of sufferings. By leveraging the hybrid nature of the Kurds, the governing regimes have capitalized on the ideological, political, religious, and social differences of the Kurdish-Yezidi population, along with tribal disputes, to further "divide and rule" Kurdish society (Halliday 2006: 16; Entessar 1992: 2). Thus, these ruling regimes have colonized the minds, occupied the land, and appropriated the culture of the Kurdish-Yezidi segments, thereby determining their past, present, and future (Aksoy 2013).

The Kurdish population came to a critical juncture with significant attention from the international state community and the public, especially in light of the rise of the IS, its genocide against the Kurdish-Yezidi segment, and their active armed engagement in a dynamic fight against the IS in Syria and Iraq since 2014. Furthermore, Kurds in Syria are struggling to transform the new Syrian state; Kurds in Turkey are assisting in the replacement of the authoritarian regime with a democratic government; and Kurds in Iran are playing a critical role in overthrowing the Iranian regime under the slogan "Jin Jîyan, Azadî" (Woman, Life, and Freedom). The Kurds in Iraq played a pivotal role in the 2003 downfall of the former Iraqi regime. Despite their dynamic and transformational role in the Middle East, the Kurdish elites including party and tribe actors have remained politically fragmented and have lacked a coherent movement with collective attempts to create and govern their own future (Gurses et al. 2020). The Kurdish-Yezidi groups have continuously revolted in a variety of ways against the denial and oppression practices of various governing regimes in their native countries, but their attempts have failed to implement their political goals. However, the armed clashes and repression by the ruling states resulted in waves of refugees escaping to the shores of Europe and other parts of the globe.

The Yezidis are non-Muslim and heterodox Kurds with their own religious system based on orally transmitted tradition. They speak Kurmancî, a predominantly Kurdish dialect, and are distributed across the Kurdish region that includes Iraq, Turkey, Syria, Georgia, Armenia, and the European diaspora, particularly in Germany. The population with the Yezidi belief worldwide is estimated to be approximately 500,000 (Kreyenbroek and Omerkhali 2021). While the majority of the Yezidi segment identify as ethnic Kurds, there are some critical Yezidi voices who claim that the Yezidis are a separate ethnic group, setting themselves apart

1 INTRODUCTION 11

from Muslim Kurds based on their religion, which they refer to as Serfedîn or Ezdîtîyatî (Fuccaro 1999; Omarkhali 2014; Kreyenbroek and Omerkhali 2021). Within this context, Omarkhali (2014) observed that many Yezidis in Iraq identified as Arabs to protect themselves from the persecution of pan-Arabists under the Ba'ath regime. However, Kurdish national movements with distinct ideologies and political goals, such as the PDK, the PUK, and the PKK, which place a lesser emphasis on Islam, regard Yezidism as the original Kurdish religion and Yezidis as inseparable parts of the national Kurdish struggle and Kurdistan as a whole (Allison 2001: 38–42). Similar to ethnic Kurds, Yezidi Kurds are considerably fragmented due to their caste structure and identification, which is comprised of religious leaders, Pirs, Sheikhs, and Mirids—ordinary worshipers (Kreyenbroek and Omerkhali 2021).

There is no written literature or a recorded holy book for the Yezidi Kurds, and there are scant historical documents on the origins of their religion (Kreyenbroek and Rashow 2005; Fuccaro 1999). Kurdish-Yezidi community members and Western academics view the Yezidi religion from various perspectives. While some claim that Yezidism originated in ancient Mesopotamia and had significant influences from Gnosticism and Manichaeism, many others contend that Yezidism originated in ancient Iran and has some ties to the Roman Mithraist religion (Kreyenbroek and Rashow 2005). Others point out that Yezidi Kurds are an Arab ethnic group and are descended from Yezid Ibn Mu'awiyya, the Umayyad caliph who is credited with founding the organization (Izady 1992: 153–157). In the twelfth century CE, Sheikh Adi, an ancestor of the Umayyad Caliph Merwan, arrived in Kurdistan, bringing with him certain traces of the Yezidi faith. This occurred around the time of the discovery of Yezidism in Kurdistan. However, the Yezidi tradition is pre-Islamic yet has some linkages to major global faiths such as Islam, Christianity, and Zoroastrianism (Fuccaro 1999; Kreyenbroek and Rashow 2005: 3). Yezidi Kurds, along with Yarsans, Dersim Alevis, and Shabaks, are thought to have shared a significant number of cultural and religious traditions with other pre-Islamic Kurdish populations (Kreyenbroek and Omerkhali 2021: 534). These pre-Islamic groups have been considered to be ethnic Kurds. The majority of Kurds, however, were forced to convert to Islam as a consequence of their defeat by Arab settlers in the Battle of Jalawla in 632 (Mustafa 2021).

Muslim settlers intensified the persecution of Kurds who practiced religions other than Islam, such as the Yezidi worshipers. Under Ottoman rule, due to their non-Islamic beliefs, Yezidi Kurds were subjected to numerous atrocities at the hands of these rulers and even traditional Islamized Kurdish chieftains such as Bedir Khan Beg and Mir Muhammad of Rawanduz (ibid.). The Ottoman-Turkish explorer Evlîya Celebi reported the mistreatment, disdain, and prejudice of Yezidi Kurds. He dehumanized Yezidi Kurds in his book *Seyahatnâme* by portraying them as barbaric, disobedient, aggressive unbelievers who worshiped the black dog (Tezcür et al. 2021). Like this, Yezidi Kurds were depicted in the *Sharafnama*, the most significant work on the history of the Kurds, as suspicious groups that were punished due to their non-Islamic beliefs (ibid.). Particularly, Yezidi Kurds have been accused of being "devil worshippers" by the Muslim Turks, Muslim Arabs, and some Islamized Kurdish tribes. This derogatory term has been used to justify genocidal policies and practices against the Yezidi Kurds (Izady 1992; Fuccaro 1999; Bengio 2012; Omarkhali 2017). Consequently, the Muslim Ottoman rulers killed a large number of Yezidi Kurds, while a substantial number of them escaped to Georgia and Armenia or were forcibly transferred there. From the period of the Ottoman Empire until the emergence of, and most recent onslaught by, the Islamic State in 2014, the Yezidi Kurds were exposed to genocidal policies, exploitation, and practices and thus have been the victims of Turkish and Arab Muslims, as well as a few Islamized Kurdish tribes. Yezidi Kurds have recorded 74 distinct incidents of genocide and displacement since the Ottoman era, including both pogroms and massacres (Ferman) (Gatzhammer, Hafner, and Khatari 2021). As a result of ongoing genocide, victimization, and suffering, Yezidi Kurds are being forced to abandon their ancestral homeland and seek refuge in other countries, primarily in Europe and Germany.

EMERGENCE OF KURDISH-YEZIDI REFUGEE MOVEMENT

Kurdish-Yezidi refugees have been a continual migrant flow since this population's failure to carve out their state and exercise cultural and political autonomy in their homeland. The Kurdish-Yezidi population is subsequently subjected to repressive treatment and assimilation by the Turkish, Persian, and Arab regimes. Yet, these oppressive policies and assimilationist strategies did not provide the anticipated outcome in regard to resolving the Kurdish-Yezidi question. In contrast, the strategies to eliminate Kurdish-Yezidi identities through assimilation into the superordinate nations have not only failed but have also created the conditions for violent conflicts in the wake of Kurdish-Yezidi population uprisings against regime policies. These violent clashes prompted the displacement and evacuation of the Kurdish-Yezidi community, which sought asylum in European states. Currently, the number of Kurdish-Yezidi refugees in Europe exceeds two million, according to estimates from various Kurdish-Yezidi diaspora leaders and Kurdish institutions (Dag et al. 2021). Since Kurdish-Yezidi refugees are not legally recognized as a separate and distinct immigrant population or as a particular ethnic or religious minority, these estimates do not correspond to the actual numbers, and it is thus impossible to verify their accuracy. The rationale for underrepresentation and denial of Kurdish-Yezidi refugees in European nations reflects the repressive policies of governments in their countries of origin, which adjusted assimilation procedures, designating these subjects as Turks, Iraqis, Iranians, or Syrians. As a result, the European governments do not recognize the ethnic and religious identities of the Kurdish-Yezidi minority; instead, they register them in accordance with the nationalities that their home countries' ruling regimes have granted them, which deny their identities. According to Laizer (1996: 193–194), origin states are at the foundation of the denial of the Kurdish-Yezidi population:

> Kurds travelling as Turks, Arabs or Iranians on papers issued by these governments feature on immigration statistics solely by these same descriptions [...] no separate figures are available for the Kurdish population of Western Europe and other countries. Not only has Kurdish origin been masked prior to leaving Turkey, Iraq, Iran and Syria, it is also hidden from the moment of arrival on foreign soil [...] Kurds are identified as nationals of the country in which they were reduced to minority status after 1924.

The inadequate representation of the Kurdish-Yezidi refugee community is further compounded by an overall lack of understanding of their requirements and challenges. For example, Kurdish-Yezidi refugees have frequently been subjected to prejudice, particularly by Turkish and Arab immigrants from their home countries. However, since these ethnic and religious components are not acknowledged, these incidents are not recorded. Additionally, the leaders of Kurdish-Yezidi organizations were unable to persuade authorities in European nations to acknowledge and provide services in the Kurdish language. Instead, Kurdish-Yezidi refugees are required to use services in Turkish and Arabic languages.

The Kurdish and Yezidi refugee movements have historically evolved through four periods since the turn of the twentieth century, each of which included the means of their escape, decisions about their destination nations, and solidarity for survival. During the first stage, which covers the years 1900–1960, Kurdish intellectuals were exiled to Istanbul or other countries outside of Turkey by the Ottoman government and following Kemalist administrations. The Ottoman Empire aggressively persecuted religious groups in the early twentieth century. This caused a substantial number of Yezidi Kurds to flee directly in search of a new, secure home in Georgia and Armenia (Omarkhali 2017). Countries of exile provided shelter for Kurdish-Yezidi refugee groups, allowing them to engage in cultural activities and publish critical works. The second stage consists of Kurdish refugees who fled Turkey, Iraq, and Iran in response to three incidents between 1970 and 1990. The first development was the postwar economic recovery of the European states, which depended on the recruitment of low-cost and unskilled labor forces from Turkey and southern European nations, notably in the 1960s due to labor shortages (Ammann 2000: 121). The Turkish government encouraged a number of Kurdish immigrants to work as guest workers in Germany and other Western European countries. Within the framework of assimilation and dehumanization strategies, successive Turkish governments sought to incentivize Kurds to leave Turkey's predominately Kurdish regions (Timar 1998: 34). The Turkish government aimed to depopulate Kurdish territories in Turkey by expelling as many ethnic, Alevi, and Yezidi Kurds as possible (Timar 1998: 33–35; Skubsch 2000: 105–106). The second event is the defeat of the Kurdish movement in Iraq in 1975, when the American and Iranian administrations abandoned Mustafa Barzani's movement for their own ends. Subsequently, the Saddam regime initiated the Anfal campaign against the Kurdish movement, expelled Kurds from their ancestral homeland, and spurred their mass exodus. Kurds fled, seeking refuge predominantly in the United Kingdom and other countries in Western Europe (Wahlbeck 1999: 72). Iranian Kurds were also persecuted, especially after the Islamic Republic was established in 1979 after the monarchy had been overthrown and replaced by a regime that did not recognize Kurdish claims for autonomy. Along with expanding its repression of Kurdish activists in Iran, the Mullah regime began to pursue and assassinate Kurdish dissident leaders in European cities. For instance, leaders of the Kurdish PDK-Iran (a party with its headquarters in Iran) were assassinated in Berlin and Vienna. The vast majority of Iranian Kurds fled to

France and other Western European nations (Ammann 2000: 131; Hassanpour and Mojab 2005: 221–222; McDowall 2005: 456–457). The third incident that led to the forced exodus of Kurdish-Yezidi refugees from Turkey, especially those who were already political activists, was the coup d'état by the Turkish military on September 12, 1980. They were persecuted as a result of their participation in activities that aided the Kurdish cause. Following the military coup in Turkey in 1980, politicized Kurdish-Yezidi activists sought shelter abroad to escape Turkish persecution, mostly in Sweden but also in other countries in Europe. There, they resumed their political activities and began organizing Kurdish labor forces (Emanuelsson 2005). The third wave of Kurdish-Yezidi refugees arrived in the 1990s, when the PKK and Turkish military clashed, resulting in evacuating, looting, and burning of thousands of Kurdish villages (Çiçek 2017). The Turkish military forcibly removed more than three million Kurdish-Yezidi inhabitants from their villages and towns. This resulted in enormous and recurring waves of Kurdish refugees seeking refuge in Turkish metropolitan areas and subsequently in Europe throughout the 1990s. A significant number of these displaced people were ultimately successful in their attempts to survive. The final stage, from the late 2010s to the present, refers to the displacement of Kurdish-Yezidi refugees as a result of the dramatic and rapid re-escalation of violent conflicts between the PKK and the Turkish army since 2015, the Syrian civil war, and IS' occupation of large territories in Iraq and Syria, which drove Kurdish and Yezidi segments into Europe. A significant number of the escaping Kurds-Yezidis subsequently settled as refugees in a number of states in Europe.

KNOWLEDGE PRODUCTION AND KURDISH-YEZIDI REFUGEES

For an understanding of how Kurdish-Yezidi refugee realities are influenced by epistemological assumptions, we must look at the process of knowledge production, comprising its content, practices, purpose, and dissemination. Social constructivism asserts that reality is subject to social negotiation. On the basis of this claim, reality is not fixed, and the production and reproduction of knowledge about reality are a function of humans' lived experiences and interactions with their social environments (Magalhães and Sumari 2022). This knowledge is mediated to familiarize us with the reality of objects and to unearth unknown facts and new information based on their experiences, values, norms, and practices. However, the political and social positions, cultural and educational context, and access to resources in the institutional space of mediators are crucial aspects when using the experiences of the objectified to understand their realities.

In this context, Kurdish-Yezidi refugees have been studied in a number of academic publications as well as at international conferences and workshops hosted by highly esteemed institutions in Europe and the United States. Many of these platforms have been used by certain mainstream researchers to address refugee narratives about their experiences, contexts, actions, and emotions as empirical and experimental data for analysis, interpretation, and to generate new theories in an effort to produce knowledge about how to integrate refugees and regulate their conduct—a process that excludes these subjects. That is, these forced refugees are interviewed as empirical subjects without being recognized as collaborators capable of contributing to theoretical and conceptual frameworks of knowledge production. They are utilized as a source of experimental data, but they are not considered co-producers of theories and concepts. Consequently, Kurdish-Yezidi refugees have frequently been marginalized in the knowledge production process. Their participation has only been limited to data collection, which undermines the presentation of their realities and the expression of their perspectives in institutional settings. Furthermore, the scarcity of unbiased information about Kurdish-Yezidi refugees in relation to the source of their displacement as a result of copious amounts of official propaganda by Middle Eastern states makes it difficult to obtain "unofficial" information about what transpires on the ground (Scalbert-Yücel and Ray 2006). Thus, the refugees in question are unable to assert their voices and tell their own narratives about their experiences. Instead, three epistemes—Western-centric humanitarianism, state-centric methodological nationalism, and colonialism—shape refugees' knowledge of their lived experiences, circumstances, and political and social realties. While the humanitarian perspective continues to portray these and other refugee subjects as pitiful objects dependent on the humanitarian assistance of contemporary western (European) actors, the state-centric perspective perceives them within the framework of their integrability to be useful for the labor market and controllability for the security interests of nation states (Wimmer and Schiller 2002). The colonial episteme prevails over the categorization of refugees via the dominance of institutional contexts and the exploitation of refugees' narratives about their experiences and details (Mayblin and Turner 2021). These epistemes hegemonize refugee knowledge production while dissociating refugee context from their experience, pushing against their organic perspectives, and calling into question their epistemological agency, which is depicted as unscientific and subjective. However, the section that follows will focus on an alternative form of refugee-centric knowledge that seeks to provide us with an in-depth understanding of the world of the marginalized Kurdish-Yezidi refugees.

In regard to refugee studies, I understand humanitarianism as neoliberal assistance governance that intervenes, motivated by compassion and empathy, often via individual efforts to rescue the lives of refugees as helpless, wretched, and pitiful objects (Benton 2016). Humanitarianism does not just pertain to individuals risking their lives to help refugees in crisis situations; it also encompasses governmental assistance agencies, civil society, and scholarship. While humanitarian aid is crucial for saving lives and raising consciousness through the production of knowledge, it also functions as a hegemonic and colonial apparatus of Western states and their agencies applied to "non-white bodies," including refugees, to maintain their passive victimhood by undermining and even eliminating their "selfhood," "agency," "alternative form of knowledge," and self-presentation (Hassouneh and Pascucci 2022). As passive victims, refugees' perspectives are clouded, and their knowledge production capacity is severely disqualified since they simply exist as physical objects deemed as incapable of thinking, representing, or governing themselves (ibid.). Subsequently, they are unable to be scientific due to their subaltern status, which has been imposed, for instance, on subordinated communities throughout the colonial and nation-state eras (Memmi 1974: 139 and Bulhan 1985: 82). They are characterized as individuals who lack scientific skills but are contingent on assistance and who perpetually exist in an unequal relationship with national citizens or researchers because they rely only on their humanitarianism, compassion, and empathy without real autonomous agency (Fleischmann 2019). Consequently, the capacity of refugees to generate their own knowledge is questioned, while their narratives of experience and context are appropriated. I've observed face-to-face discussions at numerous local and international conferences and workshops and read, for example, in the co-edited volume *Methodological Approaches in Kurdish Studies: Theoretical and Practical Insights from the Field*, how Turkish and Western scholars, in particular, emphasized the "vibrant field" in the Kurdish Studies Series by referring to panels at international conferences, including the International Studies Association (ISA) or the Middle Eastern Studies Association (MESA). Then they imply that the voices of Kurdish-Yezidi subjects, including refugees, are audible and visible.

However, these scholars disregard those who represent the subjects, leaving aside the exclusion of these concerned subjects, whose representation remains in the hands of non-Kurdish-speaking scholars who only encountered the subjects in question during their field research. In my opinion, this point of view and study oversimplify the complexities of refugees' historical, political, and social origins and fail to stimulate awareness of their unmediated circumstances. The refugee subjects' knowledge of the truth is concealed and inadvertently denied. From a humanitarian standpoint, this body of knowledge eradicates the presence of refugees' selfhood and leaves out significant details about what drives refugees to flee their home countries in their own words, what their escape narratives are, how they build their identities, what shapes their social interactions and gender roles, how they view their conditions in exile, how they deal with social and structural difficulties in their host countries, and how domestic politics affects their lives. These concerns, including those involving conflicts, persecution, displacement, and the production of Kurdish-Yezidi refugees by Turkish, Arab, and Iranian governments, are glossed over and ignored.

State-centric episteme, which has been identified as methodological nationalism, is another prevalent approach that influences the production of knowledge and how we interpret Kurdish-Yezidi refugees through the prism of nation states. This approach correlates societies with nation states, which are deemed to be the natural units of migration studies and analysis. It confines migration and refugee issues to the preservation of national borders, the security of states, and the integration of refugees within the framework of labor market needs and national interests (Wimmer and Schiller 2002). In other words, the historical and contemporary theories of migration and integration, as well as refugee policies, have been presented to us via the lens of nation states, shaping our views on migration studies (Magalhães and Sumari 2022). However, state-centric scholarship promotes the nationalist assumption, serving national states while denying knowledge production from refugees' viewpoints as unscientific for failing to satisfy institutionalized academic standards. This kind of state-centric study remains uncritical and unreflective while also simplifying the complex contextual, political, and social realities that refugees undergo (ibid., 27). Multiple studies also examine the topics surrounding the Kurdish-Yezidi refugees through the gaze of governmental institutions and from a state-centric viewpoint (Scalbert-Yücel and Ray 2006). These studies contribute often to the promotion of official narratives of ruling Turkish,

1 INTRODUCTION 19

Arab, and Iranian governments by glossing over the vital role of ruling states in refugees' painful experiences of persecution, displacement, and abuse at the hands of state regimes and institutions. In these studies, they compared the oppression, displacement, and torture used by the Turkish government to generate the Kurdish-Yezidi refugees to their own tragedies caused by natural disasters like earthquakes and floods in Turkey. Thus, they view the repressive policies of Turkish states that have led to the displacement of Kurdish-Yezidi refugees as misfortune (Dag 2020). This approach derogates the traumatic experiences of forced Kurdish-Yezidi refugees regarding their displacement, exile, and conditions, distorts the political and social reality of concerned refugee subjects, and conceals the Turkish state's repressive and discriminatory role and policy. In this sense, state-centric knowledge decontextualizes the reality of Kurdish-Yezidi refugees, ignores the historical factors that led to their refugee status, and disconnects their circumstances from their contextual and political realities, depoliticizing the Kurdish issue. State-centric scholarship not only misrepresents the social and political circumstances of Kurdish-Yezidi refugees and reinforces the nationalistic assumptions represented by nation states, but it also colonizes the production of knowledge about these refugees.

Colonialism is the third powerful episteme influencing knowledge production about Kurdish-Yezidi refugees and dominating academic and political forums. Two characteristics of colonial episteme include, but are not limited to, the "domination" and "exploitation" of migration studies (Mayblin and Turner 2021). These colonial characteristics are the primary component of the colonial research process for knowledge production regarding the cultural and social realities of refugees. Domination is associated with actions of occupying and controlling the content and processes of knowledge production in the institutional sphere of dissemination, such as publishing houses, journals, workshops, and conferences. The researchers who are associated with the colonial approach serve as gatekeepers, deciding what should be published or presented and what should be disregarded. Along with a large number of other Kurdish academics, I contend that certain Turkish editors typically support works that are favorable to their viewpoint in terms of upholding power supremacy as well as uncritical research. Several young female and male Kurdish academics who are underrepresented outside of traditional academic fields and lack access to resources have told me about their encounters with Turkish book series and journal editors who purportedly envisioned assisting the Kurdish academics with getting their monographs or journal papers published. However, these editors implied that the Kurdish academics would agree to have them co-author their own publications, which downplay intellectual criticism of the colonial structures and ideology of the Turkish state. I have encountered these colonizing approaches, for instance, in review reports of my works that reproduce the coloniality of knowledge. They cast doubt on the originality, credibility, and authenticity of the interview data that I gathered from disadvantaged refugee interviewees in their own languages and impose a standardization of my works, ignoring the harsh facts of Kurdish-Yezidi refugees and their cultural background. I have seen it myself and heard from several other Kurdish academics about how researchers with such colonial approaches dismiss their critical works as "unscientific," "generalized," and "gossip." This undermines not only the scholarship of Kurdish-Yezidi researchers but also the narratives of refugee subjects. These approaches associate Kurdish-Yezidi refugees with their compatriots in Kurdistan, who are viewed as "uncivilized" or "backward" minorities in the context of security and terrorism research in the Middle East or as Turkish, Arabic, or Persian "immigrants" abroad. Voices of refugees that are critical, contextual, reflective, and based on first-hand experience of persecution, displacement, and abuse are quickly disregarded in their studies. These researchers with colonial ambitions continue to colonize, monopolize, and control knowledge by attempting to disqualify the knowledge production of Kurdish refugee scholars and question the narratives of ordinary refugees. This strategy resembles the way colonizers delegitimize indigenous knowledge to gain further control over it (Wane 2014).

I contend that certain Turkish and non-Kurdish actors continue to have a significant influence on Kurdish studies, eradicating the voices of Kurdish-Yezidi scholars and distorting the ontological and epistemological assumptions and realities of Kurdish-Yezidi subjects. The first two authors of the co-edited book *Methodological Approaches in Kurdish Studies: Theoretical and Practical Insights from the Field* (Baser et al. 2019) make a number of claims in their introductory chapter about the growing field of Kurdish Studies, but they do not reflect on their own positionalities and ignore the fact that Turkish scholars dominate these studies and resources, treating Kurdish-Yezidi populations and refugees as objects in their own views. They disregard the impact of formal state ideologies on their professional education and socialization in general. For instance, these authors applaud the existence of an academic Journal of Kurdish

1 INTRODUCTION 21

Studies without considering who is in charge of it. In this context, the Kurdish scholar Nilay Gündoğan Gündoan wrote a short piece about the dramatic demise of this journal. She drew attention to an incident in which Ibrahim Sirkeci, a Turkish scholar who owned the *Journal of Kurdish Studies*, sold it to a predatory publisher without informing the editorial board in advance, who then published non-peer-reviewed articles on the journal's website (2023). Thus, Turkish scholars hegemonize both the space of Kurdish-Yezidi representation and the subject matter of knowledge. They examine the themes influencing the identities, histories, cultures, experiences, and perspectives of Kurdish-Yezidi populations and refugees while silencing their voices by removing any possibilities and venues for self-description, self-representation, and self-interpretation by the subjects in question.

The exploitation of narratives of Kurdish-Yezidi population and refugees about their reality and lived experiences reduces their function to that of objects of experimental data sources, eliminating their active participation in knowledge production and excluding them from reflective interpretation and analyses of these data as well as from recommendations for policymakers. Within this context, the Kurdish Women's Freedom Movement in the diaspora, for instance, has addressed its criticism of certain scholarship that uses Kurdish women as experimental objects for data analysis while ignoring their voices as "equal partners" when contributing to knowledge production (Jadaliyya Reports 2021). Additionally, several Kurdish academics have shared their experiences of exploitation and discussed on the mailing list of the Kurdish Studies Networks how they felt abused throughout the data gathering, translation, and transcribing processes while being left out of the interpretation and analytic processes that underlie knowledge production and theorization. The lived experiences of Kurdish-Yezidi refugees are used as crude experimental data that is normalized and disassociated from the ruling politics of colonial states, geopolitical contexts, and historical contexts, as well as the hierarchical power relationships between the concerned researchers and the researched subjects. This is done either intentionally or unintentionally to represent colonial scholarship. Colonial research consequently distorts the cultural and social reality of colonized populations, including refugees, subjecting them to abuse and marginalization and excluding them from their own self-representation in political decision-making about how their reality and lives are affected (Darder 2019: 15). Consequently, their cultural, historical, and epistemic truths and traditions are silenced and condemned

22   V. DAG

for failing to meet the modern standard of superordinate societies (Smith 1999). In this approach, subaltern communities' production of knowledge is erased in addition to being rendered invisible, decontextualized, and discarded. Disenfranchized populations are forced to define themselves via the prism of colonial episteme, perpetuating alienation and subalternity. Thus, colonial research frames and promotes colonial politics to deny indigenous populations the right to experience their cultural, historical, and social realities in accordance with their customs, values, and norms. These scholars who advocate the colonial approach also have a further objective, which is to safeguard their entrepreneurial interests. Accordingly, they remain committed to controlling the institutional space of knowledge production and exploiting the data of subjugated and oppressed populations as well as refugees. They seek to uphold their hierarchical and subordinate position of power by utilizing the different advantages of education, foreign languages, and "direct access to resources and institutions" (Mayblin and Turner 2021).

This colonial research is in harmony with the Middle Eastern governing regimes' colonial policies and the political and cultural standards that are prevalent in the vast majority of "modern" European cultures. It exploits and trivializes the tragic experiences of Kurdish-Yezidi refugees by focusing on their labor-force integration while ignoring the history of relationships between the Kurdish-Yezidi population, European powers, and Middle Eastern ruling states. Even Edward Said failed to recognize how the Turkish, Arab, and Iranian states use their own internal colonial gazes to abuse the indigenous populations and their natural resources, usurp their cultures and lands eradicate their identities, and repress their representative bodies. Said, for instance, believed that Christians and Kurds in the Middle East were exploited as instruments by Western colonial powers to further their own oriental policies there (2003: 191). Instead of acknowledging the legitimacy of autonomy and cultural demands made by these marginalized indigenous multiethnic and multireligious populations for their political and cultural rights, Said's assertion is reminiscent of the official discourses of the Turkish, Syrian, Iranian, and Iraqi institutions. Academics who are state-centric and colonial adopt Said's stance, condemning foreign military interventions in authoritarian Middle Eastern states while ignoring internal colonialism as a phenomenon of dominance and exploitation that institutions and academics promote and impose on Kurdish-Yezidi culture, history, and social structures, resulting in waves of refugees who are compelled to flee their traditional homeland. The colonial episteme undermines the subjects' understanding of historical occurrences, context, and political and social processes in both the home countries and the new hosting surroundings. Detaching the plight and precariousness of Kurdish-Yezidi refugees in Europe from the repressive events, tyranny, and devastation caused by Middle Eastern governing regimes and politics renders it impossible to understand the processes that produced them. While three epistemes, namely humanitarianism, methodological nationalism, and colonialism, exclude Kurdish-Yezidi refugees from knowledge production about their narratives resulting from their lived experiences and misrepresent their ontological questions, the following section will present an alternative type of refugee-centric and organic episteme that includes the direct participation of refugees in depicting, interpreting, and analyzing their narratives about their lived experiences through oral history and storytelling means.

REFUGEE-CENTRIC EPISTEME AND KURDISH-YEZIDI SELF-REPRESENTATION

Refugee-centric episteme represents an organic but informal approach to knowledge production from below, which can be identified as an alternative or counter-knowledge to state-centric and colonial epistemes. Refugees generate narratives—the articulation of social interactions between people and political events and social environments (Hamelink 2016)—regarding their lived experiences of statelessness, political oppression, social discrimination, racism, and exile, as well as their desire for social justice and the continuation of their cultural and traditional practices abroad in their own words. By doing this, refugees not only reclaim their voices for active participation in the process of counter-knowledge production and push against the erasure of their cultural, historical, and social values, but they also contribute to the democratization and decolonization of knowledge. Refugees serve as both subjects and objects of their narratives by experiencing, witnessing, describing, analyzing, and interpreting incidents and crises. They tell us in their own voices and languages who they are, why they have experienced what they have gone through, and how they struggle to restore their cultural, historical, and social realities beyond the perception of their physical bodies. Telling stories in their own words signifies that refugees gain the ability to recite, define, and interpret their organic truths based on their lived experiences and do not rely on certain researchers to represent them and develop discursive and interpretive evaluations of their realities, which might ultimately result in their alienation. Storytelling, used by colonized indigenous, and oppressed communities, functions frequently as "decolonizing approaches" and counter-narratives because it involves testimonies, restoring community spirit, and remembering the traditional relationships between community members and lands and social settings prior to their colonization. (Muñoz 2019: 64). The marginalized, despite their perception as academically "disqualified," untrained, and illiterate subjects, utilize oral narrative as an original and vibrant means of knowing and transmitting it to the following generation. It has an emancipatory impact on the content, practices, and context of knowledge, eliminating the colonizing and subjective role of mediators as those who tell us about their objects. Thus, oral storytelling has a high potential for the recovery of feelings of estrangement in pursuit of emancipation and provides an alternative mode of knowledge production for the disenfranchised, who refuse to be identified as inferior, primordial, wretched, and unfortunate subjects.

The refugee-centric version of knowledge has been formed by indigenous, decolonizing, and feminist scholarship (Haraway 1988; Smith 1999; Darder 2019; Smith et al. 2019; Wane et al. 2019). Despite cultural, historical, social, and structural differences, indigenous, colonized, and socially marginalized communities share analogous experiences of disenfranchisement, deprivation of power over their geographic and social spaces, and lack of self-representation. They are frequently confined to physical bodies that are subject to control and regulation and relegated to the margins of mainstream societies. Furthermore, Donna Haraway's concept of "situated knowledge" is essential for locating, positioning, and situating epistemologies, highlighting the need for concerned communities to be heard and their reality claims to be rendered visible (Haraway 1988; Magalhães and Sumari 2022: 30). Haraway asserts that "situated knowledges require the object of knowledge to be pictured as an actor and agent, not as a screen, a ground, or a resource, and never finally as a slave to the master that closes off the dialectic in his unique agency and his authorship of 'objective' knowledge" (1988: 592). In the context of situated knowledge and inspired by disenfranchised epistemes, refugees, despite their marginalization in mainstream societies, constitute often neither servants nor sources but rather owners of their experiences and creators of their knowledge. They foster our understanding of their world in their own words. They describe, interpret, and analyze themes, narratives, and events to create meanings that allow us to gain insight into their oppression as a result of their cultural, political, and social realities and traditional ways of living and knowing. In this way, refugees offer, through their personal accounts, an understanding of their lived experiences that state-centric and colonial forms of knowledge have concealed, excluded, and rendered unknown. By rejecting their representation through the lens of "master narratives" and from the perspectives of colonial "others," they affirm their self-representation in an effort to advance a new understanding of their values, identity, and social world.

Refugee-centric episteme is predominantly transmitted through oral history and testimonies based on refugees' own first-hand accounts of their experiences. Researchers of underprivileged communities, including social movements, minoritized people, and oppressed and colonized societies, have embraced oral history as a tool for empowerment that allows them to take control of their historical narratives and the authority to interpret their histories (Bishop 1995; Ritchie 2015: 128; Muñoz 2019). Oral history highlights the narratives and perspectives of the disenfranchized on the periphery of society in an effort to draw attention to their plight and promote social equality and justice (Janesick 2010: 104). In other words, oral history is an effective means for outsiders to assert their identities by expressing their genuine narratives, which continue to influence their cultural and social existence. In this sense, oral history empowers refugees to reclaim control over their historical and contemporary realities from researchers supported by colonial power structures. In this way, refugees exercise epistemic agency and provide us with illuminating accounts of their past circumstances, connecting them with their current situation and deciphering the causal conditions that influence it. Oral history also disrupts the power imbalance in the knowledge production process, in which refugees are at the mercy of humanitarian, state-centric, and colonial interpretation and scholarship. Regardless of their educational background, access to institutional resources, or privileges, refugees have the ability to construct descriptive and analytical narratives in their native language. They contest the institutionally produced, standardized, and interpreted texts and official documents about themselves, which frequently fail to reflect the perspectives and realities of refugee subjects. Together, refugee-centric knowledge and narratives may assist policymakers, academics, and the public in better understanding the subjugated conditions encountered by refugees without making broad descriptive and interpretive assumptions about them. With its content and methodologies, refugee-centric episteme can offer new vantage points for emancipatory and reflective knowledge about refugees from their own perspectives and based on their lived experiences and their present circumstances.

Oral history has been utilized by the Kurdish-Yezidi population to preserve their identity, culture, and history despite widespread illiteracy and policies of colonization, assimilation, and prohibition (Tamadonfar and Lewis 2023: 86–100). The marginalized segments of the Kurdish-Yezidi population, primarily women, were empowered through storytelling to participate in historical and social activities, recall agonizing and joyous incidents, and articulate their demands and desires (ibid.). However, we lack the first-hand voices of Kurdish-Yezidi refugees through storytelling that provides readers with insight into their lived experiences instead of relying on policy-driven statistical data. Refugees in books paint a vivid picture of the actual circumstances that prompted them to flee or be expelled from their home country. They express what it entails to be the "victimized" objects of state discrimination and marginalization in Turkey, Syria, Iran, and Iraq, as well as the risks one takes when deciding that an escape journey through Greece and Italy to countries in North and West Europe is their best chance for survival and that of their families. They also demonstrate how they navigate the bureaucratic obstacles of a delicate asylum process while learning a completely new language and cultural norms. They additionally talk about how newly arrived and long-term refugees and diaspora members support or do not support one another in the countries where they have settled. Finally, the Kurdish-Yezidi refugees reflect on how they (re)construct their identities in exile and mobilize for homeland affairs from afar. These stories, taken together, provide an intimate and first-hand understanding of why Kurdish-Yezidi refugees leave their ancestral homeland, as well as the courage, intellectual wit, emotional dexterity, and political dispute required to do so while remaining active actors in their fight for political justice. Through storytelling, Kurdish-Yezidi refugees' narratives connect the past and present, their ancestors and the new generation, and the homeland and receiving states in a cultural, political, social, and geographical context. They are fundamental to identifying the historical events, social and political conflicts, violence, state repression, discrimination, exclusion, maltreatment, and colonization that have influenced the backgrounds, experiences, and ways of life and knowing of refugees. Indeed, the repercussions of events and politics in their home countries follow them to their host countries and sometimes appear to impede the establishment of their new lives in the new environment. Collectively, these anecdotes and recollections serve as testimonies and preserve these narratives for future generations. And, by taking a closer look at Kurdish-Yezidi refugees and how immigration regimes, asylum procedures, integration policies, and welfare benefit systems operate in different European countries, we can see how bureaucratic procedures shape the identities, relationships, and integration processes of refugees in different ways. This insider perspective also exposes the contradictions in European immigration policies and systems, which we should look at if we wish to develop and enact a sustainable and equitable policy for asylum seekers in Europe.

Process of Interviews and Data Collection

Interviews serve as indispensable tools for ethnographic researchers to gain insight into the historical context, culture, and social structures of participants, as well as their motives, actions, and interactions, to examine and comprehend the overall picture and the entirety of societies. The researchers use interviews to explain their arguments and assumptions. Interviews are required if researchers are seeking to "understand participants' perceptions or learn how participants come to attach certain meanings to phenomena or events" (Taylor and Bogdan in Berg 2001: 72). Researchers expand and deepen their understanding of the community under research through "in-depth interviews" (Angrosino 2005: 44) and are frequently inspired to pursue avenues of interest. Thus, researchers typically rely on interviewees who have pertinent knowledge about the investigated subject or are experts in the subject under study. However, this imbalance of power may shift once the interview data is in the possession of the researchers, and they have interpreted and analyzed it. During this process, they run the risk of failing to leave free room for interviewees to express their feelings and minds as they try to shoehorn refugee-narrated responses into their pre-established assumptions and arguments (Ritchie 2015: 16). Consequently, the data gathered through interviews may be less insightful and original when illustrating refugee narratives. However, interviews conducted within the context of oral history become written and documented texts, with their originality and veracity derived from the narratives of the subjects of the research. Interviews and their recordings are an essential component of oral history because they elicit original knowledge from interviewees about their lived experiences and events in the past, which frequently shape present and future developments (Abrams 2010). Oral history interviews afford interviewees a voice to address their first-hand experiences without general assumptions, references to prediction, or evidence (Janesick 2010: 104). Moreover, oral history interviews play a crucial role in redressing the imbalance of power between interviewers, researchers, and interviewees, whether researched or refugees, to shift the power balance from interviewers to interviewees and democratize and decolonize the production of knowledge (Ritchie 2015).

As part of the H2020 Project "Migration Governance and Asylum Crises" (MAGYC), I conducted and recorded a variety of interviews with Kurdish-Yezidi refugees between 2018 and 2020 throughout 17 urban and border cities. The interviews were conducted in Berlin, Landshut, and Munich in Germany; Stockholm, Malmo, and Lund in Sweden; Vienna and Salzburg in Austria; Bornholm in Denmark; Paris, Nice, Antipas, and Cannes in France; and Rome, Bari, Grosseto, and Ventimiglia in Italy. My field research included 230 semi-structured and in-depth interviews with recently arriving and long-term Kurdish-Yezidi refugees, asylum applicants, and naturalized refugees from Turkey, Syria, Iraq, and Iran. Leaders, activists, dormant members of the Kurdish diaspora, and isolated exiles were among the interviewees, whom I met through pre-established contacts and a snowball sampling. However, due to space limitations, I was able to present 129 interviews, involving 108 male and 21 female Kurdish-Yezidi refugees. However, the quantity of interviews is less significant as all individual stories become collective narratives about oppression, statelessness, refugeehood, racism, and denial, as well as lack of recognition, structural obstacles, exile, homeland politics and responsibility. As a former Kurdish refugee, I was able to seamlessly establish contact with Kurdish-Yezidi refugees and diaspora members due to our shared experiences of persecution in the homeland and challenges in countries of settlement, as well as our abilities and knowledge of the Kurdish language, Kurdish cultural and normative codes, and in-depth understanding of the way of life. I then conducted 15 to 20 in-depth individual and group interviews in each city. Each interview lasted between 15 minutes and two hours. The interviews were carried out in German, Turkish, and Kurdish (Kurmancî and Sorani dialects). My native language is Kurmanjî, and I also speak and understand the Soranî dialect. I am also fluent in German, English, and Turkish, which has at times been beneficial, especially while editing this book. Perhaps most crucially, as an attentive researcher, I can understand the "language of emotions" that, given common experience and self-reflection, can be attributed most particularly to refugees (Mahmud 2022). All of these features place me in a unique insider-outsider position as both a refugee researcher and a community researcher. More on this in a moment.

I organized my interview questions into four categories: diaspora leaders, refugees in metropolitan regions, refugees in rural areas, and group interviews. My interviewees recounted various incidents stemming from their encounters with persecution and displacement in their homeland, as well as their escape journeys. They also expressed the difficulties and tensions they endured in their countries of residence because of their legal status, social and political positions, and encounters with prejudice, racism, and other uncertainty. The majority of matters covered by the Kurdish-Yezidi refugees are explanatory and pertain to problems and concerns about their community. I interviewed diaspora leaders about their organizations' histories, the different types of services they provide, their interactions with refugees, the challenges and constraints of their services, their cooperation with authorities, and their homeland-related activities. I interviewed refugees in urban areas, focusing on their experiences in their home countries, their narratives about smuggler escapes, their connections to diaspora organizations and the services they received from them, the challenges they encountered during the integration process, and how their homeland affairs impacted their daily lives. In the third category, I interviewed refugees about what prompted them to escape and how they perceive their ongoing process of integration in the absence of diaspora networks. I also raised questions about whether they obtain support services in terms of language lessons, housing and employment opportunities, and general information for their orientation. I endeavored to understand how refugees meet their requirements during the adaptation process without relying on diaspora structures. In the final category, I focused on the interaction between diaspora leaders and refugees to gain insight into how diaspora leaders and refugees recognize one another and identify their demands and interests.

For the purpose of selecting interviewees, I chose interlocutors on the basis of their legal status, generations, gender identities, occupations, employment types, and statuses. I also took into account their levels of language skills in their new societies, education, housing situations, years of their immigration, countries of their emigration, their positions within diaspora organizations, and their ties to pre-existing Kurdish-Yezidi communities in terms of political affiliation or kinship, as well as cross-border

30   V. DAG

relationships with family or friends outside of their original cities of settlement. The identities of the Kurdish-Yezidi refugees, the names of the cities in their home countries, and the labels of the Kurdish organizations with which they have been involved or that I interviewed have all been anonymized to prevent any negative consequences for the interviewees and their families. The individual identities and names of their institutions are less significant than their collective voices and general messages, which are powerful, representative, and insightful because many Kurdish-Yezidi share similar collective experiences and common concerns rooted in the conditions and statuses of both their home and host countries.

My Positionality as a Refugee Researcher in the Process of Knowledge Production

In this research project, I take on the role of a refugee researcher with a Kurdish background. However, I do not consider myself an insider or an outsider researcher if the insider/outsider researcher dichotomy is defined based on political or religious community membership. The Kurdish-Yezidi refugees and population are heterogeneous subjects in relation to their tribal, political, religious, and social boundaries, despite the fact that these boundaries are not fixed and are subject to constant transformation. They are diverse as a result of their multiple dialects, multiple religions, multiple communities, urban and rural origins, and multiple actors with conflicting political agendas and ideological orientations. Despite my shared experiences of persecution, torture, imprisonment, and exile, I do not feel a sense of belonging to any of the political, religious, or social groups of the Kurdish-Yezidi population. Hence, I am neither an insider nor an outsider, as I do not identify with any subgroups, yet I express my exile and Kurdish background. I am intimately familiar with the cultural, historical, and linguistic facets of the Kurdish-Yezidi population and the social interactions of refugees on a daily basis, as well as how they relate to one another. Therefore, I was able to pose different and more specific questions than researchers from outside the Kurdish-Yezidi population would ultimately ask to gather information. Researchers from outside the society under investigation may not be aware of its cultural and social norms and customs since they are confronted with "different problems and pose different questions" (Zinn-Baca 2001: 159). However, I benefited directly from having access to a variety of knowledge sources

1 INTRODUCTION 31

produced by leadership and ordinary members of the relevant refugee and diaspora communities, as well as from being familiar with certain cultural norms, taboos, and unofficial power structures within the community in question. I also had permission to conduct the interviews that energized and facilitated the field research process (Unluer 2012: 5). My familiarity with the Kurdish-Yezidi refugee communities enabled me to obtain direct insight into their lived experiences, historical context, motivations, and communal lives. Finally, as a refugee researcher, I have the unique capacity to establish immediate contact with relevant individuals and networks for interviews without being concerned about developing trust and rapport with participants. Although the insider perspectives of researchers are frequently contested due to drawbacks in relation to "duality, overlooking certain routine behaviors, making assumptions about the meanings of the events, and not seeking clarification, (...) closeness to the situation hinders the researcher from seeing all dimensions of the bigger picture while collecting data" (ibid., 6), I did not run into these difficulties because the refugees' narratives in this book are uninterpreted and expressed in their own words. I view every refugee I have interviewed as an equal co-author when it comes to the description and interpretation of their experiences.

In the course of this project, I defined my role as a refugee researcher and co-author to facilitate my interlocutors' ability to express themselves in their native languages while also serving as a translator of both language and emotion, which was essential in the processes of interviews and their recording as well as their composition for the completion of this book. The vast majority of Kurdish refugees struggle to express their experiences and problems in both their native language and other languages. This is mostly a consequence of their experiences with assimilation, trauma, and, in many instances, torture, as well as the ban on speaking Kurdish in their home countries, intimidation by their ruling regimes, and being stripped of an education. They have also been residing in countries outside of Kurdistan without a legal status for more than half of their lives, with the implications of being unsheltered, unprotected, and vulnerable. They live a "life in transit," where they are constantly "on the move" physically, psychologically, and emotionally. Most refugees have an enormous ability to emotionally voice their experiences of oppression, migration, and overall memories, despite the challenges and anxiety of verbalizing their feelings.

As a former refugee, I understood the accounts of my interviewees with compassion, intuition, and introspection. I also share their accounts of persecution, imprisonment, and escape from my countries of origin, along with their experiences of prejudice, racism, and exile in countries of settlement. Consequently, my first-hand knowledge enabled me to access the ineffable sentiments of my interlocutors while also providing historical and political context for their origins. Language is, without a doubt, an indispensable tool for conducting interviews. I am fluent in several Kurdish dialects, Turkish, German, and English and have served as an interpreter for Kurdish refugees in Germany and the United Kingdom, translating between Kurdish and Turkish and German and English. As the interim editor, it is imperative that I collect, translate, transcribe, structure, and reconfigure interviews. In this role, I determined which interviews to leave out, include, and categorize, but this process was limited to the intricacies required to contextualize the stories of refugees so that they were readable, authentic, and flowing. Without attempting to theorize the statements of the Kurdish and Yezidi populations, I provided a descriptive analysis for each chapter to enable readers to understand the context of the events that they talk about and that have shaped their lives. In contrast to the majority of academics, I did not treat refugees and their narratives as experimental data or sources for the building of theories or the interpretation and production of knowledge. The narration and interpretation of their own accounts were within the power of the refugees. In other words, the Kurdish-Yezidi refugees, who are both the objects and subjects of their descriptions and knowledge, are delegated the power of narration and interpretation. Together, my life experience as a former refugee and a refugee researcher, my language skills, my profound understanding of the Kurdish-Yezidi population, and my professional achievements as a scholar uniquely qualify me to carry out this work. It also situates me to combine the refugee interviews, translate them, put their narratives in context, and produce insightful findings about their lives. I translated all of the interviews into English over the course of 11 months. My translation strategy aimed to render my interlocutors' words as faithfully as possible, adhering as closely as possible to the original and literal sense, while translating whole metaphors, proverbs, and expressions according to their value and sense in English rather than providing a literal translation from their source language. Most importantly, I have made every effort to authentically preserve the emotional language that was vital to my interlocutors' self-expression and self-presentation.

Without a doubt, the interviewing process was highly emotional for me. As a refugee researcher with first-hand knowledge of the situation, I could not help but feel powerless as my interviewees described their devastating and perilous circumstances and sobbed as I listened, observed, recorded, and subsequently transcribed and translated their emotionally charged words. Certainly, my personal narrative had an influence on how I listened to and processed the stories of the Kurdish-Yezidi refugees I interviewed. In the Kurdish-Yezidi context, these emotions and memories include the social misery that comes with being unidentified and unrecognized as human beings (as displaced and abandoned refugees) in terms of not having a country of their own, not having access to basic resources, and living in the shadows or on the margins of the societies they live in every day in Europe. These circumstances had a profound impact on my approach, viewpoint, positionality, and self-reflexivity when I conducted the interviews, and they elicited my own traumatic memories and emotions of suffering. However, my intention in sharing these types of emotional narratives is not to evoke feelings of pity, remorse, or victimhood within the context of humanitarianism in either my readers or the refugees I interviewed. Rather, I urge a reading of these narratives as a moment and an opportunity to recognize these refugees' struggle for survival and against injustice, coercion, and victimization resulting from the policies of authoritarian regimes or governing nation-state institutions. Refugees' attempts to create a political space of equal expression, presentation, and encounter are what remain most urgent and significant in light of their past and current tragedies. Therefore, the first step in determining what we should do with these stories in terms of good policy is to understand what occurred to them. As a refugee researcher who believes that all academic work is politically motivated, I hope that exposing these accounts will disrupt the politically motivated silence and denial surrounding them. And at the policy and academic levels, more historically and politically informed and reflective approaches could be adopted to see, hear, and feel these oppressed refugees, who are now able to tell their own stories. The hope expressed in this collaborative book is to advance this intimate knowledge of and connections among policymakers, scholars, and refugees.

The decolonial methodology that underpins this oral history project seeks to fundamentally and profoundly dismantle the conventional, centralized, depoliticized, and decontextualized perspective that has been used to produce knowledge about Kurdish-Yezidi refugees. Overriding the hegemonic lens of the detached, uncritical, and unreflective researchers, this approach seeks to privilege the voices of the marginalized (both of

34   V. DAG

my interlocutors and undoubtedly also of mine), while also being attentive to the unique access of my position to acquire and share my interlocutors' stories. My additional objective is to deliver knowledgeable and informed critiques by using the training that I received as a researcher in the fields of political science and anthropology. This training has served to further sharpen my critique of the knowledge production process in which refugees experience exclusion and underrepresentation. As I conducted my research, I thought about how, under the guise of modernity, these scientific disciplines have frequently undermined the authenticity of refugees, labeling them as "subaltern communities" in terms of how they construct their identities, their cultures, and their truths while developing definitional and theoretical concepts and understandings of refugee reality and conditions without a word from them about them. Given my own biography, some may be tempted to doubt the objectivity of this investigation. However, as a refugee researcher, I perceived my position as inextricably entangled with oppressive experiences and sought to expand definitional concepts about refugees to produce and disseminate authentic and original data for a greater awareness of the refugee experience. Therefore, this book has also provided me with an opportunity to reflect on my own experiences, cope with my memories as a former refugee, and then place them critically on the outside as a researcher using my intimate knowledge.

Structure of the Book

This book is a collection of oral stories from and about Kurdish-Yezidi refugees living in exile in multiple countries (Austria, Denmark, France, Germany, Italy, and Sweden). It offers an open platform to a variety of refugee populations speaking Sorani and Kurmanjî and adhering to Yezidi, Alevi, and Sunni religious principles, as well as originating from different geographic regions within their home countries, namely, Iran, Iraq, Syria, and Turkey. In their own words, Kurdish-Yezidi refugees and diaspora members address their experiences from the homeland, their escape journeys, and the integration processes in their receiving countries. The self-narratives in this book are rich in regard to multifaceted topics that provide insight into the realities of Kurdish-Yezidi refugees in Europe and their Middle Eastern compatriots' circumstances. By giving priority to first-person accounts from underrepresented and subaltern subjects, the book takes an all-encompassing approach to the field of migration and Kurdish refugee studies in terms of indigenous joint authorship and the critical

1 INTRODUCTION 35

forms and contents of refugee-centric knowledge through oral history and testimonials within the framework of decolonizing methodologies.

In addition to the opening and concluding chapters, this book is broken into six further chapters that, considering as the whole, describe and analyze the historical context and diverse experiences of Kurdish-Yezidi refugees.

The second chapter, "Homeland Conditions: 'Speaking Kurdish Was a Crime,'" looks at the cultural, historical, political, and social conditions of various Kurdish-Yezidi segments in Kurdistan. Here, refugees describe how these conditions impacted their way of life and invoke the impetus for their departure. This ranges from the evacuation of their towns and villages to political participation, persecution, torture, and imprisonment. This chapter depicts the conditions to which the Kurdish-Yezidi population was subjected as a result of the repressive policies of the governing regimes in Turkey, Syria, Iran, and Iraq, which ultimately led to their escape.

In Chap. 3, "Escape: 'I Had Seen the Deaths of My Children with My Own Eyes,'" refugees recount the details of their escapes from their countries of origin and their quest for alternative means of escaping their home countries. They critically discuss their encounters and interactions with smugglers, emphasizing their journeys through transit countries. They reveal their troubles with authorities, abandonment, and powerlessness, all of which have long-term consequences for their mental and physical health as well as their orientations in new environments. Refugees and asylum seekers outline the difficulties that arise in obtaining asylum and how this undermines their ability to get residence visas in the countries where they are received.

The fourth chapter is headed "Asylum Processes and Challenges: 'We Neither Die nor Live but Receive Some Breath.'" Refugees emphasize the unwelcoming and ill-informed attitudes of authorities and point out that their legal statuses are intertwined with discrimination and obstacles in their orientations and perspectives in their new environments of settlement. Refugees and asylum seekers suffer from distinctive experiences, highlighting the significance of their legal standing and resident permits. Furthermore, they touch on the role of pre-established diasporic communities in the asylum claim process in terms of translation, address registration, housing, and employment.

In Chap. 5, "Toward Integration: 'We Cannot Achieve Integration Without Struggle,'" refugees discuss the obstacles and opportunities they face during their adaptation and settlement in host countries. They highlight the difficult issues that arise in relation to housing shortages and labor markets, language skills, structural barriers, and the inability of authorities to comprehend the background and requirements of refugees. Additionally, refugees stress the negative psychological effects of social isolation, the difficulties associated with adjusting to host nations' cultures and social structures, and bureaucratic obstacles to family reunion. Refugees appreciate the significance of diaspora organizations in urban areas for supporting them in conquering hurdles and creating opportunities. Refugees in urban regions frequently express their dissatisfaction with diaspora organizations due to ignorance and a lack of competence.

In the sixth chapter, "Self-Governance from Below: 'Self-Help Services Are Necessary to Mitigate Our Suffering,'" refugees refer to their relationships with other members of their communities. These include narratives regarding relationships between newly arrived refugees or asylum seekers and pre-established refugees, specific problems within the Kurdish diaspora community relating to generational conflicts, identity construction, solidarity provision, and social conflicts, as well as solutions to these various issues. With these narratives juxtaposed, the chapter facilitates a discussion among refugees in urban regions about the cultural and social functions of diaspora organizations that serve as social capital spaces for them. In the chapter, the interviewees also draw attention to how the diasporic organizations fall short of mediating between different refugee subgroups to meet their shared needs, resolve interpersonal disputes, and advance peace, cohesiveness, and welfare.

The topic of "Exile: 'I Have Not Dreamed of Being Here Since I Still Live There'" is covered in the last chapter. Kurdish-Yezidi refugees discuss their exile circumstances in relation to their estrangement from and yearning for their homeland. Cut off from their homeland, refugees suffer the adverse implications of exile; it affects their mental state, their social relationships, their ability to concentrate on their mundane tasks and lives in receiving countries, and it causes undesirable changes in their behaviors. Uncertainty, precarity, despair, and marginalization are part of their exile-related situations. This is particularly evident among Kurdish-Yezidi refugees in Italy and France. They imply that exile is dynamically intertwined with the homeland and invoke refugees' motivations to maintain strong ties with their compatriots. Consequently, they organize various individual and collective events in favor of homeland politics. The diaspora organizations, called home of Kurds, appear to alleviate the repercussions of exile when they provide a space for refugees to interact and express themselves, exchange their experiences, and establish relationships. This chapter sheds light on the interactions between exiles, refugees, diaspora organizations, and their homeland affairs. Finally, refugees express their displacement-related emotions and aspirations for their return, traditional lives in the homeland, and families.

The concluding chapter takes a critical look at the effects of humanitarian, state-centric, and colonial studies on understanding the social world of Kurdish-Yezidi refugees. It suggests that collaborative research with the participation of refugees in conducting studies and disseminating the knowledge is vital to understanding the issues, constraints, and opportunities facing refugees and the people in their home country. In this context, I summarize the findings with references to the refugees' own views regarding the origins of refugee production, obstacles to adaptation, exile, and the homeland issue to illustrate the crucial role of these topics in the lives of Kurdish-Yezidi refugees.

REFERENCES

Abrams, L. 2010. *Oral History Theory*. London and New York: Routledge.

Aksoy, O.E. 2013. Music and Reconciliation in Turkey. In *The Kurdish Question in Turkey: New Perspectives on Violence, Representation and Reconciliation*, ed. C. Gunes and W. Zeydanlioglu, 225–244. Oxon and New York: Routledge.

Allison, A. 2001. *The Yezidi Oral Tradition in Iraqi Kurdistan*. Surrey: Curzon Press.

Ammann, B. 2000. *Kurden in Europa: Ethnizität und Diaspora*. Münster: Lit Verlag.

Angrosino, M.V. 2005. *Projects in Ethnographic Research*. Long Grove: Waveland Press, Inc.

Baser, B., M. Toivanen, B. Zorlu, and Y. Duman, eds. 2019. *Methodological Approaches in Kurdish Studies: Theoretical and Practical Insights from the Field*. Lanham, Boulder, New York and London: Lexington Books.

Bengio, O. 2012. *The Kurds of Iraq: Building a State within a State*. Boulder and London: Lynne Rienner Publishers.

Benton, A. 2016. Risky Business: Race, Nonequivalence and the Humanitarian Politics of Life. *Visual Anthropology* 29 (2): 187–203.

Bishop, A.R. 1995. Collaborative Research Stories: Whakawhanaungatanga. PhD Thesis, Presented to the University of Otago, Dunedin.

Bulhan, A.H. 1985. *Frantz Fanon and the Psychology of Oppression*. New York: Plenum Press.

Çiçek, C. 2017. *The Kurds of Turkey: National, Religious and Economic Identities*. London and New York: I.B. Tauris.

Dag, V. 2017. Stateless Transnational Diaspora Activism and Homeland Politics: Motivations, Opportunities and Challenges A Comparative Case Study on the Mobilisation of Stateless Kurdish Diaspora Activists in Berlin, Stockholm and London. PhD Thesis, Submitted to the Free University of Berlin.

———. 2020. Decolonising Kurdish Refugee Studies: The Need for a Critical, Reflective and Emancipatory Approach. Refugee Research Online. Available at: https://refugeeresearchonline.org/decolonising-kurdish-refugee-studies-the-need-for-a-critical-reflective-and-emancipatory-approach/ (Accessed 8 April 2023).

Dag, V., C. Craven, and F.B. Adamson. 2021. Mapping the Kurdish Refugee Community and Diaspora in Europe: Case Study. *Report Deliverable* 5.2, EU H2020 Grant 822806.

Darder, A., ed. 2019. *Decolonizing Interpretive Research: A Subaltern Methodology for social Change.* London and New York: Routledge.

Edmonds, C.J. 1971. Kurdish Nationalism. *Journal of Contemporary History* 6 (1): 87–106.

Eliassi, B. 2021. *Narratives of Statelessness and Political Otherness: Kurdish and Palestinian Experiences.* Cham: Palgrave Macmillan.

Emanuelsson, A. 2005. *Diaspora Global Politics: Kurdish Transnational Networks and Accommodation of Nationalism.* PhD Thesis, Presented to the Göteborg University, Göteborg.

Entessar, N. 1992. *The Kurdish Ethnonationalism.* Boulder and London: Lynne Rienner Pub.

Fleischmann, L. 2019. Making Volunteering with Refugees Governable: The Contested Role of 'Civil Society' in the German Welcome Culture. *Social Inclusion* 7 (2): 64–73.

Fontana, B. 1993. *Hegemony and Power: On the Relation between Gramsci and Machiavelli.* Minneapolis and London: University of Minnesota Press.

Fuccaro, N. 1999. *The Other Kurds: Yazidis in Colonial Iraq.* London and New York: I.B. Tauris Publishers.

Gurses, M., D. Romano, and M.M. Gunter, eds. 2020. *The Kurds in the Middle East: Enduring Problems and New Dynamics.* Lanham, Boulder, New York and London: Lexington Books.

Halliday, Fred. 2006. Can We Write a Modernist History of Kurdish Nationalism? In *The Kurds: Nationalism and Politics,* ed. Faleh A. Jabar and Hosham Dawod, 11–20. London, San Francisco and Beirut: Saqi.

Hamelink, W. 2016. *The Sung Home Narrative, Morality, and the Kurdish Nation.* Leiden and Boston: Brill.

Haraway, D. 1988. Situated Knowledges: The Science Question in Feminism and the Privilege of Partial Perspective. *Feminist Studies* 14 (3): 575–599.

Hassanpour, A. 1992. *Nationalism and Language in Kurdistan, 1918–1985.* San Francisco: Mellen Research University Press.

1 INTRODUCTION 39

———. 1994. The Kurdish Experience. *Middle East Report* 189 (24). Available at: http://www.merip.org/mer/mer189/kurdish-experience (Last accessed on 26 August 2023).

Hassanpour, A., and S. Mojab. 2005. Kurdish Diaspora. In *Encyclopaedia of Diasporas Immigrant and Refugee Cultures Around the World, Volume I Overviews and Topics*, ed. M. Ember, C.R. Ember, and I. Skoggard, 214–224. New York: Springer.

Hassouneh, N., and E. Pascucci. 2022. Nursing Trauma, Harvesting Data: Refugee Knowledge and Refugee Labor in the International Humanitarian Regime. In *Refugees and Knowledge Production: Europe's Past and Present*, ed. M. Kmak and H. Björklund, 199–2014. London and New York: Routledge.

Izady, M.R. 1992. *The Kurds: A Concise Handbook.* Washington, Philadelphia and London: Crane Russak.

Kartal, C. 2002. *Kurdistan und der Grundsatz der Selbstbestimmung: Der Rechtstatus der Kurden im Osmanischen Reich und in der modernen Türkei.* Hamburg: Kovak.

Khatari, D. 2021. Die Massenvernichtung der Jesiden in Sintschar, Baschiqa und Bahzani. In *2021. Ferman 74: Der Genozid an den Jesiden 2014/15- Analysen- Interviews- Dokumentatonen*, ed. S. Gatzhammer, J. Hafner, and D. Khatari, 117–136. Baden-Baden: Ergon Verlag.

Kreyenbroek, P.G., and K. Omerkhali. 2021. Kurdish' Religious Minorities in the Modern World. In *the Cambridge History of the Kurds*, ed. H. Bozarslan, S. Gunes, and C. Yadirgi, 533–549. Cambridge, New York, Melbourne and New Delhi: Cambridge University Press.

Kreyenbroek, P.G., and Khalil J. Rashow. 2005. *God and Sheikh Adi are Perfect: Sacred Poems and Religious Narratives from the Yezidi Tradition.* Wiesbaden: Harrassowitz Verlag.

Laizer, S. 1996. *Martyrs, Traitors and Patriots: Kurdistan after the Gulf War.* London and New Jersey: Zed Books Ltd.

Magalhães, P.T., and L. Sumari. 2022. Methodological Nationalism and Migration Studies: Historical and Contemporary Perspectives. In *Refugees and Knowledge Production*, ed. M. Kmak and H. Björklund, 19–37. London and New York: Routledge.

Mahmud, B. 2022. *Emotions and Belonging in Forced Migration: Syrian Refugees and Asylum Seekers.* Oxon and New York: Routledge.

Mayblin, L., and J. Turner. 2021. *Migration Studies and Colonialism.* Cambridge: Polity Press.

McDowall, D. 2005. *A Modern History of the Kurds.* 3rd ed. London and New York: I.B. Tauris & Co Ltd.

Meho, L.I. 1997. *The Kurds and Kurdistan: A Selective and Annotated Bibliography, Bibliographies and Indexes in World History.* Westport, Connecticut and London: Greenwood Press.

40   V. DAG

Memmi, A. 1974. *The Coloniser and the Colonised*. London: Earthscan Publications Ltd.

Minahan, B.J. 2016. *Encyclopedia of the Stateless Nations: Ethnic and National Groups Around the World*. 2nd ed. Santa Barbara, Denver and Colorado: Greenwood Press.

Mouffe, C., ed. 1979. *Gramsci and Marxist Theory*. London, Boston and Henley: Routledge and Kegan Paul.

Muñoz, M. (Xicana Tejana). 2019. River as Lifeblood, River as Border: The Irreconcilable Discrepancies of Colonial Occupation From/With/On/ Of the Frontera. In *Indigenous and Decolonizing Studies in Education: Mapping the Long View*, ed. L.T. Smith, E. Tuck, and W.K. Yang, 62–81. New York and London: Routledge.

Mustafa, M.S. 2021. *Nationalism and Islamism in the Kurdistan Region of Iraq: The Emergence of the Kurdistan Islamic Union*. London and New York: Routledge.

Nisan, M. 2002. *Minorities in the Middle East: A History of Struggle and Self-Expression*. 2nd ed. Jefferson, North Carolina and London: McFarland & Company, Inc. Publishers.

Omarkhali, K., ed. 2014. *Religious Minorities in Kurdistan: Beyond the Mainstream*. Wiesbaden: Harrassowitz Verlag.

———. 2017. *The Yezidi Religious Textual Tradition: From Oral to Written: Categories, Transmission, Scripturalisation and Canonisation of the Yezidi Oral Religious Texts*, 1–19. Wiesbaden; London and New York: I.B. Tauris Bloomsbury Publishing Plc.; Harrassowitz Verlag.

Jadaliyya Reports. 2021. Open Letter to the Public: About the Article 'Beyond Feminism? Jineolojî and the Kurdish Women's Freedom Movement. In *Jineolojî*. Available at: https://www.jadaliyya.com/Details/42819 (Accessed on 24 July 2021).

Janesick, J.J. 2010. *Oral History for the Qualitative Researcher: Choreographing the Story*. New York and London: The Guilford Press.

Ritchie, D.A. 2015. *Doing Oral History*. Oxford and New York: Oxford University Press.

Romano, D. 2006. *The Kurdish Nationalist Movement: Opportunity, Mobilization and Identity*. Cambridge, New York, Melbourne, Madrid, Cape Town, Singapore and Sao Paulo: Cambridge University Press.

Romano, D., and M. Gurses, eds. 2014. *Conflict, Democratization and the Kurds in the Middle East: Turkey, Iran, Iraq and Syria*. New York: Palgrave Macmillan.

Said, W.E. 2003. *Orientalism*. London: Penguin Books.

Scalbert-Yücel, C., and M.L. Ray. 2006. Knowledge, Ideology and Power. Deconstructing Kurdish Studies. *European Journal of Turkish Studies* 5 (5). https://journals.openedition.org/ejts/777 (Accessed 5 February 2022).

Skubsch, S. 2000. Kurdische Migrantinnen und Migranten im Einwanderungsland Deutschland: Wie werden sie von der Pädagogik und Bildungspolitik wahrgenommen? PhD Thesis Presented at the Universität—Gesamthochschule- Essen.

Smith, L.T. 1999. *Decolonizing Methodologies: Research and Indigenous Peoples.* London, New York and Dunedin: Zed Books Ltd. and University of Otago Press.

Smith, L.T., E. Tuck, and K.W. Yang, eds. 2019. *Indigenous and Decolonizing Studies in Education: Mapping the Long View.* New York and London: Routledge.

Tamadonfar, M., and R. Lewis. 2023. *Kurds and their Struggle for Autonomy: Enduring Identity and Clientelism.* London: Lexington Books.

Taylor and Bogdan in Berg, B.L. 2001. *Qualitative Research Methods for the Social Sciences.* 4rd ed. Boston, London, Toronto, Sydney, Tokyo, Singapore: Allyn and Bacon.

Tezcür, G.M., Z.N. Kaya, and B.M. Sevdeen. 2021. *Survival, Coexistence, and Autonomy:* Yezidi Political Identity after Genocide. In *Kurds and Yezidis in the Middle East: Shifting Identities, Borders, and the Experience of Minority Communities,* ed. G.M. Tezcür, 77–99. London and New York: I.B. Tauris Bloomsbury Publishing Plc.

Timar, F. 1998. Die Wahrnehmung der Kurdischen MigrantInnen in Deutschland—durch die Brille der Türkischen Politik?. *Kurdische Migranten in Deutschland: Problemfelder Hintergründe Perspektiven und die Rolle der Nichtregierungsorganisationen,* ed. Navend—Kurdisches Informations and Dokumentationszentrum e. V., 33–46. Bonn: As-Druck.

Unluer, S. 2012. Being an Insider Researcher While Conducting Case Study Research. *The Qualitative Report* 17 (58): 1–14.

Vali, A. 2003. Genealogies of the Kurds: Constructions of Nation and National Identity in Kurdish Historical Writing. In *Essays on the Origins of Kurdish Nationalism.* Costa Mesa: Mazda Publishers, Inc.

Wahlbeck, Ö. 1999. *Kurdish Diaspora: A Comparative Study of Kurdish Refugee Communities.* Hampshire and London: Macmillan Press Ltd.

Wane, N.N. 2014. *Indigenous African Knowledge Production.* Toronto: University of Toronto Press.

Wane, N.N., M.S. Todorova, and K.L. Todd, eds. 2019. *Decolonizing the Spirit in Education and Beyond: Resistance and Solidarity.* Cham: Palgrave Macmillan.

Wimmer, A. 2002. From Subject to Object of History: The Kurdish Movement in Northern Iraq since 1991. *Kurdische Studie* 2 (1): 115–130.

Wimmer, A., and N.G. Schiller. 2002. Methodological Nationalism and Beyond: Nation State Building, Migration and the Social Sciences. *Global Networks* 2 (4): 301–334.

Yeğen, M. 2006. Turkish Nationalism and the Kurdish Question. *Ethnic and Racial Studies* 30 (1): 119–151.

Zinn-Baca, M. 2001. Insider Field Research in Minority Communities. In *Contemporary Field Research: Perspectives and Formulations*, ed. R.M. Emerson, 159–166. Long Grove, IL: Waveland Press.

CHAPTER 2

Homeland Conditions: "Speaking Kurdish Was Equal to a Crime"

The recent exodus of Kurdish-Yezidi refugees from their traditional homelands in the Middle East into exile in European states is the result of political, social, and violent conflicts in their home countries. The emergence of the Islamic State, the collapse of the so-called peace process between the PKK and the Turkish state, the growth of an authoritarian Turkish state, and Turkish incursions into the neighboring, war-torn states of Syria and Iraq are just some of the political and violent events that have led to forced migration since the beginning of the 2010s. The forced migration and exile of Kurds-Yezidi people since their statelessness in the Middle East after the collapse of the Ottoman Millet System in the early 1920s have nonetheless been an everyday occurrence of their lives. The Kurds, a multireligious and multilingual population, were unable to unite around an overarching goal that would have overridden the chieftains' tribal interests and allowed them to form their own state or exercise autonomy. Several factors contribute to the failure of tribal actors to represent the common interests of the diverse Kurdish-Yezidi population under conflictual and tumultuous conditions and in the face of political upheavals. Internally, these factors include the absence of common Kurdish-Yezidi voices, the paucity of written civic literature, even though this population possesses a great deal of oral traditions in the form of Dengbêj (singing storytelling), and intra-community animosity in the form of tribal competition for resources and territories (Tamadonfar and Lewis 2023; Hamelink 2016). External factors include the diverse geopolitical interests of governing

© The Author(s), under exclusive license to Springer Nature Switzerland AG 2024
V. Dag, *Voices of the Disenfranchized*, Mobility & Politics, https://doi.org/10.1007/978-3-031-46809-4_2

43

powers, specifically the colonial French and British mandates, their dividing and ruling policies in the region, as well as the antagonistic policies of the newly emerging Turkish, Iranian, and Arab rulers.

Since the establishment of the contemporary Turkish, Arab, and Persian states, there have been multiple Kurdish uprisings against the oppressive policies of the governing countries. The Sheikh Said rebellion in Diyarbakir in 1925 and the Said Riza uprising in Dersim in 1938 against Turkish governments are two of the most important Kurdish uprisings. Other uprisings include the Simko Shikaki rebellion in 1926, the Qadi Muhamed uprising against the Iranian-Persian rulers in 1946, the PDK movement against Iraqi governments since the 1930s, and the Kurds in Syria since the 1960s against Syrian regimes (Jwaideh 2006). Since 1980, Kurdish-Yezidi national movements have established themselves in Turkey, Iraq, Iran, and Syria. These movements have revitalized Kurdish identities, enhanced political awareness, and rallied the Kurdish-Yezidi populace in opposition to the governing administrations of the aforementioned states (Romano 2006). Even though Kurdish actors still harbor intra-community animosity toward one another, they are attempting to defend Kurdish rights and freedoms through a variety of methods. The PDK in Iraq, albeit rhetorically, seeks to carve out a nation state that can defend Kurdish rights, whereas the PKK has abandoned the concept of a Kurdish nation state and seeks to obtain constitutional recognition of cultural Kurdish rights and self-governance outside the model of a sovereign state (Gunes 2012; Voller 2014). Meanwhile, neither actor has yet accomplished their objectives. Since the establishment of the states above, however, the efforts of Kurdish actors have frequently been thwarted by the draconian actions of the governing powers. For instance, the Turkish massacre of Alevi Kurds in Dersim in 1938, the atrocities of the Syrian Pan-Arabists against Kurdish children burned in a cinema in Amude, Syria, in 1960, and the genocide committed by the Ba'ath regime of Iraq via Anfal operations against the Kurds in Iraq in 1988 are still fresh in the minds and hearts of Kurdish-Yezidi people. As a result, the traditional Kurdish way of life in rural and urban areas, as well as their culture, names, identities, social structures, and local self-governance, have not only been less tolerated by the ruling regimes but have also been subject to forced assimilation and erasure (McDowall 2005; Jwaideh 2006; Tejel 2009). To put it another way, the current regimes impede the freedom of social and cultural expression of the Kurdish-Yezidi population, as well as its political and cultural sovereignty. Kurds are required to abandon their cultural identities and

2 HOMELAND CONDITIONS: "SPEAKING KURDISH WAS EQUAL TO A CRIME"

assume the national identities that are assigned to them. The rejection of imposed policies by various Kurdish population segments resulted in oppression, exile, and displacement. Most Kurds and Yezidis became refugees in their own homeland after fleeing their birthplaces and villages to cities or metropolitan centers inside Turkey, Iraq, Iran, and Syria, and subsequently overseas to European states.

Kurds in Turkey have been persecuted and targeted by governments since the establishment of the Turkish state, and their cultural and linguistic rights remain far from constitutional recognition, with the suppression of Kurdish parties, organizations, politicians, and ordinary citizens, as well as the denial of their cultural rights. Since 2015, when the AKP (Justice and Development Party) lost its hegemonic position due to the success of the pro-Kurdish-Yezidi HDP (Peoples' Democratic Party) and the formation of a coalition with ultranationalist Turkish groups under the MHP (Nationalist Movement Party) (Gunes 2019), this strategy has become more aggressive. While thousands of Kurds have been imprisoned and the Kurdish-Yezidi reality has been degraded, the Kurds have played a vital role in challenging the AKP hegemony in the 2018 and 2023 Turkish presidential and parliamentary elections. Similarly, the Iranian government has subjected the Kurds to systematic discrimination by outlawing Kurdish languages and detaining, imprisoning, and executing a large number of activists. For instance, a Kurdish teacher called Zahra Mohammadi received a five-year jail term from an Iranian court in 2022 for teaching the Kurdish language in Iran's Kurdistan Province (Medya News 2022). Later that year, in September 2022, the Iranian regime's morality police murdered a 22-year-old Kurd girl named Jîna M. Amînî. International and domestic outcries followed Jîna's death. Kurdish-Yezidi actors, including the PDK-I, Kurdistan the PJAK (Kurdistan Free Life Party), and the Komalah (Komala Party of Iranian Kurdistan), urged a general strike throughout Kurdistan Province, inspired by the Kurdish slogan "Jin, Jîyan, and Azadî!" (Woman, Life, Freedom). This protest movement spread from Kurdistan to other Iranian provinces, including West Azerbaijan, Gilan, Tehran, Qazwin, Isfahan, Mashhad, and Baluchistan, and to many Western nations. Thus, the Kurds in Iran have become an important domestic challenger against the Iranian Mullah regime, with international repercussions.

Since the foundation of the Syrian state, the pan-Arab regime has been ruthlessly oppressing Kurds in Syria. In the early 1960s, hundreds of thousands of Kurds were stripped of their citizenship rights and have since lived as stateless subjects devoid of basic social, civic, and political rights (Tejel

2009: 61). They were forced to leave their villages and towns by the Syrian regime and were replaced with Arab people (ibid.). In a manner comparable to the plight of the Kurds in Turkey, the Kurdish language and culture were outlawed and denied. Nevertheless, with the outbreak of the Syrian civil war and the emergence of the Islamic State, the Kurds, as the most pre-organized segment of the Syrian population, obtained the opportunity to seize control of a substantial area of Syria following their conflicts with Islamist jihadists and certain elements of the Ba'ath regime (Dag 2023). Moreover, the Syrian Kurds evolved into the primary regional force of the international coalition fighting the Islamic State and played a crucial role in the military defeat of radical Islamist organizations, including the Islamic State and its affiliates (Knights and van-Wilgenburg 2021). Furthermore, they have established self-governance and incorporated multiethnic and multireligious communities into their constructed progressive and democratic paradigm that promotes gender equality and grassroots democracy (Knapp et al. 2016). They also defy Bashar al-Assad's regime to reinstall his authoritarian rule over Syria. However, their future is uncertain because their status is unrecognized and their partnership with the United States and other international actors, including members of the anti-IS coalition, is confined to military cooperation and precludes any political support for the Kurds to obtain a recognized status.

Finally, the Kurdish-Yezidi population of Iraq was the victim of genocide by the Pan-Arab regime led by the late dictator Saddam Hussein. It used chemical weapons on Kurds as part of its Anfal genocidal campaigns, which Saddam Hussein labeled "spoils of war" (Romano 2006). In this background, Saddam's troops gassed 5000 Kurds, including women, children, and the elderly, in the town of Halabja in 1988. Saddam Hussein's anti-Kurdish-Yezidi campaigns consisted of mass exterminations, the murder of approximately 180,000 people, the devastation of 3000 communities, and the exile of millions of civilians (Kelly 2008). Kurds provided the most support against Saddam and played their part in dismantling his dynasty and reconstructing the Iraqi federal state in 2003 (Tucker 2004). The control and dominance of tribe structures under the Barzani and Talabani clans over the political affairs of the Kurdistan Region have had little positive impact on the economic and social conditions of the Kurds. These ruling dynasties have been repeatedly accused of high levels of nepotism and corruption (Phillips 2019). Thus, sources of persecution for Kurdish-Yezidi refugeehood from Iraq for cultural, ethnic, and religious reasons under Saddam's rule have been replaced by persecution by clan

2 HOMELAND CONDITIONS: "SPEAKING KURDISH WAS EQUAL TO A CRIME"

parties of their Kurdish-Yezidi oppositions and dissidents for criticizing the clans' economic and social negligence and corruption.

Last but not least, the Kurdish-Yezidi population was the target of the Islamic State's most horrifying crimes in 2014 in Syria and Iraq. Following IS' genocide in the Shengal (Sinjar) region of Iraq in August 2014, the Yezidi Kurds suffered not only the massacre of thousands of their children, who were either killed or taken as hostages to be sold as sex slaves in Arab nations, but also the destruction of many of their towns due to IS attacks and anti-IS operations (Khatari 2021). According to Kreyenbroek and Omerkhali (2021: 536–37), 300,000 Yezidis were compelled to leave their homes and seek refuge in neighboring nations. While several Yezidi Kurds were killed in their attempts to reach secure refugee camps, many others were able to escape to European nations. Currently, the majority of these refugees dwell in refugee centers in the KRI (Kurdistan Region of Iraq). They are unable to return to their towns and villages, which are now the subject of ongoing Turkish airstrikes as well as a battle for dominance between rival Kurdish actors, including the PDK and PKK-supporting forces, the Iraqi government, and Hashd al-Sha'bi Iranian militias (Miserez 2020). Currently, internally displaced Yezidi refugees live in Iraqi refugee camps among other internally displaced refugees, and they are routinely attacked by Islamic Arabs and Islamic Kurds in Iraq, who claim them to be "devil worshipers" (Hosseini 2020). In other words, whereas all different segments of Kurds themselves have been subjugated and minoritized by governing states due to their cultural and ethnic particularities, the Yezidi Kurds are persecuted due to their non-Muslim faith and have become an oppressed minority within and among minoritized Kurds in Iraq. The Kurdish-Yezidi refugees in various European countries explain how statelessness, discrimination, and immigration have influenced their identities and altered the trajectory of their lives.

THE ROOTS OF DISCRIMINATION

We were forced to leave our native land and sought refuge in Istanbul.
—Merdem—France (2)

Kurdish families have many members who once lived on very fertile grounds, owned many fields, and had robust farming livestock. So, they had a lot of resources and their own way of living in the homeland. They also were embedded in very warm community structures and social relationships in Kurdistan. However, many families left these traditional and well-grounded ways of living and their wealth in the agriculture sector due to their political struggle for the liberation from colonization of their land. These large families encountered economic difficulties to accommodate and feed their children when they were forced to leave their homeland and had to escape to metropolitan cities. We were also one of these Kurdish families that were forced to leave their native land and seek refuge in metropolitan Istanbul due to the war in the 1990s. I became a refugee for the first time in Istanbul, where I was under heavy pressure because of my Kurdish identity. I could not speak Turkish but acquired the language with an accent. My Kurdish identity and my Turkish accent were the sources of my discrimination at the hands of Turkish children. I had to fight for a way to get along with these different conditions, as the arrival of a Kurdish child in such a large city means the start of a difficult life. In parallel with these heavy conditions of a new life, the economic struggle of my family and social changes were additional factors that aggravated my situation. Many Kurdish families would not have to leave their homeland and face economic hardship if they had not encountered political problems and the lack of recognition of the Kurdish identity.

While struggling economically in Istanbul, we faced adaptation requirements that the Turkish system imposed on us. For example, there were poor outskirts in Istanbul where hijacking, murder, drug deals, rape, and kidnapping were predominantly ignored and even promoted by the Turkish authorities. However, the authorities kept a sharp lookout for rich neighborhoods and ensured that rich people were safe. This example demonstrates that the state has always neglected, crushed, and exploited poor people while protecting and promoting the interests of rich people. This policy has encouraged me to question this system. When I was growing up like a Kurd, I started to search for my political Kurdish identity and discover it more and more. In Istanbul, there were pro-Kurdish political parties and institutions engaging in the search and struggle for the Kurdish identity. I also joined a political group and started to take part in political activities in my neighborhood in order to protect my environment, friends, and neighbors. However, the response of the Turkish system to this kind of activism was torture and imprisonment. This system approved the deployment of any means possible against individuals to intimidate and stop them from struggling for justice.

As a consequence of my political engagement, I was imprisoned in 2006. This happened three months after my marriage. The Turkish police

2 HOMELAND CONDITIONS: "SPEAKING KURDISH WAS EQUAL TO A CRIME"

first forced me to work for them as a spy to collect information from Kurdish political parties and organizations in Istanbul. They wanted me to betray my values, people, and national struggle and change sides to serve the Turkish state. Within this context, the Turkish police asked me to apply for the repentance law according to Section 221 of the Turkish Law Code. I rejected this offer and was tortured and beaten in many different ways, endlessly. I experienced this inhuman brutality at the hands of the Turkish authorities. In prison, I witnessed and observed the dirtiest face of the Turkish state and lost my full empathy and hope to understand the Turkish state. I realized the barbarity the authorities demonstrated against the Kurds through their acts and behaviors. I contracted tuberculosis in the Turkish prison and then caught pneumonitis. When I was conditionally released after four years, I had limited opportunity to secure employment as I was designated by the Turkish state as a terrorist. The Turkish authorities have always looked at my criminal record and have told me that I have been blacklisted by the government. I worked as a scrap dealer for three or four months during the judicial process. Normally, I had an occupation—working as a plumber. I had my own shop, and my economic situation was good before I was imprisoned. I had been sentenced to 22 years of lifelong imprisonment because of all my legal activities, such as press releases and democratic actions. I had no other choice but to escape to Europe and look after my family.

It was common in Turkey to be discriminated against for our Kurdish identity....
   —Mir—Italy

The reason why I escaped to Italy was because of my military service: I was assigned to Kurdistan in Eastern Turkey. I did not go to the obligatory military service, and so I was a criminal for three months. In the end, I reported for duty. During my conscription, I was at a military base where the officer was a Kurd too. He complained about how we Kurds are allocated to Kurdish regions while the Turks are assigned to western Turkey— places like Istanbul and Izmir. The administration favored soldiers who were relatives of the MHP's or AKP's Members of Parliament. These people were offered a safer place, while we were sent to dangerous places. In Eastern Turkey, the army wanted us to encounter our guerrilla friends. I spent 12 months in Eastern Turkey doing military service, but it was difficult because we could not speak Kurdish. When we started speaking

50   V. DAG

Kurdish, they arrested us and put us in a cage to torture us. The soldiers called this cage the disco. They humiliated us and did not allow us to speak Kurdish because they accused us of being traitors. They insulted us, but we told them that we were not voluntarily in the military but were forced to be there by authorities. Once, when I spoke Kurdish, I was arguing with a soldier from Rize (a coastal city in the Turkish Black Sea Region). I was punished and forced to act as guard for eight hours, four at night and four during the day, for longer than a month. When my conscription was over, I joined my family in Gaziantep, where they'd moved. I applied for a job there in a textile factory. I was invited to an interview, at which the first question they asked me was whether I was Kurdish or Turkish. I responded that I am Kurdish. The employer refused to offer me a job because of my Kurdish identity. It was common in Turkey to be discriminated against because of our Kurdish identity when we were refused employment. We could not obtain employment and failed to respond to the material and spiritual problems of my family.

The Turkish state was hostile to us.
    —Mervan—France

With my family, I was actively involved in the Kurdish struggle against the oppression and colonization of the Turkish state. For instance, one of my brothers and many of my relatives were martyred while struggling with the Kurdish freedom movement. I have been arrested several times by the Turkish state, and my family was constantly under Turkish repression in the 1990s. Our village was burned, and we were forced to leave the Kurdish region in 1995. Some of my family members escaped to Antalya and the others to Istanbul. I migrated to Antalya with two of my brothers and stayed there for seven years. In 2000, we returned to our village within the framework of the Return to Village and Rehabilitation Project that the Turkish state had introduced. However, the Kurdish struggle continued to a different extent. In 2008, we were forced to leave our village again and moved to the city center of Mardin. I started to set up my business in 2014. I decided to get involved in politics when the PKK leader Abdullah Öcalan sent out his letter for peace, democracy, and equality, which was read on March 21, 2013. The Kurdish and Turkish people, along with the world, saw this as a positive process. In 2014, I ran to be a council member during a local election and was elected for Mardin's municipality. In June 2015, the AKP lost power at the national election—what I consider

2 HOMELAND CONDITIONS: "SPEAKING KURDISH WAS EQUAL TO A CRIME"

to be the only democratic election in Turkish history. After the loss of the AKP, we thought the peace process would continue, but the AKP-led Turkish government stopped the peace process and started a new war. It increased the pressure on us and the rest of the Kurds. As a reaction, the Kurdish youth started a resistance in Mardin and built barricades to defend themselves against the Turkish military forces. However, the Turkish forces launched extensive attacks with all their might and razed six boroughs in the Mardin area to the ground. During this curfew, we moved to our village until the ban was over. After four months, we returned to the city center, but our house had been demolished. The Turkish soldiers plundered everything they found, took away all the stuff they needed, and destroyed the rest of our furniture and items in the flat. We could not use anything anymore. I rented a flat in another neighborhood. The Turkish government ousted the Kurdish mayors and council members and replaced them with trustees. I was also removed from my duties. After I was removed from the council, I continued my political engagement in the Mardin region. Around 40,000 or 50,000 people were internally displaced to other towns and cities, and thousands of civilians were imprisoned and killed. When the TOKI (Mass Housing Development Administration) started to build mass housing, they found many bodies that had been killed and dumped by the Turkish forces. Nobody knows how many people got lost there. The loss was both material and spiritual. Nevertheless, we did not give up our struggle but continued according to our possibilities.

The repression of the Turkish state was so severe that many people did not dare pass the street in which the office of the DBP (Democratic Regions Party) was located. I continued to visit its office but was arrested twice during this time by the Turkish counter-terrorism units. They did not have considerable evidence but accused me of attending the funerals of Kurdish guerrillas and writing press releases. I was not involved in any kind of violence but carried out democratic activities. However, the Turkish forces intensified repression and intimidation. The Turkish interior ministry filed a suit against me for my political activities during my position as a councilor within the framework of counter-terrorism. In addition, my family had problems with the Turkish state during the 1990s. The Turkish state was hostile to us. Our criminal records were already registered, and the Turkish cops found everything about me when they put my name through their database search engine. I realized I would either be arrested and put in prison or must escape from Turkey.

52   V. DAG

I left first for the Kurdistan Region of Iraq, but I could not manage my life there as conditions were very unpleasant. I sold my house for half the actual cost and borrowed a large amount of money. I contacted a smuggler group and agreed with their conditions and payments. So, they enabled us to escape from Turkey. Finding refuge was the only way to save our lives. Otherwise, I would have ended up in prison. The Turkish authorities have filed many suits against me and launched raids on my family after my escape. There is also an outstanding warrant against me in Turkey. I told the French Office for the OFPRA (Protection of Refugees and Stateless Persons) that they are the state and can dig out my stories too. The Turkish police officers have raided my house three times since I left my homeland. They have established a military perimeter and sit for many hours in front of my house. They interrogated my wife about my activities and whereabouts. These are the psychological and political problems we face. I have been put in prison twice: once for 35 days and again for three months. I was not scared to go to prison, but I was responsible for my family and children. My age was another factor. I consulted with my family and assessed the situation to decide whether I should opt for prison or refuge, but I decided for refuge, which we found better than prison. It is hard for us to be in exile, but I still think being a refugee is better than being in prison.

> *We can be everything in Turkey, but we are not allowed to be Kurds.*
> —Serdest—Sweden

In the 1990s, the Turkish state burned our village in Kurdistan, and we had no choice but to migrate to western Turkey—Istanbul. In 2010, our situation deteriorated in Istanbul because we remained loyal to our Kurdish identity. It also deteriorated because of my brother's detention. Subsequently, we decided to return to Kurdistan, where we barely had a moment of peace because the Turkish security forces destroyed half of our town in Mardin during the trench warfare in 2015. Many Kurdish youth and civilians were jailed and killed, and our houses were razed to the ground by Turkish soldiers and other Islamic groups. For example, those involved in killing the Kurdish children and youth had long beards and could not speak Turkish. The government deployed these people, and we think they were IS members. We have witnessed the cruelty of the Turkish state and how they have brutally killed our children, youth, and women. They have burned many people alive. My sister was taking pictures of victims to send and disseminate these documents among international human rights institutions. However, she was arrested and accused of taking pictures of these incidents without the permission of the soldiers.

In the 1990s, the Turkish states burned our village, and we migrated to Istanbul, where we could not endure the hard economic and political conditions. Therefore, we decided to return to Mardin in 2010. However, the state destroyed half of Mardin in 2015. We were not allowed to leave our houses. Those involved in the destruction in Mardin were not only Turkish soldiers but also many Islamic groups.

In addition, since I was a Kurdish musician, I performed at the Kurdish weddings in Mardin. I was also well-known to the Turkish security forces, who detained me in 2016 at the Newroz celebration, cut off my fingers to prevent me from playing the saz, prohibited me from performing Kurdish music, and threatened to do likewise in the future. It was a tragedy. Since I was injured and felt threatened, I decided to leave my children and wife behind and take a flight to Sweden. It was hard to escape Turkey, but I had to buy a fake travel document with a lot of money from smugglers. The Turkish authorities let me flee because, as the Erdogan regime keeps urging us, either love or leave the country [ya sev ya terk et]. They wanted me to leave the country since I did not love it. We can be everything in Turkey, but we are not allowed to be Kurds. A few days ago, I had a phone conversation with my son. He said that he also wants to leave Erdogan's country. I told him that he lives in Kurdistan, which is thef Erdogan's country. Yet, the Turkish authorities do not care where we take our departures to; they just want us, the Kurdish dissidents, to leave Turkey. I resumed the production of my music in Sweden after my fingers were treated. I live in Sweden, away from my children and wife.

Our worst enemy is not Arabs or Turks but the Kurds themselves.
    —Serger—Italy

We have escaped from Kurdistan. Our problem is not the Iraqi government, which does not govern over us in any way. Rather, it is the ruling families in Kurdistan. There are two dominant mafia-like political parties that are much worse than the Saddam regime, even though Saddam has killed, oppressed, and hurt Kurdish people. These are the Barzani and the Talabani families. The Kurdish people are in pain, and they leave their homeland for Europe because they have fallen into the hands of these mafia families. We did not imagine that the sons of Saddam Hussein, Uday Hussein and Qusay Hussein, would be an inspiration for the sons of Jalal Talabani and the sons and nephews of Masoud Barzani, who destroy Kurdistan and make Kurdish people poor and weak. These two political parties encourage Kurdish enemies to bomb Kurdistan. One brings Turkey, the other brings Iran and the PMF (Popular Mobilization Units). (These parties have divided Kurdistan into two social classes—one part consists of millionaires, and the other consists of destitute people who do not have food to eat. This is a fact.) Why do you think Kurds run away from Kurdistan today?

On the other hand, we have the problem of the PKK, which kills two Turkish soldiers and causes the invasion of the Turkish state to come and destroy all the Kurdish villages. Therefore, the Kurdish people escape to Europe and become wretched. They accept whatever happens to them. A month ago, a ship sank, and Kurdish children died at the hands of an Afghani human smuggler. Kurdish children die every day. The reason they die is because they escape from these mafia-like families, who have sold out the Kurds to Iran, Iraq, and Turkey. I do not aspire to obtain asylum in Europe, as I prefer to comfortably live in Kurdistan. I would not exchange one meter of Kurdistan for the whole of Europe, but life in Kurdistan is not bearable because of the ruling Kurdish mafia-like parties. They expect us to be their slaves, and if we refuse their demands, we face humiliation, arrest, and terrorism. I fought for Kurdistan against the Saddam regime in the hope that Kurdistan would become liberated. I had never considered that Kurds would oppress themselves, which is much worse than the Arab oppression against the Kurds. Therefore, I think our worst enemy is not Arabs or Turks but the Kurds themselves. They let their Kurdish brethren suffer. For example, the budget of South Kurdistan is enough to cover the entire living costs of all Kurdish people. However, we cannot find a job in Kurdistan while Bangladeshis are offered jobs and they earn 50 to 100 dollars every day. We would be thankful to make 20 Euros a day in Italy.

Constant Persecution

I was on my soil but lived as a permanent refugee.
    —Ihsan—Italy (2)

I am from North Kurdistan and have lived in Turkish metropolitan cities for 20 years. Over this period, I have been actively involved in democratic politics and actions. While I was engaged in legal activities in 2007, I got caught up in police operation and put in prison. Before I was jailed, the Turkish forces targeted patriotic activists and patriotic Kurdish businessmen. It was a state crackdown against Kurdish businesses to destroy the Kurdish economy and intimidate Kurdish patriots. The operation was a joint project of the Gülan Movement and the AKP in 2007 against the Kurds and was one of the largest operations started before the KCK (Kurdistan Communities Union) operation. When I was released from prison after about two years, I represented the Human Rights Association in the Aegean region. However, the Turkish state filed several suits against me and confirmed my 11-year prison sentence. The court ordered my arrest, but I left the Turkish metropolitan area. I had many opportunities to escape to Europe, but my choice was to go to the Kurdistan region of Iraq, where I wanted to resume my legal and democratic engagement. I considered this region to be a part of free Kurdistan, which had already achieved a partial status in any case, and I am a Kurdish person. As soon as I arrived in Kurdistan, I started my political and legal engagement in Hewler (Erbil, capital city of Kurdistan Region of Iraq) for four and a half years. However, I faced the repression of the PDK at the request of the Turkish state. They insulted and threatened me several times. My name appeared in the media a few times when I was among activists in Hewler who faced death threats at the hands of the Parastin—the intelligence service of the PDK. My lawyers were told that I must leave Kurdistan, otherwise I would be extradited to the Turkish state. If the Parastin forces would not extradite me to the Turks, they would not be responsible in case I were assassinated. In this way, they posed a death threat. This is why I left Hewler and moved to Sulaymaniyah, in the Kurdistan Region of Iraq. After I left, the PDK forces launched an operation and arrested 40 of our friends who were engaged in democratic and political activities in North Kurdistan but escaped to South Kurdistan. They spent two months in prison in South Kurdistan, while some others were extradited to the Turkish state or left on a minefield. There was no difference between the repressive concept of the Turkish state and that of the PDK against the Kurdish patriots. They are from different eggs but from the same hen. I moved to Sulaymaniyah, where I lived for one and a half years, but the hitmen of the PUK started to wake up and employ the same concept. I was also arrested many times, and my name appeared often in the media. This was my refugee experience when I escaped to Turkish metropolitan cities, first to Hewler, and this time to Sulaymaniyah. I was on my soil, but I lived permanently as a refugee. Although the land and history that belonged to our ancestors were ours, the existing mindset forced us to live as refugees. Since the Zenyari—the intelligence service—started to intimidate me and would not let me live in peace, I did not have any other choice but to not live in Kurdistan anymore. I called my family and discussed this with them. My family and siblings sold their houses and put together their belongings to pay for my journey of escape to Europe. After my adventure in South Kurdistan, I found myself in Europe, which was not my choice. I think that Europe is the reason for the practices and the foundation for what is happening in South Kurdistan—Europe is responsible for the worst situation in the Middle East and all the tears and pains of its people. Although Europe has created chaos, poverty, and a dividing mindset in my own homeland, I fled to that same Europe to seek refuge and asked Europeans to provide me with a shelter.

My body could not resist these pains and sufferings anymore....
—Serbaz—Italy

I am from a village in the Botan area. I was a child during the hottest political period of the Kurdish struggle. Because of its weakness towards the Kurdish struggle, the Turkish state discriminated against and mistreated Kurdish civilians. The Turkish army started to burn down villages in Kurdistan. Our village was burned and demolished too. Many civilians were killed by anonymous murderers in the service of the Turkish state while launching fierce attacks on Kurdistan. Tansu Ciller, the Turkish Prime Minister at the time, conceded that the Turks had reoccupied Kurdistan. Against the repression and attacks of the Turkish state, my family and other villagers were forced to leave our village and become refugees. At that time, I was 11 years old. With my family, we escaped to South Kurdistan and settled in a refugee camp, but later moved to the Makmur area. In order to receive legal status as politically persecuted refugees in Iraq, my family members and all of the older people started a hunger strike

2 HOMELAND CONDITIONS: "SPEAKING KURDISH WAS EQUAL TO A CRIME" 57

that lasted 60 days until the Iraqi authorities accepted our request. Initially, these authorities wanted to deport us to Turkey, but we rejected this plan. Since the Turkish state had stripped us of our Turkish citizenship, we were granted political asylum by the UN as a result of our struggle. After we were granted political asylum, we did not receive any support apart from the Kurdish movement. The internal Kurdish conflict and the military operations of the Turkish state forced us to relocate our camps and become refugees several times on the soil of Kurdistan. In total, we had gone through seven different camps until we settled in 1998 in Makmur, where we relied on Saddam Hussein, a name that all Kurds know very well. We should ask ourselves why we entrusted ourselves to Saddam Hussein, who was a dictator, oppressed the Kurds, and committed genocide. The answer is that the oppression and persecution of the PDK and Barzani forced us to rely on Saddam Hussein and seek shelter. We escaped to one of the Kurds' largest enemies. The conditions of being refugees under his control were very hard. As individuals, family members, and residents in this camp, we experienced grave and desperate circumstances. We were beaten and killed; we fled and feared. I was a child and grew up under conditions of refugeedom—a condition that meant we lived permanently in the shadow of violent conflicts. For example, when we would put up the tent for the school, we also had to dig our trenches and bunkers at the same time to protect ourselves from the Turkish airstrikes and Barzani forces in Kurdistan. We have been permanently suffering and facing oppression. In the process of my continuous refuge, many tragic incidents happened to me. I lost my father, and my sister was killed while she was a part of the Kurdish struggle. It was very hard when I had to shoulder the responsibility for my family too. My body could not resist these pains and sufferings anymore because it has reached its capacity. I started to have serious health issues and could not get medical treatment in the homeland. I decided to come to Europe and become a refugee.

Kurdistan and Baghdad are lovely places, but not for us Yezidis.
    —Xeyal—Germany (2)

We walked for many days without food, drink, or clothes to escape IS' genocidal acts against us Yezidis in 2014. We initially sought refuge in the Kurdistan region of Iraq following the massacre. We then paid smugglers to traffic us to Europe. We have managed to flee but could not take our children, who live currently in abandoned Shengal (Sinjar). Our situation was not bearable, as we lost everything in Shingal. There is nothing left out there. Our houses were grazed to the ground and plundered. The Arabs cut off the heads of our people. They abducted our 9 years old girls and took many hostages. We could not risk going back. If Shengal would not have been destroyed, I would have lived there with my children now, but we cannot return to Iraq. We have gathered many severe experiences and lost everything. In Germany, our situation has even deteriorated because we were told that Germany is the place of human rights and justice for women and children. We have arrived here but have not witnessed any of these rights yet. The German authorities told us that Kurdistan is beautiful, and we can live there. I said yes, Kurdistan and Baghdad are lovely places, but not for us Yezidis. I said that these territories are strange to us, and we live in refugee camps and other people's lands. Shengal is our homeland and belongs to us, but it has been destroyed. Our underage girls and children are hostages over there. There is nothing more difficult in the world than this situation. We can never forget this trauma.

We knew that Turks mistreated Syrians.
   —Erdehan—Denmark

I am from Afrin but grew up in Taqa, near Raqqa (Syria), where I lived for 50 years. I got married shortly before the civil war in Syria broke out. After my marriage, I lived with my family for a while but then moved out to be on my own, as our culture requires it. I moved to Aleppo and lived there for three years. It was controlled by the Free Syrian Army, and the war never ceased. I have witnessed how the regime forces left-over barrel bombs on top of us. We could not work in the olive fields anymore because of the war. I went to Afrin with my family, which was under the control of the Kurdish forces. It was safer and more stable than the other parts of Syria. I stayed in Syria until 2014. Some of our neighbors escaped to Iraqi Kurdistan as the route to Kurdistan was open. They stayed there for a year, and we went to see their house. They told us to get employed in Kurdistan. We decided to go and see what was going on in Kurdistan, as we had already decided to leave Syria. It was hard to leave, but we could not imagine what the Arabs would do with us—perhaps kill us. We decided to escape from Syria as a family, leaving no one behind.

My sister, who moved to Kurdistan before me, suggested that we travel to Kurdistan. I went to Kurdistan and spent ten days there but could not get a resident permit. I was very stressed and had to decide whether to

2 HOMELAND CONDITIONS: "SPEAKING KURDISH WAS EQUAL TO A CRIME" 59

leave to go back home [to Afrin] or to Kirkuk since my neighbors lived there. We had never seen the Kurdistan Region of Iraq in reality; it was only in our dreams. We decided to travel to Kirkuk, where we could find more job opportunities. We asked my father to join us since we had employment and could settle, but he refused. Nevertheless, we sent him some money. We spent two years in Kirkuk, but my sister and brother wanted to go to Turkey even though we were all doing well. My father wanted us to come back to Syria. We decided to go to Turkey and cross the border towards Afrin, but the DAES had already occupied many regions. We could not cross the Turkish border as there were many soldiers. It was dangerous to go to Afrin, and we also did not want to stay in Turkey since we knew that Turks mistreated the Syrians who wanted to escape to Europe. We decided to join the refugee wave to escape to Europe. With the help of a smuggler, we managed our trip from Kirkuk to Denmark within nine days.

LANGUAGE OF EMOTIONS

Speaking Kurdish became equalized with crime.
  —Oramar—Austria

Kurds lack cultural, linguistic, and political recognition and have been permanently oppressed and discriminated against by colonizing regimes or Kurdish tribes. We have always lived with fear, worry, and trauma. Due to this treatment, we are mentally less stable. This causes a lack of confidence and a failure to express ourselves. Our problem of expression has historical dimensions. For example, I was born and grew up in a Kurdish village, and I could not speak Turkish until I was seven years old. For me, Turkish was the discovery of a new world, language, and people. As soon as I started going to school, Kurdish—our mother tongue—was banned. However, this ban was not confined to school but was also extended to speaking Kurdish on the streets, in parks among friends, and at home with my siblings. For example, the teachers entrusted us with the task of reporting and spying on those pupils and siblings who spoke Kurdish on the streets and at home. In school, we were beaten by teachers after having been reported to them since we were constantly told that we were not allowed to speak Kurdish. So, our language was banned. With other pupils and classmates, I was constantly mistreated and tortured every day for speaking Kurdish. Since we could not express ourselves in Turkish alone and had to compulsorily use some Kurdish words, we were, for example, slapped twice in our faces. I was clever in school and could perform well on my own, but when the teachers asked me to solve a task, I was blocked and could not read. Therefore, I have never liked my teachers. Since they have beaten me every day for speaking Kurdish, nothing has remained for me to like them.

We developed allergic attitudes towards the Turkish state and its system as a result of these colonial atrocities and practices, which limited my life to my village. I thought my village was the world, and I knew this world only through the lens of my own village. For example, when the rainbow appeared after the rain, we ran to catch it, but we could not reach it. At this point, I realized that the world is much greater than my village. When I was growing up, I traveled a lot around the world to find out how great and diverse it was. This means if we do not have our own state but are ruled by another alien regime, we become traumatized, mentally sick, and incompetent to express ourselves. To put it differently, the colonizing regime cut off our tongues and paralyzed our brains, leaving us unable to think. Accordingly, the Turkish teachers used violence against us to suppress and banish our feelings and prevent us from speaking Kurdish and articulating ourselves. This was not only my experience, but rather those of all my classmates and my generation in the Kurdish region. I wanted to study but did not have any opportunities to go to university as it was impossible in the Kurdish region, which was ruled by the Turkish regime. Therefore, when Kurdish refugees arrive in these European countries, they cannot easily express themselves and address their issues. They feel inferior and wretched as they were not offered any opportunities in Turkey and were forced to remain behind.

Additionally, we were given Turkish names, while our original Kurdish names were changed. I have, for example, two children whom I named Welat (homeland) and Bawer (belief) because I am in Austria. However, these Kurdish names and identities are forbidden in Turkey, and the Turkish state institutions have been deployed as an instrument of oppression and repression against us Kurdish people, our identity, and our culture. This repression continues in different forms at the hands of Turkish institutions abroad and has an impact on the integration of the Kurdish refugees [in host countries]. This disturbs the pattern of our integration into a new society. In order to overcome this repression, the education of the Kurdish refugees plays a crucial role in their integration. However, it is difficult to obtain this integration as Kurdish immigrants live from day

2 HOMELAND CONDITIONS: "SPEAKING KURDISH WAS EQUAL TO A CRIME" 61

to day and do not know what awaits them the following day or, in the case of their deportation, what will become of them. Many asylum seekers could end up in prison when they are deported, as they are politically persecuted in Turkey. They might face many troubles when they are deported. These worries mentally affect asylum seekers and refugees prevent their integration and might even lead to their deaths.

The problem of the Kurds is hidden in their emotions.
—Serhat—Italy

I have an Arabic name and a Turkish family name, but I am a Kurd. My parents could not speak Turkish at all. I was forced to go to a school where we were taught Turkish. It was impossible to speak Kurdish, let alone study it. Anyway, I went to a Turkish school for four years but received a five-year certificate because I was a hard-working pupil. Since my father was religious, he wanted me to be an imam. Therefore, he decided to send me to the Medrese (a religious school for becoming an imam), but I ran away from this school as my father's wish was against my will. I cried because I was used to going to normal school where I liked math, physics, technology, history, and medicine, which I wanted to study. However, when I was at religious school, I was provided Arabic books to read and memorize, but I did not understand anything. I lost one and a half years. I was supposed to learn not only for a year but for 200 years about how to wash corpses, perform ablutions, and where the direction of Mecca is. Therefore, I left the school and ran away to Istanbul, where I started working on construction sites with my mother's relatives. However, I did not disclose my Kurdish identity and always kept it secret because I was scared to tell anyone that I was Kurdish. Nevertheless, the Turks knew that I was a Kurd from Kurdistan. They were hostile towards me for this reason. They'd say to me in Turkish, "you bum Kurd" (*Ulan Kürt*). I swallowed everything because I didn't want trouble. I had to put up with what they said to continue my life peacefully. We were also made to forcefully accept the Turkish identity: we could always read on our mountains and fields in Kurdistan, phrases like "Turk, be proud, work, trust" (*Türk, Ögün, Çalis, Güven*), or "happy is the one who says I am a Turk! (*ne mutlu türküm diyene*)," and "Speaking Turkish means speaking a lot!" (*Türkçe konuş çok konuş*).

At 16, I escaped to Europe. My destination was Austria, but I was arrested by the police when I arrived in Italy. The cops took my fingerprints and released me, but I was not aware of the consequences of this detention as I was still a child. I continued to immigrate to Austria, where I was arrested. Subsequently, the Austrian cops deported me to Italy by plane, where I was arrested. They found out that I had applied for asylum in Italy based on my fingerprints. I was granted toleration upon my arrival, and it was suggested that I apply for asylum in order to secure my stay in the refugee camp in Italy, but I did not know what asylum meant. When I went to the Police Headquarters (*Questura*), by the immigration Office (Ufficio Immigrazione), I saw a script that said that every human being is equal before the law, without mentioning Italians, English, Germans, Arabs, or other people. I was very happy to see this script and almost cried because we were used to reading only "Turk" almost everywhere and were not considered human beings in Turkey. However, in Italy, we read that the law is for everyone to be equal. I asked myself if this was the place I had been looking for. After three months, I realized that it was only a theory and not the truth. I laughed about this. I have been living in Italy for 19 years, but I still do not believe in this script.

I decided to stay in Italy, learned the language, and started to work as a translator for Kurdish and Turkish asylum seekers. For my work, I gathered a lot of information about their numerous experiences escaping persecution, oppression, and discrimination. However, the situation of the Kurds is unique, and it is difficult to understand it. There are asylum seekers from Afghanistan, African countries, and Arab countries, and they can express in their own language why they are seeking asylum, but it was difficult to understand the situation of the Kurdish asylum seekers. Often, the question is raised about the reason that Kurdish asylum seekers cannot speak their own language but speak other languages. I think the Kurds were banned from speaking their Kurdish language in the homeland and forced to speak other non-Kurdish languages. Therefore, they fail to express themselves in other languages in an appropriate way. I think if someone can speak the language of emotions, they will understand the situation of the Kurds very well, because it is an awful tragedy. The problem of the Kurds is hidden in their emotions, but they cannot bring them out or articulate them because they feel ashamed. When some Kurdish asylum seekers are invited to interviews for their asylum, they tell authorities to speak in Turkish since they can identify themselves better, but it is not true since they cannot express themselves in Turkish either. Their lips get dry, they scratch at their hair, and they get blocked since they do not know what to say. They become mute. When I am there for my translation

2 HOMELAND CONDITIONS: "SPEAKING KURDISH WAS EQUAL TO A CRIME"   63

service and witness their dilemma, I feel like I am about to cry. I curse those people who put the Kurds in this situation. The way in which the Turks banned Kurds from speaking their own language is unprecedented in the world.

We become nervous when we start expressing ourselves in custody....
   —Kerwan—France

Due to our experience of oppression, we become nervous when we start expressing ourselves in custody upon our arrival. We live in constant fear. We come from Kurdistan and identify ourselves as Kurds, but both are denied. If someone's request is denied, how can they express themselves? We have been brutally treated, discriminated against, and oppressed for years; our language and history have been banned. It is very painful when I cannot now express myself in my mother tongue. We are forced to express ourselves in a strange language that causes us many psychological problems. We go to school in Turkey in a foreign language when we are five or six years old. The teachers are foreigners, but they force us to adapt to their strange culture and language. Kurdish lives start to be chameleon-like, changing colors according to our new environments because we are constantly forced to imitate the other and adapt our ways of living to theirs. In this process, we encounter many contradictions and start to develop something like a personality disorder. We do not have the resources to surmount these challenges, and we have many doubts about our lives and futures when we do not have our residency permits. My residency permit's absence has a severe negative impact on my life. To live freely and work legally, a residency permit is an inevitable condition. Therefore, we do not feel comfortable and pleasant because we do not possess the permit. It is also uncertain whether we will be granted residency permits or not. We have been waiting for years for our asylum case, but we have not been invited to interviews. We do not know how long we still need to wait for the court date in our asylum case. Consequently, we take each day as it comes, cannot work, rent a flat, and have normal lives. We are still young, but we will have to marry, set up a home, and build a future. However, we cannot do anything because of the problems related to our residency permits. Our philosophy for living is as if we would not have lived yesterday, and we will not live tomorrow. Many of our friends have partners or are married but live away from their wives and children. These are very serious

64 V. DAG

problems for the Kurdish immigrants and have severe psychological effects on their lives.

STATELESSNESS

Due to statelessness, we are all dispersed and live abroad as refugees....
—Ardan—Italy (2)

We Kurdish people do not have individual issues but share common political and economic problems that are related to the failure of the Kurds to create their own state. Therefore, the reality of Kurdistan is obvious, and there is no need for propaganda. Due to statelessness, we are all dispersed and live abroad as refugees, but we are part of the reality of our people in Kurdistan. So, we are not Turks but rather Kurds and live with one national identity and culture. It is not possible to live with two national identities and cultures. Otherwise, we would not be ourselves anymore. We cannot leave our essence and be something else. We are those people who grow up with a culture that affects our way of dressing, eating, customs, and a sense of morality that has been inherited from our ancestors. We have a Kurdish reality that we cannot deny, and even if we deny our reality, we cannot adapt to a new society because we do not belong to ourselves anymore and appear strange to receiving societies. Since we are a society with collective national elements, we face the same destiny. For example, we have been economically poor for hundreds of years because of the colonization that has become a reality in Kurdistan. Since we have been colonized we have been striving for control over our resources. Therefore, our unemployment rate in Kurdistan is over 80 percent, and these people must struggle against the poverty and starvation that have been imposed on them by colonial regimes. However, we are people who have always been involved in struggles and conflicts against colonial politics and statelessness. Thus, our problem is very comprehensive and deep, but in the end, we are refugees abroad because we share the collective destiny of statelessness and colonization.

...this was the identity of statelessness.
—Aynur—France

The circumstances in Turkey were very difficult and unbearable, when I recall my psychological situation there. I also faced many challenges

2 HOMELAND CONDITIONS: "SPEAKING KURDISH WAS EQUAL TO A CRIME" 65

before I arrived here. The first two-year period on my arrival in Europe was even worse and more exhausting, but then I started to gradually adapt to my new life. I can interpret this time as an asylum seeker in a liminality as the best of a worse situation and a lesser evil compared to my circumstances in Turkey. I was able to manage some issues here in terms of my adaptation, especially after I was granted asylum. I had to escape from Turkey because our identity is not recognized there and we do not have our own state, while the authorities here know we have escaped here because we do not have our own state. Accordingly, the French authorities leave us with the feeling that they will not grant us asylum and a basic right to live, even though we are stateless and do not have a recognized identity. In reality, there is no difference between the logic in relation to our statelessness in France or that in Turkey. This is my interpretation. As a matter of fact, when I received the ID card for my refugee status in my hand, I sat down and told myself that this was the identity of statelessness. It is a different ID card.

These European countries are aware of our dilemma—that we are Kurds, persecuted and without our own state—but we struggle to retain these identity cards. I did not commit any crime, was a student at the university, but I am Kurdish, and attended 8 March or Mayday events to claim and defend my Kurdish identity. However, although the authorities here are familiar with these circumstances, they ensure that I only have a life once I receive their ID card. Their logic means that I exist but only when the authorities want me to exist, because they do not treat us as human beings until we receive their ID cards and asylum rights. Actually, we do not exist normally, but exist only because our destiny is at the mercy of authorities. In the end, they tell us that we either have to receive their ID card or have to leave, but we also make a lot of effort by submitting many documents that they require in order to decide whether we are lying so as to receive these ID cards. Allegedly, these European countries present themselves as democratic countries which pretend that they have human values, which entice us to seek asylum. However, they impose on us their own conditions and ID cards without which we do not have any opportunities and rights to live and work here. These rights are basic and essential to organize our daily lives and survive. Therefore, here is a lesser evil compared with conditions in Turkey.

66   V. DAG

Being stateless is a great pain that I experience permanently!
—Mavan—France

We are stateless refugees. Statelessness is a kind of humiliation and inferiority, implying the fact that we are crushed and are worthless. We are stateless, and our origins and identities are questioned. Therefore, being stateless is a great pain that I experience on a daily basis. My pain is rooted both in my country of origin and in my country of settlement. Due to statelessness, we do not exist. People without a state are like houses without a roof. Everyone comes in and out for their own interests. This house is abandoned. This also applies to our homeland, which is the place of our ancestors. Our homeland is like the womb of our mother, where we feel pleasant and secure. My homeland is also my village, where I was born and raised, spent my childhood and adulthood, and formed my dreams and reality. I fell to the ground too when I was horseback riding. I also know that I need three cubic meters of space for my grave when I die. I need to pay for it everywhere in the world, but the only place for which I do not pay is in my village, where I am accepted. Even if I die here, my children will spend a lot of money to bury my body in my homeland.

REFERENCES

Dag, V. 2023. The Implications of Turkish Interventions in Rojava for US and EU Foreign Policies. *The Commentaries* 3 (1): 51–69.

Gunes, C. 2012. *The Kurdish National Movement in Turkey: From Protest to Resistance.* London and New York: Routledge.

———. 2019. *The Kurds in a New Middle East: The Changing Geopolitics of a Regional Conflict.* Cham: Palgrave Macmillan.

Hamelink, W. 2016. *The Sung Home Narrative, Morality, and the Kurdish Nation.* Leiden and Boston: Brill.

Hosseini, S.B. 2020. *Trauma and the Rehabilitation of Trafficked Women The Experiences of Yazidi Survivors.* London and New York: Routledge.

Jwaideh, W. 2006. *The Kurdish National Movement: Its Origins and Development.* New York: Syracuse University Press.

Kelly, M.J. 2008. *Ghosts of Halabja: Saddam Hussein and the Kurdish Genocide: Saddam Hussein and the Kurdish Genocide.* Westport, Connecticut and London: Praeger Security International.

Khatari, D. 2021. Die Massenvernichtung der Jesiden in Sintschar, Baschiqa und Bahzani. In *2021. Ferman 74: Der Genozid an den jesiden 2014/15- Analysen-*

2 HOMELAND CONDITIONS: "SPEAKING KURDISH WAS EQUAL TO A CRIME"

Interviews- Dokumentatonen, ed. S. Gatzhammer, J. Hafner, and D. Khatari, 117–136. Baden-Baden: Ergon Verlag.

Knapp, M., A. Flach, and E. Ayboga. 2016. *Revolution in Rojava Democratic Autonomy and Women's Liberation in Syrian Kurdistan.* London: Pluto Press.

Knights, M., and W. van-Wilgenburg. 2021. *Accidental Allies: The U.S.–Syrian Democratic Forces Partnership Against the Islamic State.* London, New York, Oxford, New Delhi and Sydney: I.B. Tauris.

Kreyenbroek, P.G., and K. Omerkhali. 2021. Kurdish' Religious Minorities in the Modern World. In *the Cambridge History of the Kurds*, ed. H. Bozarslan, S. Gunes, and C. Yadirgi, 533–549. Cambridge, New York, Melbourne and New Delhi: Cambridge University Press.

McDowall, D. 2005. *A Modern History of the Kurds.* 3rd ed. London and New York: I.B. Tauris & Co Ltd.

Medya News. 2022. Kurdish Teacher in Iran Jailed for Teaching Kurdish to Kurds. (online), Available at: https://medyanews.net/kurdish-teacher-in-iran-jailed-for-teaching-kurdish-to-kurds/ (Last accessed 10 May 2023).

Miserez, D. 2020. *Trauma and Uprooting.* Leicestershire: Matador.

Phillips, D.L. 2019. *The Great Betrayal: How America Abandoned the Kurds and Lost the Middle East.* London and New York: I.B. Tauris.

Romano, D. 2006. *The Kurdish Nationalist Movement: Opportunity, Mobilization and Identity.* Cambridge, New York, Melbourne, Madrid, Cape Town, Singapore and Sao Paulo: Cambridge University Press.

Tamadonfar, M., and R. Lewis. 2023. *Kurds and their Struggle for Autonomy: Enduring Identity and Clientelism.* London: Lexington Books.

Tejel, J. 2009. *Syria's Kurds: History, Politics and Society.* Oxon and New York: Routledge.

Tucker, M. 2004. *Hell Is Over: Voices Of The Kurds After Saddam.* Guilford: Lyons Press.

Voller, Y. 2014. *The Kurdish Liberation Movement in Iraq.* London and New York: Routledge.

CHAPTER 3

Escape: "I Had Seen the Deaths of My Children with My Own Eyes"

Penaber (Original language in Kurdish)	Refugee (translated version in English)
Karwanek wa dîsa bi rê ket	Here again, another caravan has set off.
Bûn wek koçeran û felaket	Like nomads they face calamity
Xeml û xêza wan karwana reş in	The color and ornaments of the caravan are black.
Bi derd û kul pey hev dimeşin	They walk one after another in pain and grief.
Penaberin penaber	They are refugees! Refugees!
Wek koçera der bi der	They wander like homeless nomads.
Welat welat digerin	From one country to another
Bûne wek teyrê bêper	They look like wingless birds.
Heywax li min, heywax li min	What a pity! What a pity!
Penaber in koçer in	Refugees and nomads
Heywax li min, heywax li min	What a pity! What a pity!
Wek teyrê bêper in	They look like wingless birds.
Karwan karwanê kul û derdan	This is the caravan of pain and grief.
Dev ji mal û milkê xwe berdan	They left their homes and belongings.
Digerin wek koçeran der bi der	They wander like homeless nomads.
Rih û can û milkan tev li ser dan	Their bodies and souls are all they have.
Karwan karwanê penaberî	It is a refugees' caravan.
Ronahî li wan bûye tarî	Light has become their darkness.
Nizanî ne dikenin ya digrîn	It is hard to know whether they cry or laugh.
Nizanî ne sax in yan mirî	It is hard to know whether they are alive or dead

Source: Lyrics and music by Aram Tigran 2009, translated by the author

© The Author(s), under exclusive license to Springer Nature Switzerland AG 2024
V. Dag, *Voices of the Disenfranchized*, Mobility & Politics,
https://doi.org/10.1007/978-3-031-46809-4_3

70   V. DAG

The lyric *Penaber* reflects well on the refugee dilemma of the Kurdish-Yezidi population, which has been pushed into the position of refugees in their own traditional homeland. Their migratory patterns are often similar: Kurdish-Yezidi refugees first become such because they flee from their birthplaces, then from their villages to towns or large cities, then to other locals inside the borders of their ruling states (specifically in Iraq, Iran, Syria, and Turkey), or to European countries as a result of persecution and displacement within their own homeland. These repressive events determine the fate of the Kurdish-Yezidi population and are fundamental to the exile of their politicians, intellectuals, leaders, and activists. They undergo the same exodus and refugeehood that their ancestors did under past empires like the Iranian Safavid or the Turkish Ottoman empires, as well as current regimes like those in Iran, Iraq, Syria, and Turkey.

The Kurdish-Yezidi have moved from country to country, shedding mixed tears of laughter and anguish because of their liminal, exiled state, unable to distinguish between their dreams of tranquility in receiving states and the persecution-related horrors they experienced in their homeland. The authoritarian and ultranationalist rulers in Turkey, Iran, and Syria push these ethnically and religiously othered refugees to leave their traditional homelands to escape miserable living circumstances, oppression, and torment. They not only lose their property and homes, but they also become mute bodies suffering in silence. The tragic experience of the Kurdish-Yezidi refugees is reflected in *Penaber*'s gestures toward the repressive conditions in their homeland: their interactions with smugglers, their search for new countries to obtain asylum rights and settlement requirements, and their commitment and ties to their compatriots. For many to continue existing, they seek the services of smugglers to flee their home countries, exposing themselves to grave risks that oscillate between death and survival, and when smugglers traffic asylum seekers overseas or through treacherous terrains, they walk a razor's edge.

Since the beginning of the 2010s, surges of conflict-driven refugees from Kurdistan have utilized the services of these human traffickers to escape persecution by the regimes or paramilitary forces in their home countries and arrive in Europe.

Many Kurdish-Yezidi dissidents who are engaged in political disputes with the governing authorities in their homelands cross their borders with the support of smugglers to reach adjacent nations, where the function of the borders shifts from separating to safeguarding them. Turkey is a significant destination for asylum seekers seeking smuggling networks due to

3 ESCAPE: "I HAD SEEN THE DEATHS OF MY CHILDREN WITH MY OWN EYES"

its central location between Iraq, Iran, Syria, and Europe. These human traffickers offer services to desperate people seeking asylum as commodities because they generate substantial profits with minimal investment risk. Smugglers do not incur losses when commodified asylum seekers perish in severe conditions or are arrested by border guards while seeking to survive. The smugglers guarantee their smuggling fees in advance and do not care whether asylum seekers arrive in safe countries or not. Therefore, smugglers routinely abandon asylum seekers in perilous circumstances, resulting in the deaths or imprisonment of many of these subjects, while others must rely on the solidarity of their peers to survive. Kurdish-Yezidi refugees told me that they rely on mutual solidarity to support one another along their escape route. This endeavor, which lasts longer than just their flight and continues in their destination countries in North and West European countries, depends on the mutual solidarity that refugees offer to other refugees. Solidarity is the primary source of their incorporation into their pre-established networks. The Kurdish and Yezidi refugees describe how human traffickers treated them and how they relied on one another to survive in their final destinations.

SMUGGLER NETWORKS

...it took me months before I could find a reliable smuggler network....
—Merdem—France (2)

I made decisions about whether to go to Europe, but it was not an easy decision to put into action since I did not have the means necessary to get out of Turkey. However, I was fortunate enough to inherit a home that my family had owned for many years. It was necessary for me to sell my house to save not only my own life but also the lives of my family members. I paid the smugglers with the money from the sale of the property, yet even this was insufficient because it was necessary to hire trustworthy smugglers. There are two types of smugglers: the first type works with and is supported by the Turkish government to get rid of problematic people like me so that we may all go to hell. The second type of smugglers that engage in human trafficking are the ones who collect the money from the asylum seekers. They then leave these asylum seekers in the middle of the sea, where they are left to either perish or become bewildered in the wilderness. Finding a trustworthy smuggling network took me several months. I had the good fortune to meet these traffickers, who set up my departure on a cargo ship for Italy. I was in the hull of this ship with 13 or 14 asylum seekers. We were shivering down there because it was the midst of winter. Because of the sub-zero conditions, I entertained the thought that we might not make it to Italy alive. After 18 days of being frozen in the ship's hull, we finally made it to Italy. However, this was not the end of our problem. I arrived in a country where I did not speak the language and was evidently in a very precarious economic position. In spite of these challenges, I had the feeling that I was devoted to the struggle for my survival because I was also committed to the rescue of those who I had left behind and to continuing my search for hope.

> *...we fled from death yet simultaneously confronted it in the process of our flight!*
> —Saman—Italy (2)

Smugglers tyrannize us when it comes to money. While smuggling us from Turkey to Greece, they defrauded us of enormous amounts of money. They do not believe in God and have no pity in their hearts. They take advantage of our vulnerable positions and exploit us when they are aware of our challenges. I attempted to use the ferries and fly out of Greece on six separate occasions, but neither of those attempts was successful. Because I could not depart via these means of transportation, I sought to escape Greece in other ways. I met a smuggler and traveled to Albania. We had to flee the authorities who were tailing us before arriving in Albania—it was like something out of a movie. We spent roughly 15 to 20 days in a clandestine and illegal hotel in Albania until I recruited another smuggler. We were often questioned about whether we were Turks everywhere we went. We avoided identifying as Kurds out of concern that Albanians, who adore Turks, may find out and send us to Turkey. We met smugglers there and paid them to help us cross the border into Montenegro, but we were apprehended and returned to the police station in Albania. The officials pushed us to sign a document, which I refused to do. I also refused to provide my fingerprints and apply for asylum. However, I was disheartened when my companion returned to Greece and then Turkey, where he was detained and imprisoned.

The Albanian authorities detained me for the third time and informed me that I would be deported to Turkey since I was unable to leave the country. So, I pulled out a knife and closed the door behind me. I warned him that both he and I would be killed if he went through with deporting me back to Turkey. We did not have a translator; therefore, I was unable

3 ESCAPE: "I HAD SEEN THE DEATHS OF MY CHILDREN WITH MY OWN EYES"

to explain myself, and they were unable to understand me. With the knife, I scratched the inside of my throat and bled. I told him that there was no possibility for him to survive in that room. He screamed, but I shut the door, preventing anyone from entering. I instructed him to provide a translator even though I had locked the door to prevent guards from entering since I would be executed if I were deported to Turkey. A translator arrived and requested that I sign a document so that I could be transferred to the refugee camp. I did not sign anything, but we ultimately agreed that I might be housed in a refugee camp without signing anything. After spending three days in this refugee camp, I was able to successfully flee the facility. I do not remember how it happened, but I ended up talking to a woman from Albania who was fluent in English. In return for money, this woman persuaded her parents to smuggle me into Montenegro, where I spent a month. I then continued to Bosnia and Herzegovina, where I also spent two days. I negotiated with smugglers to take me from one country to the next without success. They were possibly not professional smugglers. I used my phone's translation to ask them how much they wanted. They requested 100 euros, but I countered with an offer of 200 euros: 100 euros in advance and another 100 euros upon my arrival in Croatia.

In Croatia, I was arrested twice. The creation officers were harsh and battered me. They smashed my phone, confiscated my 700 euros, and repatriated me to Bosnia and Herzegovina. I resumed my journey to Croatia but was arrested once again in a forest. It cost me between 600 and 700 euros each time I was detained. I didn't have any money and had to rely on my family, who borrowed it from other relatives and friends. My adventures began in Bosnia and Herzegovina and Slovenia, where I was detained twice. Police dogs had already caught us, so we were unable to escape. The police assumed I was a smuggler after I was caught three times with different groups. I countered this claim and informed them that Bosnia and Herzegovina had many refugee applicants. I constantly joined new groups, but if they let me leave, they'd never run across me again. If not, I would bring a new group with me next time because I have memorized the route. They did not let us leave and instead demanded that we sign a document to be transported to a camp for refugees. However, we were detained for a day before being hauled away in the middle of the night. We opened our eyes at the Zagreb detention camp before being deported to Bosnia and Herzegovina.

74   V. DAG

Every time we attempted to cross national borders, the journey took 12 days, and we ran into a variety of wild animals. I once came upon a bear who nearly ripped me apart. We fled from death yet simultaneously confronted it in the process of our flight. My family prayed for me every day. In the end, my family wanted me to return to Turkey and turn myself in because they wanted to see me alive, even if it meant sending me to prison. They were concerned about whether I was dead or alive every time I embarked on a journey and lost communication with me for 15 or 20 days. I caused them significant emotional and psychological distress. However, I had already removed Turkey from my thoughts, and returning there would result in death. I was sentenced to a 13-year prison term even though I had nothing to do with the crime for which I was condemned. The Turkish authorities attach me to every other crime since I am a Kurd and have previously received a jail sentence. In this way, the Turkish authorities were satisfied. The Turkish authorities would still hold me accountable if I were in Turkey right now, even if I hadn't done anything wrong or if someone had made an accusation against me.

Finally, I ran across a smuggler and agreed to a deal with him. He drove me right up to the Italian border. In total, he smuggled me securely from Bosnia and Herzegovina to Italy in 12 days. On that final journey, I was not detained. This cost me a substantial amount of money. This has placed myself and my family under a lot of stress because we borrowed money, and I spent it all before I got to Italy. I had just 20 euros in my pocket when I arrived in Italy, which was insufficient to cover the bus fare. I requested that my family send this money, but I lacked the necessary legal documents. While I was standing in front of the railway station, I noticed that one of the kebab shops had a name in Turkish. I walked in, explained my predicament to the employee, and requested if I could use his identity to collect this money from my family. He confronted me with yelling and screaming, accusing me of being there to turn his life into hell. A refugee from Pakistan was listening to us as we were talking in his kebab shop. He knew some Turkish because he spent some time in Turkey. He approached me and assured me that he would be able to assist me and that my family could transfer the money in his name. He was able to obtain the money and hand it on to me. When he informed me that he prays every day, I immediately assumed that he must be a kind and helpful guy. After my family had transferred the payment, they texted me the confirmation of the transaction code which I presented to him while waiting in line at Western Union. He suddenly claimed that he needed to use the bathroom

3 ESCAPE: "I HAD SEEN THE DEATHS OF MY CHILDREN WITH MY OWN EYES" 75

since the queue was too lengthy and that I could wait there until he returned. I had just arrived in Europe, and I was nervous due to my destitution and immense hardships en route. I never expected him to deceive me, yet he withdrew this money from another Western Union and vanished. I called my brother to halt the transfer and explained that I had been cuckolded. My brother was late at Western Union, and the money was gone. Apart from my mother, I had no one else to seek money from because my brothers are not wealthy and must support their children and families.

I was hungry and exhausted. I spent two days sleeping on the streets without food. I had a sleeping bag and slept without fear or worry wherever I felt safe. I called a friend of mine who was in Venice. He advised me to meet him at the Kurdish association in Rome. After many difficulties, I arrived in Rome and looked up the address of the Kurdish association on my phone's map application. I arrived at the Kurdish association and explained my predicament to some peers, but they were in the same predicament and were unable to offer much assistance. It's safe to say that we're all victims here. If a person has better circumstances and certain prospects, he or she will not seek assistance from the Kurdish organization since he or she does not rely on it. Perhaps, they will have a cup of tea, ask about us, and then leave. The Kurdish Association provides a safe haven for people who are impoverished, underprivileged, or otherwise disadvantaged. For me and other Kurdish asylum seekers, it is an important entrance. Apart from a friend who told me about a Kurdish organization in Italy that could be willing to put me up for a few days, I had no friends or family in the country.

...the smuggler fled, taking my money with him!
 —Ihsan—Italy (2)

I was forced to flee to South Kurdistan as a fugitive since I was not legally permitted to leave Turkey. My only chance of reaching South Kurdistan was with the help of smuggling networks. Therefore, I had to rely on them. However, we are all aware of the fact that the Turkish intelligence service, known as the MIT, maintains control over the refugee waves, smuggling networks, and routes into South Kurdistan, Rojava, and the entire region of the Middle East. Nevertheless, I had no alternative but to put my future in the hands of a smuggling network. Yet, I exercised caution and negotiated a substantial quantity of money with a smuggler in

South Kurdistan to smuggle me to Europe. My family was the one who collected this money. However, the smuggler fled, taking my money with him. We could not find him, and there was nothing we could do. My family managed to scrape together yet another significant amount of cash and hired another smuggling network to transport me to Europe via South Africa. However, they never bothered to take me across the continent. Instead, they abandoned me in South Africa. I was unable to flee South Africa because I was trapped there. When I arrived in Johannesburg, I did not know anyone and could not speak English. Even though they had originally planned to send me to Switzerland, Germany, or France, this smuggling network abandoned me at the end of the globe to my own fate. However, after my family's intervention, they told me that I could choose Italy, Spain, and Greece rather than the original countries. And they said that if I was dissatisfied with any of these countries, they would simply alter their phone numbers so I could no longer contact them, as they were unable to bring me to other countries. I had also lost all my travel documents, so I was stranded in Johannesburg. Consequently, I reluctantly chose to travel to Italy because I had no other option. They assisted me in traveling to Italy, but I was detained upon my arrival. I had no choice but to submit an asylum application once the authorities took my fingerprints.

> *My children had passed away, yet their bodies came back to life!*
> —Afran—Germany

We fled to Germany because we were left with no other option. We had to endure considerable amounts of trouble on our way here. I had already left Qamishli by the time fighting broke out between Kurdish forces and the Syrian government in 2004. During that period, I was sentenced to six months of imprisonment. After my release, I fled to Lebanon, where I remained until 2017. I was unable to travel to Turkey, Iraq, or Kurdistan from Lebanon. At that time, Turkey did not allow citizens of Syria to enter without first obtaining a visa. I requested a visa through the representative of the Kurdistan Region of Iraq. The Iraqi Kurds also denied my visa. I could not provide a guarantor, or a significant sum of money as requested. I found out that Iranian visa requirements do not apply to Syrian nationals. We flew to Iran with my family, despite not knowing anyone there. Only one smuggler I knew via phone claimed he could get me out of Iran. We also spent three days in Iran. It was extremely difficult for us to leave

Iran for Turkey. My children had passed away, yet their bodies came back to life. I witnessed their suffering with my own eyes. It was quite cold, and we were sleeping outside in the mountains. If we had stayed there for another day, they almost certainly would have perished. The extreme weather made my children incapable of speaking. On the other hand, we believed that once we arrived in Turkey, we would be free from all these hardships.

We spent one week in Turkey before embarking on a boat journey. We were on the water for more than four hours. We were terrified that we would not be able to make it through the night at sea. Nevertheless, God assisted us in escaping to Greece, where we lived in tents for 11 months. My children had skin rashes because of the infections that were spreading in the refugee camps. Hot water was not available to us. It was snowing, so we had to take cold showers. There was no electricity, and things were in a terrible state overall. The sole saving grace was that the officials smiled at us. They indicated that they could only offer us a smile and assist us in surviving. After 11 months, we were granted asylum, but we departed for Germany. We believed we had arrived in paradise when we first came to Germany and compared our circumstances to those in other countries. We did not have to live in tents. We resided in a room with four walls. Hot water was also available. My children are secure while receiving necessary medical care. However, when we went to court, we were informed that we had to return to Greece since we had been awarded refuge in Greece, not Germany. We informed the authorities that we felt obliged to seek asylum in Greece since the Greek authorities warned us that we had no option but to provide our fingerprints or be deported to Turkey. We had no other choices available. In short, they made our lives miserable.

...human trafficking violates our social, moral, and ethical principles!
—Yekdan—Italy

Kurdish asylum seekers describe how human traffickers treated them cruelly when they arrived at our office. We attempt to intervene as effectively as possible. We always support Kurdish asylum seekers because human trafficking violates our social, moral, and ethical principles. We acknowledge their efforts to aid Kurdish asylum seekers who are fleeing for their lives, but human trafficking is an abhorrent and immoral practice that we reject. Our organization also offers workshops on human trafficking that explain why we oppose it and work to prevent it. Some individuals may also discuss the positive aspects of human trafficking, and we can appreciate their point that politically persecuted activists would be unable to escape if smugglers did not operate. This is a debatable topic, but we cannot defend human trafficking if the negative aspects outweigh the positive ones. In any case, I believe that those who engage in the trafficking of people are fully aware of the stance that we have taken against them. Consequently, they never approach our organization or come near us. They know exactly what we would do to them if they lived among us. We would also take legal action against them if we discovered they were human traffickers. We would also notify police stations to monitor and be vigilant regarding the individuals we suspect of being involved in human trafficking. These smugglers are in no way affiliated with the Kurdish association. Kurdish human traffickers from South Kurdistan, for example, prevented Kurdish asylum seekers from South Kurdistan from approaching our organization because they were misinformed, we would deport them to Iraq. They must have some compassion before they disseminate these lies because we do not have the planes, the money, or any other legal rights to arrest and deport these refugees to South Kurdistan or Iraq. They are here as a product of violent conflicts. However, these human traffickers discredit our organization and discourage refugees from joining to continue their lucrative human trafficking businesses. They smuggle refugees and hold them hostage for a week or ten days, but on top of the smuggling expenses, they also charge them for their accommodations in a park or their food. They have created an industry out of human trafficking, which is a terrible development.

Country Search

...authorities in every country we visit arrest and deport us to Italy....
   —Sherzat—Italy

I have been granted asylum in Italy, but it provides me with no advantages. We have fought hard for our rights, but we have been unable to receive assistance because Italy is a corrupt country. The authorities assert that seven million Italians suffer from starvation, so they cannot respond to our requirements regarding how to support us. There are numerous refugees, and the authorities are unable to assist us. They tell us that we have been granted asylum rights to live in Italy, but if we are not satisfied, we are free to return to our home countries, where we face conflict,

3 ESCAPE: "I HAD SEEN THE DEATHS OF MY CHILDREN WITH MY OWN EYES"

corruption, and discrimination. We are subjected to oppression and discrimination at the hands of Turks, Arabs, and Iranians throughout the region. Therefore, we cannot return to our home countries to live normally under their oppression. We have multiple problems with our relatives since they do not understand why we fled to Italy, given that everyone is aware of how corrupt and deceitful both Italy and Greece are. However, I am obligated to reside in Italy, and it makes no difference whether I have my own apartment or slumber in the streets and parks. It's up to me to sort out my own problems. So, we left our home country with just one problem but arrived in Italy with ten additional problems and difficulties, where we receive nothing more than macaroni, which the government feeds to refugees like they do to street dogs. In Italy, refugees are not treated as human beings. Even dogs are more valued—they are fed inside houses while humans feed on the streets. I've lived in Italy for five years but have received no assistance from the government. My relatives send me money so that I can stay here, but they are unable to support me in this way on a long-term basis. Being homeless in parks in Italy exposes us to prejudice, and we have no idea how to resolve our problems.

Even though most Kurds in these cities have been granted political asylum, they are still homeless. It baffles me that we must sleep outside even though we have been granted political asylum. Kurdish refugees flee their native country and seek asylum in four, five, or even six countries. However, they ultimately arrived in Italy, where asylum has been granted. Some of our acquaintances with Italian documents have been detained in Germany and sentenced to three, four, or six months in prison for violating German law, as they are not permitted to work in Germany with their Italian papers. They are presently imprisoned in Germany. We face a year in prison in Norway and six months in Swedish prison if we dare to work there. Following the completion of their prison terms, these refugees are then repatriated to Italy. Therefore, authorities in every country we visit arrest and deport us to Italy, where the government welcomes us to live and sleep in these parks without receiving any social welfare benefits or assistance services.

The lack of social assistance and benefits in Italy is well known. We are humiliated and deeply regret that we came to Italy to seek asylum. We often become ill, even if it is not too severe, but we do not have the means to wash ourselves, so we become filthy because we are sleeping on the streets and in parks. I have been to the hospital, but I have not been treated there. After waiting seven or eight hours, doctors informed me that I was in good health. Doctors do not refer us to specialists and examine us thoroughly, as would be expected of Italian citizens. Regarding language courses, I went to the council a week ago and requested that the authorities provide me with morning-to-evening language classes. They informed me, however, that the local mayor and Italian laws have changed, and therefore they are unable to help me learn the language. So, they suggested that I study Italian with a retired woman at the church or a local charity three times a week for two hours so that I might learn two words. We are wasting our time without gaining any language knowledge. They won't allow me to attend an intense session to learn the language correctly. We are unable to find work; therefore, we continue to be homeless and sleep in public spaces like parks since we lack the language skills.

Every time that we go to the council, the officers there tell us that although they understand our suffering and issues, they are unable to assist us because they lack the authority to do so. Despite being awarded political refuge, decision-makers do not provide us with such an opportunity to regulate our lives. We're advised to go to a church for lunch, but the church requires us to obtain a number to eat. We can eat if we obtain a number, but we aren't allowed to eat without one. I frequently went to the church by myself when I was hungry, but I was told there were no more numbers. The church let 20 people inside to feed them, but it abandoned 50 others who were hungry outside. The church is unable to provide food to everyone who came to ask for it. I was thus present and allowed to eat once every two days. This occurs in Italy, even though it is considered a part of Europe. We provide meals to refugees from other countries, so they are satisfied and treated with dignity when they arrive in our country. We invite them to our home, slaughter a sheep for them, and offer them everything of value we possess. In contrast, we now live in a European country but cannot even locate a place in the pasta queue and must wait two days. This is the Kurds' misfortune: we do not have our own state and hence have no power or authority to govern our own land.

...we are like nomads!
—Mako—Italy

In 1995, I was imprisoned for political reasons in Turkey. After serving a year in jail, I was finally released, but I was unable to remain in Turkey any longer. I decided that the only option I had was to run, and I made arrangements with the traffickers to go by truck. We arrived in Trieste four

3 ESCAPE: "I HAD SEEN THE DEATHS OF MY CHILDREN WITH MY OWN EYES"

days later. When we arrived at the Customs House, the officials intended to send us back, but we hurt ourselves to appear psychologically unstable. We were let go and put in a madhouse for three days. We were prepared to hurt ourselves to prevent our deportation to Turkey, which might have meant the end of our lives. We could have faced severe repercussions in Turkey for political reasons. We were willing to do whatever it took to prevent our deportation. In addition, I was married and had five children. I had to consider my family as well. In the end, I applied for asylum in Italy after 10 or 15 days but moved promptly to Germany. However, we were unaware that, under the Dublin Treaty, we would be repatriated to the first country where we were fingerprinted. We were detained as we crossed the border into Germany, but we had already submitted an asylum request. After six months, German officials handcuffed me and extradited me to Italy. They also barred me from entering Germany, for which I was fined and forced to pay deportation and travel expenses. I returned to Italy, but the Italian authorities refused to accept me. I had to struggle through the asylum procedure until I was awarded refugee status, which was irrelevant because it did not provide us with any social benefits. However, I sold my home in Kurdistan in 2001, packed up my family, and moved to Rome. I used this money to send my children and wife to Italy. I used my own money to construct a cottage for us to live near the Kurdish association. For a few months, I lived in a 50-square-meter barrack with my children and wife. I had no choice but to construct a portable bathroom and toilet since there was no other way to house all five of my children. I was unable to rent a place and pay the rent. I then moved to the Toscano region and have since worked in the agricultural industry, where I harvest olives and fruits.

As refugees, we are like nomads. We fled our homeland because we were denied the freedom to live peacefully there. We are in Italy, yet there is no permanent and constant settlement space for us. We might be expelled from this country and sent somewhere else at the government's discretion. We are continually concerned that this country is not our home. I believe that 60 to 70 percent of the Kurdish refugees living here are sick due to psychological issues. I recently underwent heart surgery, even though I am not that old. Most people have these health problems, even though they are only 20 or 30 years old. It's already 2019, and I left in the year 1998. I am unable to go back to my home country and begin a fresh life there. I cannot attend the funerals of my parents, siblings, and other relatives if they pass away. Since I no longer have any spiritual ties,

82   V. DAG

even if I owned this planet, I could not restore them. We have lost the core of our social and cultural humanity, yet we are still attempting to live to survive. We have been alienated after living abroad for 20 years, and we cannot ask someone to say hello to someone if they visit our country. To be honest, our lives were converted into sorrow and tragedy resulting from our statelessness. This is my own opinion, and it does not imply that we are not psychologically and physically well when we can work and put money in our wallets. We are still working for peanuts to avoid begging for food and being hungry. Therefore, we must strive to subsist, as neither the government nor anyone else helps.

Survival

My wife was pregnant at the time, and our unborn child perished in her womb!
   —Serwer—Germany

I crossed the Turkish border and fled Kobanî in September 2015. We first arrived in Istanbul, then Izmir, where I came across smugglers. We were each charged 2500 euros to travel to Greece. They smuggled my family and me into Europe after I paid them to help us escape Turkey. When we arrived in Greece, the authorities refused to accept our asylum requests and promptly sent us to Hungary and other Balkan countries such as Croatia, Serbia, and Austria until we arrived in Germany, where we were detained and fingerprinted. My pregnant wife was suffering from these terrible conditions. There were 15,000 asylum aspirants, so we were forced to slumber in a hall with 200–300 other refugees or in tents outside. We decided to continue our journey and seek refuge in Norway, where we submitted our asylum applications. We were assigned to a location where we were unable to see any other people. However, we were only able to stay there for a total of three months before we had to leave. My wife was pregnant at the time, and our unborn child perished in her womb. Our fingerprints revealed to the asylum officials that we had previously asked for asylum in Germany. They asked us whether we wanted to stay in Norway or return to Germany. We decided to return to Germany and arrived in Hamburg, where we spent a month in a refugee shelter with numerous asylum seekers. After I started feeling sick, doctors determined that I had brain cancer. However, we have not been granted political asylum in the three years since we arrived in Berlin, despite the destruction of our city, Kobanî, and the loss of all our possessions.

3 ESCAPE: "I HAD SEEN THE DEATHS OF MY CHILDREN WITH MY OWN EYES" 83

They terrorized us, shattered our wills, and stripped us of our dignity!
—Amed—Austria

When I was detained, the police officers put gloves on and stripped me down—I was with a group of ten naked asylum applicants. They terrorized us, shattered our wills, and stripped us of our dignity. When I was detained in Turkey on suspicion of terrorism, for instance, the police stripped me naked, harassed me, and subjected me to brutality. We are here to seek sanctuary from terrorism, yet this makes me feel like some kind of terrorist who has come to hurt others. They undressed me and examined my genitalia, treating me as if I were a terrorist. They opened my mount for inspection. I was extremely embarrassed by the way I was treated. I was unprepared for this treatment and viewed it as hostile, mafia-like, and untamed.

The European police treated us similarly to their Turkish counterparts. They began to interrogate me, but I could not communicate in their language. They took along a Turkish translator who collaborated with the police officers and acted similarly to them. As if he were a detective, he inquired about every aspect of my life and the routes I had taken to get there. This translator operated on behalf of the Turkish government and presented me as a terrorist to European authorities. As a Turkish citizen in a foreign country, I still encounter discrimination despite my distance from the Turkish government. I was detained in every country I crossed until I was nearly returned to Turkey, where I am now wanted on an outstanding arrest warrant and might potentially spend the rest of my life in jail. Therefore, the authorities in the countries through which we traveled did not care that we were asylum applicants fleeing persecution. My predicament and appeal were disregarded. Despite these difficulties, I asked for asylum and ended up in a refugee camp where I was provided soap and linen to bathe and shave. I felt like I had rolled about in the mud and filth and that I was trapped within a prison cell. Since I had previously spent time in prison, I could not distinguish between these conditions and those of a prison; we were required to shower in a cubicle and shave. After that, we were given beds in a bunk configuration. We were also provided with suitable clothing and footwear, both of which we were also supplied with when we were imprisoned.

The way of life and organizational structure in the camp were exactly like those found in a prison. At a certain time in the morning, we were required to get up and have breakfast. If I had missed this time frame, I

84 V. DAG

would not have eaten breakfast and would have had to wait till noon. We have to wait until dinner if we are late for lunch. There was always a set mealtime, and if we missed it, we were not permitted to eat. We were allowed to be outdoors from 8 a.m. to 8 p.m., and we were required to check in to ensure that we came before 8 p.m. Being late prevented us from entering again. This corresponded to the hours of operation of semi-open prisons in Turkey. This indicated that the authorities attempted to assimilate us into the prison system by adjusting us to it. They wanted us to focus solely on food and to sever all ties to our homeland, culture, and identity to conform us to the model they drew for our integration. As a result, we were compelled, along with other refugees, to capitulate and be at the discretion of the authorities, as if we were hostages at the mercy of hostile military forces who sought to eradicate us. As a condition for my continued survival, I was required to maintain my allegiance to them in return for the impression of being held prisoner. We are required to sign the terms and conditions governing what time we sleep, go, and return to the refugee camps. We are expelled from the refugee camps if we fail to sign it three times. Only a two-day absence is permitted for each of us currently. We are facing sanctions for the third day. We are prohibited from migrating to another city or leaving our federal state under this contract unless we have a judicial or medical appointment. This means we are subjected to terrible circumstances, endure prejudice from authorities, and live in prison-like conditions.

I am looking for anything to help me stay alive!
—Cotkar—France

My father encouraged me to go to Europe because he was concerned that I might join the Kurdish guerrillas when I grew up. My grandfather solicited the assistance of his nephews as well as a close family friend who lives in France. He believed that they would assist me upon my arrival and clear the path for a new life. However, my family did not assist me in any manner upon my arrival. They only gave me an address for my asylum case, but they turned their backs on me when they failed to inform me that OFPRA had invited me to an interview regarding my asylum claim. Consequently, I was unable to attend my asylum interview. My acquaintance informed me that the OFPRA had denied my asylum application. I appealed twice to the commission in an attempt to overturn the rejection decision, but they remained adamant in their stance. During my two years

3 ESCAPE: "I HAD SEEN THE DEATHS OF MY CHILDREN WITH MY OWN EYES"

without legal documents, I did not even possess an identification card. These officials lacked compassion for my situation and constantly questioned me in an untrustworthy manner. The higher court ruled that I am recognized as a refugee from Kurdistan, a non-existent sovereign state. Since I did not have a country to which they could deport me, they determined that I was allowed to stay and live in France. They told me I could start a new life in France, but they did not grant me permission to work or the right to apply for social welfare benefits. I am still confused about why they made that decision; maybe they were implying that I should steal in order to maintain my standard of living.

Since then, 14 years have passed. I'm not sure how this time has flown, but it has not passed swiftly. I continually moved from one flat to another. I move every two years since I don't work and cannot afford to pay my rent. I am frequently evicted from my apartment if I do not pay my rent. Often, I simply abandon the premises. I sometimes work illegally for four, five, or seven days a week to pay my rent and support my living expenses. I am looking for anything to help me stay alive. When I apply for jobs, the employers always want to know whether I have a permanent residence card. I cannot rent a flat because I lack the necessary documents and funds, and I am not permitted to work. Without money, I will starve to death and be unable to eat, drink, or even stand on my own two feet. This implies that I have a lower position in our community, as if I were nothing. This attitude is unusual to me, and I was unaware of it while in Kurdistan. This is an additional obstacle I must overcome. Life in Europe is difficult. My existence depends on my ability to obtain residency here. The Kurdish association, however, gives me strength and fills me with love, passion, and optimism because I feel spiritually supported.

We take every risk without being too concerned....
—Arshin—Italy

Normally, we prefer to apply for asylum rights in West European states, but our applications are often denied unless we provide solid documents and evidence that we deserve refugee status. However, Italy does not reject any asylum applications and grants asylum rights to everyone who applies for them. As a result, refugees are free to engage in any conduct of their choice since the Italian government does not restrict their movement and actively encourages them to leave the country. I have also received my documents, but it makes no difference whether we, as exiles in Italy, have them. If we possess legal papers, we may only be permitted to leave for other European countries, where we may find alternative possibilities for illegal employment since we are not allowed to work with Italian refugee status. When the police officers take us into custody, they deport us to Italy right away. However, for us Kurdish refugees, being apprehended and deported is not a particularly pressing concern since the way we have endured suffering and been subjected to anguish has been of an extraordinary kind. Furthermore, we are unconcerned with the repercussions and will find a means to return to the countries from which we were deported to work, as we have no opportunities or viable alternatives in Italy. We do not have a long-term plan or a project to establish ourselves and conduct our lives in Italy, and we do not now have such plans or objectives. Apart from a small number of Kurdish refugees who are forced to live in deplorable circumstances, there is no Kurdish community in Italy. We take every risk without being too concerned since we have no desire to become Italian citizens. We wish to be granted indefinite leave so that we can move to Germany or another European country to swap our residence permits there. In several European states, Kurds are well organized, have established institutional structures, and are involved in a variety of activities. However, similar communities, organizations, and activities do not exist in Italy.

SOLIDARITY

...discussing aspects of friendship, collective life, and solidarity!
—Bawer—France

I was compelled to choose exile in France as a result of my political engagement in Turkey. It was impossible to live in Turkey due to police harassment and threats. I consulted with my family and informed them that I could no longer live safely and peacefully in Turkey. My family approved my escape from Turkey to Europe. I then traveled to Istanbul from my hometown, where I met a group of smugglers. I was smuggled to Greece along with other asylum applicants. However, the Greek police detained us and placed us in a dark cell in a refugee camp, where we did not see the sun for 40 days. Authorities threatened to deport me to Turkey if I did not register for asylum in Greece during my stay there. However, it was not my choice to ask for refuge in Greece, but I did not have another option. I did not trust the Greek government, which has had a strong

3 ESCAPE: "I HAD SEEN THE DEATHS OF MY CHILDREN WITH MY OWN EYES" 87

relationship with Turkey since the Ottoman Empire and was dealing with an economic crisis and an array of other issues. Since I did not believe the Greeks, I told the authorities that I did not wish to live in Greece and instead wished to move to Switzerland. They denied my request and threatened me with deportation to Turkey. They held me and many other peers as hostages in a refugee camp called Flako Refugee Camp, which cannot be adequately described in words. People left their feces all over the room, went to the toilet barefoot, and then returned to their beds to sit or sleep. They had never cleaned their hands and were covered in grime. The authorities did not permit us to use a smartphone, only a regular mobile phone, in order to prevent us from filming and documenting the dirt and filth in this refugee camp. I also met eight politically persecuted Kurdish asylum seekers in this camp.

We spent 40 days together in this refugee camp, which felt like a prison. In each cell, there were 40 male asylum seekers—Arabs, Afghans, and individuals from other ethnic groups. Some asylum seekers told us that they had not seen the sun in six months. They were disgruntled but disorganized. They even had to engage in combat to obtain some food. Nevertheless, we organized and educated them over a period of 40 days, discussing aspects of friendship, collective life, and solidarity. We described the PKK to them and the circumstances surrounding our flight to Greece. Additionally, we warned the Greek police in the camp that we had already sent a message to the outside world that we would go on hunger strike if they would not let us out. We wished to request that human rights organizations investigate the conditions of this refugee camp because we were subjected to inhumane treatment. The authorities humiliated us and treated us like animals, even though I have no contempt for animals—they are also living beings. Ten days after we sent out the warning message, the authorities took ten of us Kurdish asylum seekers from among the other asylum seekers and divided us up into five groups, with two people in each cell. After a few days, they started releasing us from this refugee camp, which resembled a prison. After being released, I was able to carry on using my smartphone and access the internet.

I attempted to communicate with friends who were released prior to me through Facebook and Messenger. Despite some obstacles, I was able to reach out to these friends and inquire about the address of the Kurdish association, called the House of Kurds in Athens, to which they referred me. However, the city was like a ghetto, and it was impossible to locate this address. Consequently, I was unable to find my route, but fortunately,

I was able to communicate my whereabouts to some friends from the Kurdish association, who were able to find me and pick me up. They brought me to the Kurdish Association, where I met several new friends who had been living in the area for two or three years. These friends offered me shelter and assisted me in obtaining a new phone card, shaving, and meeting my fundamental needs. They arranged for my journey to a refugee camp, where I came across many North Kurdish asylum seekers fleeing Turkey after the collapse of the peace process. Numerous asylum seekers from Rojava and North Kurdistan, as well as the Botan areas, were among those I encountered. In this particular camp, every single person who was requesting asylum was of Kurdish origin. The Kurds have established a modest, communal life in this container-truck-based temporary camp. I stayed in this camp for six months. During my time there, I learned how to live a community life with others by sharing resources and responsibilities. We also managed our own security and obtained food from the International Red Cross. However, this organization has stopped supplying us with food. I made the decision to escape the camp and travel to France. When I arrived in Paris, I went immediately to the Kurdish House, where I knew no one. My peers, however, welcomed me with open arms and helped me meet my basic needs by giving me food and cigarettes. I spent nearly all my time in Paris living in a district that had been predominantly inhabited by Kurds for the past three decades. There are Kurdish adults who are my age but were born and raised there. The Kurdish people there are kind and willing to help others. There is a Kurdish association here as well. It is inherent to our Kurdish culture to lead a communal and shared life. We cannot live distinct lives or be disconnected.

Asylum seekers establish their diplomatic channels and channels of cooperation....
—Ozcan—Sweden

I escaped to Sweden through Greece. During this time, I befriended many Kurdish refugees who were on their way to escape. These peers were scattered throughout various European nations, including France, Switzerland, Germany, and the Netherlands. We were in constant communication with one another and offered mutual support. Nonetheless, I have the impression that these long-distance connections are diminishing as we lose physical communication and Kurdish refugees confront many individual problems. Our conversations are dwindling, and we no longer need to assist one another. When we initially left our homeland, we maintained frequent communication because the need for mutual help was very strong. In this context, we backed each other when we requested assistance. We referred each other to Kurdish organizations. The issues for which we sought advice were associated with our asylum predicament. There were problems we wished to address and for which we had to seek advice. For instance, we were unfamiliar with asylum procedures in a particular country or unable to address other concerns, so we referred each other to diasporic Kurdish associations. Kurdish association in Greece was unavoidable for our asylum application entering Europe due to the paucity of individual contacts in Greece.

I assert that we are engaged in migration diplomacy, which concerns the immigration and asylum policies of different countries. This includes deportation, border policy, the length of the asylum procedure, and the length of the residency permit. I believe that comparable diplomacy exists between immigrants, asylum seekers, and refugees as well. When I was in Greece, for instance, I observed numerous asylum seekers asking each other which country offers the best opportunities and where they should submit asylum claims. This is a form of diplomacy between those seeking asylum. Occasionally, they asked me where to apply for asylum rights. We provide each other with information, such as the fact that asylum seekers should not seek refuge in Sweden due to its lengthy asylum procedures but that asylum applications are processed swiftly and positively in the Netherlands. Denmark is not a welcoming country for asylum seekers, but Germany and certain German federal states are. We learned this information from the refugees we encountered in Greece. They share their experiences with us, and we pass this information along to newly arrived asylum seekers. Asylum seekers establish their own diplomatic channels and channels of cooperation regarding asylum trafficking and conditions in certain European nations. In this manner, the asylum seekers encourage one another to submit their applications in countries with greater opportunities. They also share information regarding the routes they select and the smuggling networks with which they seek collaboration.

All of this is vital information that determines whether asylum claimants will die or survive. Normally, this information is considered confidential and cannot be officially retained in a single location. Several associations may possess some of this information. However, the experience, knowledge, and internal dissemination within the networks of asylum seekers are crucial for providing the information that asylum seekers require before,

90   V. DAG

during, and after their journeys to escape. We listen to multiple asylum seekers, monitor various situations, and collect information from a variety of asylum seekers. In addition, we discuss the refugee policies of these countries, their conditions, and other opportunities and obstacles shared by our asylum-seeking peers. We are aware, for instance, that the procedure for requesting asylum takes a significantly longer amount of time in this country compared to other European countries. When some asylum applicants travel through Italy, for instance, they may be unfamiliar with Italian refugee policy. If they are exhausted and out of money, they could apply for asylum in Italy and provide fingerprints. However, we encourage them to put forth additional effort to reach Switzerland. This is very important information. We also discourage them from seeking asylum in France, where there are no refugee camps and asylum applicants must sleep outside unless they have relatives who can house them. We inquire whether they have information or are in contact with Kurdish organizations that can assist in providing shelter. I have complete knowledge about the Swedish refugee policy and conditions, whereas my peers in France have the same knowledge regarding the French refugee matter. We have up-to-date information and share it with our asylum-seeking peers.

> *...we are in solidarity with each other in times of sadness and happiness.*
> —Mergewer—France

We strive to address the issues facing our Kurdish community segments, which include asylum seekers. We are aware of our problems and take responsibility for each other's concerns through a self-support service unaffiliated with any political movement or particular Kurdish group. We provide humanitarian assistance to refugees from all parts of Kurdistan, including the south, east, west, and north. I witnessed over a hundred instances of mutual self-support services. This region serves as a stopover for Kurdish asylum seekers who remain for one or two days before continuing to Germany, the United Kingdom, and other European countries. We look after them because we are aware of the circumstances surrounding them, regardless of the reasons why they are escaping. They rest for a few days in this city and have dinner for free at the Kurdish restaurant. Since all Kurdish immigrants come together at this restaurant, they meet and assist new asylum seekers. The Kurdish refugees in this area are very different from those in other places. We are all from the same town and metropolis in the Serhat region, but there are no refugees from Botan or

Amed. We are all very familiar with one another because we all work in the construction sector. Most Kurdish refugees are undocumented, adding to the myriad challenges they face. They work without documents, but it is difficult for them because several Kurdish business owners are unwilling to take on the risks associated with employing undocumented asylum seekers. They are not allowed to hire undocumented people who are applying for asylum, and if they are caught doing so, they face the consequence of being penalized with massive fines. Nonetheless, the refugee seekers without papers are given some chances to work. We assist them in alleviating some of their problems.

In general, we are in solidarity with each other in times of sadness and happiness. In the event of a death, for instance, all Kurdish refugees residing in this area pool their resources to cover funeral transportation costs or send the funds to the affected families in Kurdistan. We accept responsibility for and demonstrate solidarity with other Kurdish asylum applicants, irrespective of their participation in the Kurdish movement or struggle. We have solidarity with Kurdish asylum applicants in need due to our shared humanity, regardless of the lack of our statehood. These practices have been carried out for thousands of years, and this is one of the origins of our solidarity. If we had a state, however, we could have had a formal institution that could have coordinated these issues and made provisions for solidarity. However, being stateless means that the Kurds have greater solidarity that is not based on the functional service of state institutions but is more intimate, emotional, and founded on mutual commitment.

We are people who are filled with compassion and mercy as we assist those who have been homeless and are in need. For this reason, we do not necessarily require a state to provide us with support, as our history of solidarity predates nation states. We still possess the spirit of our history of solidarity, but a modern state could obliterate this sense of Kurdish solidarity. It is not just about human beings as Kurds but also about our landscape, our stones, and our rivers, which are also Kurdish and serve as another source of solidarity. In this manner, we support one another in France, just as we support our families and colleagues back home. We celebrate traditional Kurdish festivals as a collective group and with lots of color to preserve our culture and traditions. Even though we do not have our own organization, we maintain the distinctive social relationships that are typical in Kurdistan. We even demonstrate our solidarity with Turks who require our services. Additionally, we assist Afghani refugees. Since we Kurds are stateless and permanently subjugated, we can relate to the feelings and anguish of other marginalized populations. This also applies to Tamils; even if they are in a distant country, we remain open to them and demonstrate our sympathy and solidarity with them. We do not simply exist for our own people and love ourselves; rather, we exist for other people who have had experiences comparable to our own, even though their racial or geographic backgrounds may be categorically different from ours. This trait of solidarity is inherited in our nature and has existed throughout our history. We have created a new identity for the subjugated.

CHAPTER 4

Asylum Processes and Challenges: "We Neither Die nor Live but Receive Some Breath"

The plight of Kurdish-Yezidi asylum seekers and refugees extends beyond oppression by the ruling regimes and maltreatment by smugglers during their journey to escape persecution in their home countries; it also persists in various forms in European receiving countries throughout the asylum process. These involve their arrival and placement in refugee camps, as well as the legal processes surrounding their asylum applications. Kurdish-Yezidi asylum seekers frequently attempt to escape to certain European destination nations, such as Germany, the Netherlands, Austria, Sweden, Norway, and the United Kingdom, while avoiding transit nations such as France, Italy, and Greece. There are a number of factors that play a role in determining why Kurdish-Yezidi refugees choose to seek asylum in the countries of northern and western Europe. Some of these aspects include the availability of refugee camps, asylum-friendly legislation, the generosity of social welfare benefits and resources, as well as employment and educational prospects.

Kurdish-Yezidi asylum seekers have access to information about the refugee camp regulations and asylum policies of European governments thanks to their social capital, which consists of informal social networks and mutual trust. This knowledge is one of the key determinants of their choice of destination countries. They refrain from applying for asylum in South European nations such as Greece, France, and Italy based on the available information to them. This is because these European nations lack a consistent reception policy, refugee camps, and robust welfare systems,

---

© The Author(s), under exclusive license to Springer Nature Switzerland AG 2024
V. Dag, *Voices of the Disenfranchized*, Mobility & Politics,
https://doi.org/10.1007/978-3-031-46809-4_4

94   V. DAG

whereas Germany, Austria, Sweden, and Norway have well-established refugee camps and generous welfare systems.

Kurdish-Yezidi asylum applicants in Greece, Italy, and France frequently fail to secure reception in refugee camps and subsequently opt for a clandestine life. Even if some asylum seekers are admitted to refugee camps, they live in dismay and prison-like circumstances. Consequently, many asylum seekers in France, Italy, and Greece are forced to live on the streets rather than in refugee camps. This policy also denies asylum seekers access to health services, basic necessities, and social life, often forcing them into life-threatening situations. Even if the claims of Kurdish asylum seekers have been approved in many South European countries, including France and Italy, their approval of refugee status does little improve their situation due to weak and underdeveloped integration policies. In Italy and France, for example, Kurdish refugees are not provided with housing, language classes, job training and qualifications, or access to general resources necessary for settling in and finding a place in the new social environments. In the reception and integration processes, asylum seekers in southern European states are often abandoned, whereas their counterparts in northern and western European states are accommodated in refugee centers and provided with essential necessities. However, asylum seekers typically find themselves in refugee camps situated in isolated rural locations, away from the general population, and face additional legal and structural challenges. Therefore, they frequently voiced their discontent with the geographical locations, management practices, attitudes of the authorities, and regulations of each refugee camp.

Kurdish-Yezidi asylum seekers in North and West European nations are, to varied degrees, locked in prolonged asylum proceedings. Particularly, Kurdish-Yezidi asylum seekers from Turkey and Iraq are subject to exclusive and restricted measures by migration authorities. Their asylum claims are frequently denied, leaving them in a state of ambiguity, anxiety, and emotional distress. A significant number of applications submitted by many asylum seekers over a lengthy period have been refused, despite substantial evidence confirming their political persecution and outstanding arrest warrants issued by authoritarian governments in Turkey and Iraq. The affected asylum applicants are challenging adverse rulings on their asylum applications. However, court cases are often delayed for years, impacting the lives and perspectives of asylum applicants and forcing them into an uncertain world. These restrictive asylum policies have devastating effects on the lives of a great number of Kurdish-Yezidi asylum seekers.

4 ASYLUM PROCESSES AND CHALLENGES: "WE NEITHER DIE NOR LIVE... 95

They are subject to exploitation in the housing and employment sectors. This policy forces Kurdish-Yezidi asylum seekers into the hands of Kurdish and non-Kurdish landlords and employers who have established a clandestine system, or self-defined "dark world" in which they exploit the fragile conditions and vulnerable status of asylum seekers in question. While many landlords in this clandestine world charge high rents for the substandard, unregistered housing they rent to asylum seekers, many employers allow them to work in hazardous conditions for more than 12 hours per day at below minimum wage. Numerous employers on construction sites refuse to pay undocumented and illicitly employed asylum seekers their wage. Therefore, many asylum seekers expressed their dismay at the predicament that their economic, social, and emotional exploitation had placed them in, which was a direct effect of the reception and asylum procedures. In the next chapters, the Kurdish-Yezidi asylum seekers will delve into more detail on the integration process. In this chapter, asylum seekers and refugees of Kurdish-Yezidi background tell their own stories, in their own words, about their experiences after landing in new host nations.

REFUGEE CAMP

The authorities deal with us asylum seekers as if we are potential criminals!
—Serbilind—Austria

I live in a semi-open prison. I am like a hostage, as I am not free to leave my refugee camp and am banned from traveling abroad, obtaining employment, or learning the language. The authorities provide me with a bed in a room in a refugee camp and tell me to stay for many days and nights. I have to be inside from 9 a.m. to 10 p.m. I cannot go to the city center as I am prohibited from leaving the refugee camp. If I am absent for three days, the authorities will relinquish all my rights and kick me out of my room. My asylum seeker friends in other camps tell me that they do not dare leave the refugee camp for even one day, as they worry that they will be kicked out if the authorities find out that they were absent for one night. They will call the cops, who might start an investigation and take legal action against them, which may affect their asylum process. The guards come and check whether we are in our rooms every evening and count us every day, as in a Turkish prison. The authorities treat us asylum seekers as if we are potential criminals.

96   V. DAG

The government agencies do not care whether we are thirsty, hungry, sick, or have any other issues. They pay us €42 every week and tell us to buy whatever we want with this money, which does not even cover our basic needs. For example, I smoke, and this money is insufficient for my cigarettes, let alone for food and drink. I am also not allowed to work and earn money because I do not have permission. I can only work when I receive my asylum rights, but it is also uncertain whether and when I will receive my resident's permit. When I was in my homeland, I lived in much better conditions. For example, at least I was not hungry, but in Austria, I'm starving. This refutes the fact that nobody is starving in Europe. Asylum seekers and refugees in Europe are starving. We cannot even leave the camp with €42. Some asylum seekers might obtain illicit employment, but they are heavily exploited, and their employers end up being bloodsuckers. Generally, workers do not receive their wages, which are very low anyway. Asylum seekers are employed in refugee camps, and they are paid €1.50 per hour. Where in the world is labor paid €1.50? People would rather starve to death than work for this amount of money. Since the conditions have harmed my mental health in the refugee camp, I designate it as worse than a prison. I have already been imprisoned and am aware of what it means to live under the conditions of imprisonment. In Turkish prisons, I had friends speaking the same language and sharing the same culture. We could entertain and interact with each other. However, I now have to live with refugees from Afghanistan, Iran, Libya, and Egypt in a room. How can we understand and get along with each other? Neither our cultures and languages nor our other social attributes fit together. I do not understand what the criteria are that force these different people to live in one room. By doing this, the authorities are encouraging us to kill each other or live in a way in which we are isolated and live in solitary conditions. I feel like I am being punished, and I am instructed to stay here until they permit me to leave when I receive asylum.

Austrian citizens view us asylum seekers as criminals, animals, and non-humans. They are very arrogant and look down on us. This bothers me very much and has a very negative impact that I do not accept. That is the way society looks at us. It is as if I am being imprisoned until my asylum claim is successful. I will feel released from prison when I receive my residence permit. With a resident's permit, I will be recognized as a normal individual who can take part in life in Austria. Currently, I do not exist, but I am in a permanent state of punishment. As part of my asylum rights, I have permission to obtain employment and participate in a language course, but I will face bureaucratic issues and more paperwork after my asylum application is successful. The biggest benefits of a resident's permit would be free movement and the ability to travel to other countries. As I am on hunger strike at the Kurdish House at the moment, I am not staying in the refugee camp. I have asked for official permission to leave the refugee camp for my hunger strike, and the authority in charge of my camp approved my request. I am lucky that I have a nice manager who is not too harsh on me. I have been on hunger strike for 110 days, and I do not worry about the consequences of my action in this country. I escaped from my homeland in Turkey because I was a Kurdish politician and was persecuted for political reasons.

I suffered a lot, but I am OK with that!
   —Sinem—Germany

I feel comfortable in refugee camps in Germany, where I can see doctors and ask the camp administration for more attention as I am pregnant. We have even been allocated to a new refugee camp with better facilities, even though it was a bit hard at the beginning since the camp is not clean. I took a picture of the kitchen, which was full of dirt, and showed it to the female manager of the camp, asking her whether she would accept a pregnant woman living in such conditions. She understood my concern. I asked her to investigate this issue; otherwise, I would complain about it to other authorities. She promised to talk to other managers of the refugee camp. Gradually, these dreadful conditions improved. Nevertheless, we must accept our general life conditions. If I compare our conditions to what we went through during our journey in Iran and Turkey and our stay in refugee camps in Greece, where I thought I would not survive for another month, I now live in paradise. God alone knows what we went through during our journey, especially in Greece, where we had to collect wood to be able to cook. We baked bread on a heated iron plate. We stayed in tents. During the night, I saw snakes, scorpions, and mice in our tents. I was afraid of these animals. We have also experienced extremely cold and warm weather, and we have been offered worms in food and moldy bread. We had to accept everything we were offered to survive. We did not have money to buy our own food. I suffered a lot, but we could do nothing. I put up with these conditions because I was grateful for the survival of my children during our journey and that we escaped and didn't drown. At least they are alive. When I think of the scenes I have

98   V. DAG

experienced, I just thank God that I survived (weeping and crying). I have also seen asylum seekers who arrived in Greece safe, but they hurt and stabbed themselves to obtain asylum rights. They made themselves half-human. I did not harm myself, and I always thanked God that we did not go through this struggle.

I believe that God determines that everything should happen in a slow and patient manner. Some of my female refugee neighbors complain about conditions in the refugee camp, but I keep telling them to take it easy and tell them that everything will be fine. I remain patient and positive that something good will happen. I suffered a lot, but I am OK with that. I have been living in these conditions for two years, but I do not create any problems concerning my conditions in the refugee camp. Thank God I am with my husband and children together in Germany. Our lives are not directly threatened. We do not complain about where we are now or the conditions, we live in. I tell my family to look at what other people experience in Syria. People cannot sleep during the night because of the sound of aircraft skirmishing. At least we try to sleep well, but we are always nervous that something bad has happened when we receive a phone call from Syria. When I talk to my mother, she asks me whether I can hear the sounds of the Turkish jets on the phone. My whole family and relatives are in Syria, and we have many martyrs among our cousins, aunts, uncles, or neighbors and their children. Half of my neighbors have been killed. Therefore, I do not complain about our conditions or our room in the refugee camp. I am happy to have a room with four walls, which enables me to sleep. My room is big enough to sleep in and eat in. Nobody wants to live in this room, as you can see; however, I am happy to have it when compared to what I went through. To me, this is paradise. When we think of our relatives and speak with them on the phone, every time they say that someone has passed away or been killed, we are okay here.

The camps were depressing places rather than places of solace.
   —Dengdar—Germany (2)

We encountered difficult circumstances when we began living in refugee camps, which we could not have predicted or anticipated. The camps were depressing places rather than places of solace. Together with my children, there were eight of us residing in one room. We had no choice but to eat whatever was served to us. In Germany, everything was new to us—people, the system of government, rights, laws, and the language. We endured such depressing and difficult circumstances for more than a year. We felt alienated from people throughout this time; we couldn't speak the language and were isolated, having difficulties interacting with people. We did not know anyone, nor did anyone know us. After some time, the government offered us a flat, but we were still isolated and lacked any contacts. We are unaware of anyone who could educate us about our rights and the laws of Germany while simultaneously enabling us to communicate with one another. In other words, we feel alienated because we are cut off from our culture, our native land, our native language, and our families, who have been spread around the world. We don't even know if they're still alive because we can't see or hear each other. This is the primary cause of our feelings of melancholy. We were merely seeking to get away from the war in Syria, but we hadn't considered that we would have to go through a great deal of additional difficulties away from home. We were extremely disappointed because reality was very different from what we had imagined. Therefore, we do not have any psychological comfort; our well-being has diminished, and our suffering has intensified. It feels like we are in prison since we have lost everything. We leave for school in the morning to learn German and return home in the evening. Our lives are quite monotonous. It is especially difficult for us Kurdish refugees, who are unskilled and without a specific occupation. The problem of language has emerged as a further source of tension and has increased the amount of pressure that we are under.

Abandonment and Discrimination

...I was homeless and slept on the streets and in parks.
—Merdo—Italy

Italy was not my intended destination, but it was suggested that I apply for asylum in Italy. I was advised that if I failed to obtain asylum in Italy, I would not be able to acquire it in another country in Europe. Some of my friends have warned me that if I ask for asylum in a European country other than Italy, I may even be deported to Turkey. I needed to avoid this risk, and I also ran out of money to pay a smuggler to take me to another country. For all of these reasons, I decided to apply for asylum in Italy. In the first two months, I was homeless and slept on the streets and in parks. I stayed in a hotel with some peers for a total of 15 days and spent €20 per night. The hotel owner, however, requested my passport and other official

100   V. DAG

documents, which I did not possess. He then told me that I was not permitted to stay at his hotel and that I had to leave. I bought a tent and started sleeping outside. After submitting my asylum request, I was issued a new identification card that clearly states that I am a person seeking asylum. This identification card is not even recognized by any hotels, and it does not make any difference to my predicament in any way. This identification card does not even allow me to obtain money from my country of origin. It is not accepted by police officials, who always inquire as to what it implies. We were like fish out of water since we did not speak the language of the receiving community. I moved and stayed a couple of days in the Kurdish House, where I made friends with Kurdish refugees. I was able to talk about our common experiences and share information. I share a common culture with the Kurdish people at the Kurdish House and therefore feel very comfortable. In general, we are all in Italy as refugees for the same reasons in relation to our homeland. We can have empathy for each other and promote understanding of our problems. Moreover, we attend political activities such as demonstrations and protests in Italy because we did not have a chance to participate in such events in Turkey, where we would have been arrested and fined for doing so.

After a while, I had an accident, and my finger was broken and was subsequently put in a plaster cast. With my broken finger encased in plaster, I went to the help center and tried to explain to them with my broken Italian that I was sleeping on the streets. I was sick and could not bear to be homeless. They sent me to a refugee camp on the same day, and I was luckily received by one of our Kurdish people, who was called and informed about me. He wanted to help me when I arrived there. He provided me with a clean room and told his colleagues to look after me, as I am one of his people. He used to be a Kurdish refugee too, and he renounced his Turkish citizenship. I was granted a place in this refugee camp, and I felt very relieved. I was also offered lunch and dinner, as well as snacks in the morning. Furthermore, my expenses were reduced. Before being offered accommodation in the refugee camp, I had to struggle to survive as I could not take up employment, which is impossible to find in Italy anyway. I could not ask my family in Turkey to send me money because the value of Turkish money is very low in Italy. 500 Turkish lira, which is a lot of money in Turkey, is equal to €100 in Italy, which is nothing. I could barely survive with such a small amount of money. The social services in the refugee camp benefited me very much, and I still reside there after almost two years. I am very thankful for this. My camp has changed a few times, but it is still located in the city center of Rome. I only received food in my previous camp, but I receive food and €45 per month in my current camp. I also receive monthly transportation tickets and have health insurance. The government does not offer asylum seekers these essentials in all refugee camps. In some camps, as in my previous one, we do not receive any money, just a place to sleep and food. I heard from some friends at the Kurdish Association that there are some camps where people are only allowed to sleep during the night. The refugees are allowed to stay there from 8 p.m. to 7 a.m. without being offered any food. There is no centralized system of refugee camps, as each camp has its own rules in terms of food, pocket money, season tickets, etc., which exist in some camps but are absent in others. However, every day we receive the same food, which is pasta but not edible. Restaurants serving this food in Turkey would be forced to close, but we have to eat this food to save money and survive. We have difficulties finding jobs, making our own money, and managing our lives. I was granted humanitarian asylum a month ago, although I have still not received my ID card and passport. After a month, my two years in Italy will be complete. Receiving a resident's permit does not mean that I can also easily get a job. It is very difficult to get employment. I am now in a refugee camp and receive basic services, but I have to leave the camp in two months upon obtaining the right to asylum.

...I do not exist officially and socially, as I do not have legal status....
  —Kawa—Sweden

The Swedish government is not concerned with my background or the issues driving me to seek asylum. The government ignores what I went through before escaping from East Kurdistan, Iran. It acts according to its own rules and maintains its own interests with other states. It fosters a very good relationship with the Iranian government, too. Therefore, it refuses to grant us asylum rights and delays our applications. This restrictive asylum policy towards Kurds from Iran is not independent of this relationship. In the beginning, the authorities said that my application had been rejected because I did not have appropriate official papers to identify myself. I provided the authorities with my ID, but they said that the stamp and signature on my identity card do not match. I provided the required documents, but they came up with another argument that my birthday was in August on my ID card while my school certificate was dated March. This was a mistake by the Iranian government, not my mistake. I submitted additional documents to the authorities, but they refused to accept my documents and blamed the Iranian government's error on me. My lawyer and I explained all this to the authorities three times, but my application was rejected. The court decided that my file should be closed. As my file was closed, I disappeared for a while to avoid the authorities, who could have arrested me and deported me to Iran. However, in the period 2016–2017, executions increased in Iran, and the Swedish authorities became aware of this development. Consequently, they allowed me to appeal against this decision and reopened my file. I hired a Swedish lawyer who suggested that I could take legal action against the Swedish government in international and European courts since my legs are amputated and the Swedish authorities are aware of my health condition. I realized that the authorities are not interested in my physical condition, let alone my political situation and persecution by the Iranian regime. So, I escaped from Iran with the hope that the authorities would never reject my asylum, as Kurds from Iran are granted asylum rights, but in fact, my asylum was rejected three times. The asylum case has had a massive impact on my life.

I was wounded in Kurdistan and consequently lost both of my legs. Living with amputated legs, I cannot lead a normal life. Nevertheless, I appreciate my life more than anyone else. Without my strong will, I could have committed suicide, but I motivate myself to live because I am inspired by the Kurdish struggle in four parts of Kurdistan. The Kurds are stateless and consequently face many difficulties. Otherwise, could you imagine that your physical situation is not normal like that of normal individuals and that you do not have a residence permit, official employment, or a flat but still live in a normal way? I receive just a few Swedish krona, and I cannot live on this money. I always stay with friends at various places. I asked for a wheelchair and a car to get home in the evening, but my request was ignored for a year, and I am forgotten. Life is hard, and I have been living in Sweden for five years without legal status. I wish the authorities could tell me about their decision within a few months and that my asylum claim would be rejected, so I could quickly find a way to go somewhere else—to Rojava, South Kurdistan, or another European country. During this period, I do not have contact with Swedish people and cannot learn the Swedish language. I need urgent treatment for my injuries, but the hospital staff do not pay attention to my health conditions, and I am not relevant to them. For treatment, they must register my name, but my name does not exist because of my asylum status. I do not exist officially and socially, as I do not have legal status; I exist only physically. For this reason, they do not help me because I have not received asylum and am not officially registered in the system. My psychological circumstances have deteriorated as a result.

...I am bitterly resentful about the Austrian authorities identifying us as Turks!
—Ceger—Austria

The main reason that I escaped from Kurdistan and sought refuge in Austria was the Turkish state's accusation that I was involved in the Kurdish struggle. However, I am bitterly resentful about the Austrian authorities identifying us as Turks. We escape from our homeland because our language, culture, and identity are suppressed and denied by the Turkish state, but we are identified as Turks in this country. I keep emphasizing that I am a Kurd and come from Kurdistan, but neither the authorities nor Austrian citizens understand this reality. They do not pay attention to what we say and insist that we are from Turkey and, consequently, Turkish. They do not recognize our identity and culture. Therefore, it was hard and painful for me at the beginning due to the issue of our identity. First, we are identified as Turks and assigned Turkish identity, but I want to live as a Kurd with dignity. Yes, I do not have a state, but I have my society, culture, and history, and I am a member of a nation. I want to be known, identified with my nation, and recognized for my identity as a human being, which is my essence. I do not mean an ID card; my identity is my feelings, my language, my memories, and the hundreds of years of history that give me a sense of existence, construct my reality, and explain me in connection with my nation. This is my identity. If the authorities recognize my identity, I will certainly develop a positive attitude towards this society and believe in the fact that this government, country, system, and society recognize me as a human being with my Kurdish identity. Since I have never seen any positive attitudes or developments, I have been missing something in myself and my personality and have perceived myself as weak. In reality, my identity is denied, as I am identified as a Turk and a beggar. This leads to the fact that I keep my distance from this society. However, I have the feeling and reflection of my nation, for which I cannot produce the wrong reality, which was the case in Turkey. I have emphasized that this reality is wrong. Due to my critical opinion, the Turkish state persecuted me, and I ended up in this country as an asylum seeker.

104   V. DAG

Being an asylum seeker and living in exile is very hard. However, it is unbearable when, under these extreme conditions, my cultural, political, national, moral, and sexual identities are suppressed and denied by this government too. It is not a democratic understanding when one does not resist this policy of denial and mistreatment of us Kurds. If this government claims that it has a democratic system, it has to recognize that there are 40 million Kurdish people, and they have a language, culture, and humanity. It must recognize us with our Kurdish identity and that, though we escaped from Turkey, we have a Kurdish identity and are Kurdish. I expect this government to recognize my Kurdish identity. If I had gotten this recognition, I would not have left my homeland and escaped to another country. The Turkish state is our enemy, and we understand its hostile approach. However, this government treats us the same way. This aggravates our mental and social conditions. We are cut off from our community, homeland, culture, and values and suddenly find ourselves in an alien culture and difficult situation. Additionally, we Kurdish asylum seekers from North Kurdistan, in Turkey, are also discriminated against as the authorities here delay our asylum applications to assess and decide on our asylum cases. They usually reject our asylum cases by arguing until our verdicts in Turkey are confirmed by the Turkish high court, so we cannot easily receive a positive decision on our political asylum rights. The government perceives our reality through the lens of the Turkish state.

We suffer from this pain because we are stateless and abandoned!
      —Saman—Italy (2)

For two months, I slept outside the immigration office in order to get in and apply for asylum. Normally, when the cops arrest someone, they force him or her to apply for asylum. However, I wanted to apply for asylum on my own, but they did not let me in to claim asylum. Every day, the authorities took in nine or ten asylum seekers, but not more. After two months, I was let in to apply for asylum. When I went to the immigration office again, the officer asked me where I was staying. I responded that I sleep on the streets. The immigration office failed to offer me a place to stay in a refugee camp. They told me that I could sleep in the forest and sell drugs, steal, act as a pimp, or work as a park warden, which does not involve trouble. They rejected my application without telling me the reason. This is a weird country in which a police department does not recognize the paper and ID card issued by another department. So, I do not

4 ASYLUM PROCESSES AND CHALLENGES: "WE NEITHER DIE NOR LIVE... 105

have any rights or papers now, not even a health insurance card to see a doctor. I cannot even apply for an insurance card because the authorities require an address and formal documents, but I do not have any of these documents. I have been living in Italy for a year, and everyone who arrived with me has already been interviewed for their asylum application, but I am still waiting for my asylum interview. I don't know why the authorities deal with me like this.

I am homeless and have nowhere to sleep. I have not received any benefits from the Italian government and have lost everything here. I have been working illegally for a year without social insurance as I borrowed €12,000 in Kurdistan that I used for my escape from Turkey to Italy. My mother has been my guarantor, and having claimed asylum, I have to pay back this money within a year according to an agreement I had with my money lenders. The money I earn from one day's work feeds me for three days. I have been living in a self-made shack for seven months, where I do not have electricity and am forced to live by candlelight. Last year during the winter, my nose was running permanently because it was very cold, and I was sick every day. I could not take showers regularly or dress properly. My teeth are yellow because I could not brush them. Nevertheless. I do not want to leave this cottage, as other non-Kurdish asylum seekers might come and occupy it. In this case, Kurdish asylum seekers would not have any spaces. I have seen some people living on the streets in miserable conditions, and I am worried that I might end up like them. I started to be afraid because I didn't have any opportunities and didn't know anyone who could help. Therefore, I want to keep this place and share it with friends who are homeless too. We have mutual solidarity. In general, we Kurds live in a world in which the existing academic and political concepts fail to analyze and understand our dilemma. We are asylum seekers, suffering from poverty, statelessness, and nutrition disorders. We are unable to look after ourselves and lack the confidence to talk to people, developing a sense of inferiority as we fail to express ourselves. We suffer from this pain because we are stateless and abandoned. In addition, we are Kurds and are immediately labeled as terrorists.

....Our self-help services are necessary to stop our suffering!
—Agir—France

The government does not provide us with any welfare benefits after we submit our asylum applications, including basic accommodation. There is only one office established by the government where asylum seekers can line up to obtain an address. After having registered and submitted their files, we pop in there once a week to ask whether we have received any letters concerning our asylum cases. Otherwise, there is no other government service. Without previous contacts and ties, Kurdish families and asylum seekers cannot simply leave their homeland and seek asylum in southern France. They have some contacts and relatives who receive them, respond to their basic structural needs to manage their lives, and help them settle. Kurdish asylum seekers who do not have relatives might still receive support from pre-established Kurdish refugees based on their common Kurdish identity. The Kurds look after each other even if they do not have legal documents. As asylum seekers, we make efforts to manage our lives economically even if we do not have legal papers. For example, since we are asylum seekers without residence permits or any rights, landlords do not rent their flats to us. However, long-term refugees rent flats and accommodate four or five asylum seekers in a shared room to prevent us from being homeless, even though it is very burdensome to live with many people in a shared room. We have many problems and cannot focus on our lives, work, and commitments.

The government does not give us permission to take any employment, but we need to work and earn our livelihood. If we do not work, how can we survive? Again, the Kurdish refugees are committed to helping us asylum seekers by finding us employment at construction sites, accompanying us to the prefecture for asylum applications, and managing our paperwork. Essentially, they offer us employment to make some money and pay for our lives. This employment might be regarded as illegal, but it is vital for us to survive, have shelter, and avoid homelessness. What we do is use the self-help services that we provide to each other to respond to the failure of the government, which refuses to offer us necessary services. Even though they are not legal, our self-help services are necessary to stop our suffering. We might harm ourselves, our social environments, and even the state if we are neglected by the government and victimized, but we struggle to undertake any wrongdoing despite scant resources and opportunities. We prevent any bad situations by supporting each other to manage our lives. Many of us were traumatized in the homeland because of our activities in relation to Kurdish identity. We escaped hardship, persecution, and troubles, but are confronted with similar troubles when living in France and face many restrictions. Our experience of oppression is very challenging and occupies our lives in France too. However, we might

4 ASYLUM PROCESSES AND CHALLENGES: "WE NEITHER DIE NOR LIVE... 107

gradually overcome this mental distress rooted in the homeland when we receive our residence permits and take on employment and accommodation.

...there is no difference between our lives and those of abandoned dogs.
—Ajar—Italy

We have to make an effort to deal with our own issues because we cannot rely on any institutions in this country that abandon us. When we fail to express ourselves, we immediately feel inferior to native residents. We have always lived as refugees, and we have experienced such conditions in our homeland too, where we were perceived as not second-class but rather third-class citizens anyway. Therefore, if we compare our conditions and lives in Italy and Turkey, there are no differences apart from the fact that we have, despite oppression, a home in Turkey where we can live and sleep, while in Italy we live like dogs on the streets. In Italy, there is no difference between our lives and those of abandoned dogs. We live in a house in Turkey, while dogs live on the streets. In Italy, dogs live inside houses, and we refugees are homeless. However, we try to be hard-working and sort our lives out in Italy. Getting anything in Italy is like getting blood from a stone. Many asylum seekers have applied for asylum and given interviews, but there is still nothing official. By granting asylum, Italy gives us a right, but it encroaches upon other rights that are available to us and does not offer us a choice. In Italy, we do not receive any kind of recognition apart from existing only on paper, but nobody sees us formally. I don't know what we would do if we had not had this Kurdish House, which is like a hotel and camp where we Kurdish refugees can socialize, mix with one another, and find respect.

Refugees are seen as inhuman!
—Pesheng—France

I escaped to Europe, where I faced many difficulties in general, but the greatest hardship that I experienced was in France. I had to sleep on the streets for two and a half years. I had been provided with an address for my letters by a charity, but I could not receive them. They sent my letters back without informing me. When I asked for my letters, I was always told that they had been sent off. It was very difficult not to have a reliable address. Moreover, the authorities registered my wife as an Arabic woman who had

108 V. DAG

five children; the eldest child was older than me. I said that she was not my wife. The authorities realized that it was a mistake. I had the impression that we were let down by the authorities. I could not bear to stay in France and left for Sweden, where I spent many years. However, I was arrested there but did not apply to the Swedish authorities for asylum, even though the Swedish authorities insisted that I should claim asylum. I told them I was visiting my relatives. I did not have ID, apart from a copy of my French document, as I had lost the original document. They put me into custody for a month in Sweden, and I was deported to France, where I was only held for an hour and then released immediately. I was free in France, but I came across many difficulties.

It is a lie that there are human rights and democracy in France. You see many asylum seekers sleeping on the streets and in parks without any protection or rights. They are starving. These people receive food whose date has expired, but they do not have the choice to reject it. They are forced to accept everything that helps them survive. Many of these people accept spoiled food rather than steal it. These people are down at heel. They are people who do not deserve respect. Asylum seekers are seen as inhuman. We do not feel that we are human beings. I have even heard from many people that the authorities inject people who become mad as a consequence. These people are mentally depressed.

...we are worthless and meaningless human beings!
—Yado—Italy

Upon my arrival in Italy, I applied for asylum in Rome. I was told that the refugee camps are full and there are no places available. Therefore, I needed to find my own place. So, I started sleeping on the streets during my asylum process. I did not receive any material or spiritual support at all. I was not aware of the system here, which is very different. Everything looks normal and fine, but if you are within the system, it is very different. I suffered a lot in Italy and did not know where to start. I was hungry for many days and often felt abandoned. The way in which we are treated in Italy indicates that we are worthless and meaningless human beings. We are told to respect animals, but the value of human beings is absent, as people are not educated to respect human beings in Italy. But how can we respect animals? Animals are taken to the veterinary surgeon several times, but human beings are not taken to a hospital even once. The system in Italy is spoiled, but not just for us. Many films and plays have been made

4 ASYLUM PROCESSES AND CHALLENGES: "WE NEITHER DIE NOR LIVE... 109

about this system, which affects us two or three times more since we are refugees. It becomes harder for us, and we cannot get out of this state. If human beings are at a loose end and are abandoned, they tend to do everything possible to get lost. These conditions cause a loss of belief and destroy our existence because we do not exist anymore. Most Kurdish refugees get mentally depressed because they are helpless and abandoned. Individually, I could not work legally but began a job without paperwork, which was not the job that I wanted. However, after having been granted my residence permit, I could legally work and rent a flat. So, I was not a stranger anymore, as I was granted my residence permit, giving me normal status as a human being.

Generally, the Italians have a negative attitude towards us refugees. They think it is our fault that we left our homeland and escaped to another country in which we have claimed asylum. With the election of Salvini, Italians became more racist towards refugees. A few days ago, Italians in Napoli killed a refugee from Nigeria who was accused of theft. There is no law that says someone should be killed for their crime. I perceive Salvini's policy as detrimental to Italy. He always creates panic and an atmosphere like there is a problem or chaos in Italy, but there are not any problems. Nobody comes here to exploit or destroy Italy. Maybe this could be done from inside. However, these Italians are creating chaos to establish their specific policy, as happened in Turkey. They cause a crisis and chaos in the country, as if refugees were going to produce a bomb. Salvini's policy is like those of war-torn countries in that the ports are closed to ships of refugees, who are prevented from coming ashore. My brain does not absorb what he is doing because he presents everything as if bombs were going off each day. This affects us every day. Salvini keeps saying in a smart way that he is hunting undocumented immigrants, but he does not enlighten his society about the circumstances of documented and undocumented immigrants. He generalizes about all immigrants without informing people about their differences. There are many unintellectual people on the councils and in the immigration police who follow his statements on TV every day. The way he presents the refugee issue indicates that all refugees are criminals. That is how these unintellectual Italians understand refugees.

The authorities tell us sometimes that we have to return to our homeland because we are not wanted in Italy. They accuse us of being aggressive when we demand our rights. They always make trouble when we have issues with our papers, but we are not aggressive. We are only demanding

110   V. DAG

our rights. We refugees are deployed to carry out the dirtiest and heaviest
work that Italians would not carry out. Refugees clean the asses and the
crap out of their elderly. They are taken to the mountains to collect fruit,
tomatoes, paprika, and other vegetables. If a refugee becomes a lawyer in
Italy, this is a shocking case. I think humanity has come to an end in Italy.
If we are refugees, we cannot benefit from any welfare benefits. Our children cannot also make use of social welfare benefits unless they are Italian
citizens. I think that when our children go to school, they will learn about
laws and rights, but they are not given these opportunities. Italy is a country of discrimination. I want to pay my taxes and make my contribution to
this society. However, in this country, I have always been prevented from
doing whatever I wanted to undertake. I cannot perform a proper job
because they have formed organized groups and gangs that prevent us
from getting nice and easier employment. These gangs occupy all these
areas of employment and were given legal status and protection by the
government. There are many mafia groups that have spread all over
Europe. The money that the EU allocates to the Italian government for
refugees and the management of their lives is distributed by the government amongst the mafia-like groups and gangsters who employ us in dirty
work sectors without any insurance or legal papers. This happens under
the auspices of the government. I speak on behalf of the 80 percent of
refugees who are not aware of their legal rights or the laws, which are very
malign and evil. The Italian government has legalized crime.

EXPLOITATION

Exploitation is extremely common in Sweden!
   —Rezan—Sweden

There is a profound difference between being granted or rejected for
asylum. Within this system, what confirms our existence is an ID card or
passport, which we do not possess yet. This prevents me from participating in any social activities and being a part of life. For example, I cannot
attend a gym or take up a sport as I am not allowed to register given my
lack of a valid ID. I cannot receive or send mail or money using my own
name. I cannot plan for the next day, let alone for my future, as I do not
know what will happen to me the next day. The institutional environment
in this country, which governs my entire life, determines my future. This
will continue to be the case until I receive my resident permit. The second

serious issue is our economic situation. I have applied for asylum in this country, and for this reason I receive a small amount of money from the migration authority as a means of living: 1800 kroner. This does not even cover my cigarette expenses. Ridiculously, friends or family members are not allowed to send me money. If I receive €50 from someone as a donation, by law I have to inform the migration authority. The migration authority will cut this €50 out of my monthly expenses. This means, as an asylum seeker, I cannot go to a café to drink a cup of coffee. If I drink coffee, it means I have to waive two of my daily meals, as this is the price of a cup of coffee. In this sense, these conditions are inhumane and unbearable. I start to question the position that I have in this country and in the world. I not only question my identity and sense of belonging, but I also question my existence in this world.

Normally, not speaking Swedish is considered an obstacle to socialization, although almost every individual in Sweden speaks English. I think even if I were fluent in English, I would not be able to socialize with a Swede if it involved eating and drinking, as I cannot afford it. I not only need to find a solution to my inability to speak Swedish, but I also have to find a way to meet my economic needs. This process will last until my asylum process is completed. There are some voluntary institutions and individuals that help with certain issues. For example, they offer Swedish language courses. However, I have to pay to travel from the refugee camp to these courses. There are some institutions that pay these travel expenses, but they also have many conditions. For example, I am supposed to have lived in this city for 12 months and have not come to Sweden via another EU (European Union) country, according to the Dublin Treaty. Since I was previously in Greece, the Dublin Treaty prevents my entitlement to receive these expenses and attend these language courses. This also applies to the labor market and employment. I am excluded from participation in employment and social life since I was in another European member state and am therefore restricted by the Dublin Treaty. This restriction encourages us to live in the shadows and on the "black market." Normally, an employee is allowed to work legally for 8 hours and earn the minimum wage of 20,000 kroner. However, employers can instead employ people illegally for many hours for only 6000 or 7000 kroner. This is very common, as many asylum seekers do not have the choice to work under normal conditions because they have to survive.

Exploitation is extremely common in Sweden. Since the Swedish system officially does not permit an alternative labor system, the extremely

112 V. DAG

repressive conditions of the black market emerge as a result. Pre-established immigrants have created the black market as an alternative to the official Swedish labor market. Accordingly, Swedish citizens remain at a distance from us since we are black-haired strangers and are rejected as their neighbors and friends. This leads to the emergence of Arab, Turkish, and African ghettos. There are divisions between ethnicities and languages. There is not a Kurdish neighborhood yet, as the Kurds are divided within their own community and attach less importance to their ethno-national identity than other ethnic, linguistic, and religious communities do. In this sense, in Sweden, immigrants who are not Swedish are called black-haired strangers, their employment is called "black employment," and the job market is called the black market. Their world is described as a black world with black affairs. Even if we have our own money, we are not allowed to officially rent a flat and live independently. We have to rent a flat on the black market. We cannot register there and are not allowed to receive letters at such addresses. If the rent for these flats normally amounts to 5000 or 6000 kroner, we have to pay 9000 or 10,000 kroner since we rent them on the black market. In this way, the authorities cause asylum seekers to question whether they are human beings. This situation is very hard, especially when we are asked to integrate ourselves, since it is not only the language that is an obstacle. We might make efforts to overcome the language obstacle, but there is economic hardship. Even if we overcome these challenges, there are socialization problems that are impossible to solve as we are identified as black-haired strangers involved in black affairs.

A drowning man will clutch at a straw.
   —Ardan—Italy (2)

The Italian residency permit does not improve the lives of refugees in terms of social welfare rights because these are inadequate in comparison to those in other European nations. For instance, the government does not offer us welfare assistance to rent a flat or to study the Italian language. Even Italian citizens do not receive support from the central government. Tens of thousands of Italians, for instance, reside in squatted schools and government buildings in the center of Rome. The inhabitants of these slums are uneducated, jobless, and economically disadvantaged. Italian nationals are subjected to these dreadful conditions in their own country. Since the government fails to meet the necessities of its own people, it is impossible to provide assistance to the Kurdish refugees. We

4 ASYLUM PROCESSES AND CHALLENGES: "WE NEITHER DIE NOR LIVE... 113

cannot claim that there are no job opportunities in general when it comes to employment. Kurdish refugees may have better job opportunities because there are many Kurdish kebab and pizza shops, and Kurdish owners prefer to hire Kurdish people because the Kurdish community is closed and they can easily exploit each other. Many of the Kurdish refugees who came with me and queued for food in front of churches now own kebab shops. Those who were begging for food made efforts to start their own businesses and hire freshly arrived refugees for 10 to 12 hours, paying them €500 or €600. Refugees are employed for 10–12 hours, but they are only paid for 3–4 of those hours. Many formerly prominent Kurdish activists have also established their own businesses and now exploit Kurdish refugees more than any other employer, allowing Kurdish refugees to work with fake identification cards. The recently arrived refugees have no alternative but to put up with these circumstances. There is an old proverb that says, "A drowning man will clutch at a straw." They must cling to someone for assistance if they lack family, friends, or relatives and the government has abandoned them. This is the reality of life, and they do not have any other options available to them. We are obligated to put up with our circumstances, no matter how much we would rather not. Thus, in Italy, we are exploited and abandoned. We are unfamiliar with Europe and do not speak any of its languages. Many of our people who have fled to Italy have never visited a small town, let alone a large city in Kurdistan. They fled their villages in Kurdistan for political or economic reasons and arrived here, but they have no idea what to do. They are involved in challenging and impossible circumstances. Sometimes we are unable to rationally explain or comprehend our circumstances.

I remain outside the system and excluded from asylum rights.
   —Bekes—France

I am an undocumented asylum seeker. When my asylum claim was rejected in Austria, I then escaped to France, where my asylum application was rejected too. I feel like a new-born child in France since I cannot express myself and make myself understood. I always communicate with mime and signs. As with many asylum seekers, I came here with experience of exploitation. I was discriminated against and exploited in Turkey, but long-term refugees here are keen to exploit me too. This discrimination applies predominantly to Kurdish and Turkish immigrants, but also to other immigrants and French citizens. The life conditions and system in France force me to constantly search for alternatives and become involved in the black market as well as smuggling activities. However, if I had been a citizen from a Western County like Canada and Portugal, I would not have faced this kind of maltreatment, as the system is inclusive of citizens from the West. I escaped to France as a Kurd, but I am considered a Turk here, just as I am regarded as a Kurd in Turkey, and I suffer from Turkish exploitation and oppression. French society does not know how I was exploited in Turkey. Hence, I do not feel a sense of belonging to this country.

I permanently manage my life in a "zone of non-being," as I am a clandestine asylum seeker. I use ID cards belonging to other people and work on their behalf or engage in illicit employment in the construction sector to survive. I live on this money, rent an illegal flat, and live with undocumented immigrants. The employers pay me a low wage, while landlords rent miserable places for a lot of money. I make those who exploit my status rich. I suffer from this treatment, which is very painful. I wake up at 5 a.m., come back home at 8 p.m., and pay money for my hard labor to other people who exploit me. I do not work for myself but for those who already have legal papers and resident permits. These people with papers have created a system and maintained it to continue exploiting illegal immigrants. For example, they put five or six immigrants in their woeful flats and charge them high rents. These landlords benefit from our status and make a lot of money by exploiting the Kurdish refugees, who, at the same time, depend on landlords. A refugee can, for example, rent a flat that costs €1000. Since he is legal, he can apply for housing benefits and receive half of his rent. He can afford it, but an asylum seeker without legal documents cannot rent the same flat as he does not receive housing benefits and is not in a position to pay €900 or €1000 because he must cover his subsistence. A refugee with legal documents pays half the rent, has health insurance, and has legal employment. They have a lot of benefits, while asylum seekers like me lost everything at the beginning. We do not claim any asylum rights. In terms of employment, an employer can come and tell me his working hours and conditions and say that I am free to work if I agree with his terms. I do not have a choice but to work for him according to his terms, as I am a clandestine asylum seeker. So, I do not have any rights or life insurance, even though I live in the middle of Europe.

I remain outside the system and feel excluded from asylum rights. The European asylum system causes wretched and unjust conditions and a permanent state of fear that I will be arrested and deported. Normally, if I am an asylum seeker, I should have alternative opportunities to seek asylum in

4 ASYLUM PROCESSES AND CHALLENGES: "WE NEITHER DIE NOR LIVE... 115

any European country. However, I am not allowed to apply for asylum in a second European country when the first country rejects my asylum claim. If this happens, I will become an undocumented immigrant and have to go underground for 18 months until I am permitted to apply for asylum for the second time in another European country. I would not know what to do during this time, how to survive, or who to ask for advice or support from. I am not allowed to go back to Kurdistan as there is an outstanding warrant against me in Turkey. My escape to Europe has not paid off. I have family commitments because I am married. I recently lost my six-month-old baby, possibly as a result of medical neglect, but I am unable to speak the language and do not have the necessary legal documents to exercise my right to know what happened. We saw a doctor who said that my baby was healthy and well, but two days later the same doctor said that his heart had stopped, and he had passed away. The doctors did not pay attention to my infant, who might have been alive now if it had received proper examination and treatment. They could find out whether it could have lived. If we had not had an appointment, I could have lost my wife too as an outcome of poisoning. Normally, the child would have received an ID because it was six months old. When I tried to apply for this ID, they asked for my ID too, meaning I stopped this application process because they would have reported me to the police, and I would have faced deportation. The authorities provided me with paperwork saying that he is my child, but I did not receive his ID. I do not think there is anything more painful than this, and the pain leaves an unforgettable mark inside me. This will traumatize me when my wife is pregnant again. I will live with this fear. It is not easy to lose a child, but this is what the system imposes on me. People do not attach the same values to fellow humans as they do to animals. These human beings and systems do not give me a chance to survive and create problems that I am prevented from solving.

LIMINALITY

It is an uncertain life that I cannot control, and it is extremely difficult.
—Merxas—Austria

I have been living in this country for about four years, but my asylum case has not been decided yet. The authorities neither granted me asylum rights nor deported me. I do not think they can deport me anyway, as I

116   V. DAG

will be jailed in Turkey. However, the authorities indirectly encourage me to voluntarily leave for another country. This situation produces serious psychological and social problems, and I do not know how to deal with them. I always ask myself questions such as whether I will be granted a resident permit or deported, when I will be invited to a court interview, and how the authorities will decide my asylum case. It is a dilemma, and I do not know how to deal with it. It is an uncertain life that I cannot control, and it is extremely difficult. I do not know whether I will stay here or leave, and this liminality prevents me from focusing on my integration process and a normal life, although I want to learn the language, interact with Austrian citizens, and find a job. These questions are constantly on my mind, which has a negative impact on my mental health. For these reasons, life is very hard for me. Sometimes, I consider returning to Turkey and spending three years in prison since I have been here for four years, but nothing has happened. On the other hand, it is risky because there are many cases pending against me. Having considered all these cases, I will never get out of prison when I am in Turkey. If I knew I would spend only three years in prison, I would go back and do that. However, I do not know how many cases have ended, as I do not have a lawyer to follow them. In order to hire a lawyer in Turkey, I have to pay fees at the Turkish embassy, where I might be arrested too. I do not have any money to pay for these fees anyway. I do not care whether the Turkish authorities sentence me, but I might need these documents for my asylum cases. Both here and in Turkey, my situation is very critical. I am not the only one who is suffering, but also my children, who are traumatized and negatively influenced. I have not seen my family for many years and cannot be reunited with them. I suffer here, and my family is suffering there. My children go to school, but they can't focus because they think they might join me and leave their school. They are not certain whether they are going to move to Austria. They face this dilemma in Kurdistan. Most of my problems are related to my asylum claims.

Based on my asylum case, I do not think that there is justice in this country. I have been living in this country for almost four years, but the authorities have not concluded my case. If I am not going to be granted asylum rights, they should tell me. I consider going to court and file a complaint against the government or leaving for another county. I think their policy is unfair. I can accept that there are a large number of asylum seekers who have different purposes and not all of them have been politically persecuted. However, my situation is different, as I was an elected

4 ASYLUM PROCESSES AND CHALLENGES: "WE NEITHER DIE NOR LIVE... 117

councilor and represented people. I presented my councilor's ID to the authorities. I also had an official salary, and my economic situation was not bad. I did not come to Austria for economic reasons. I also had my own house and car in Turkey. I had a good life in Kurdistan. In addition, I had an olive farm that produced and sold olives. I was not super rich, but my economic conditions were very good. I think my case is very clear, as I have provided the authorities with many documents, and my sentence is already official in the Turkish e-government system. I have collected these documents, translated them into German, and provided them to the authorities. The last time I visited my lawyer, I told him to complain about the government's asylum policy, but he objected, saying doing so could negatively affect my asylum process. Nevertheless, I insisted on taking legal action against the authorities for this inhumane asylum policy, as I just want justice and am not attacking the government. My lawyer said that some of the Austrian laws are worse than those of Afghanistan and Turkey. Nevertheless, I submitted my letter of complaint to the judge, who asked me for additional documents. I sent these documents to the court three weeks ago, and I am waiting for a response from the judge.

For 17 years, I have been living with uncertainty....
— Kani—Sweden

For 17 years, I have been living with uncertainty in relation to my asylum case, which dominates my life in Sweden. I cannot undertake any transnational activities as my asylum status restricts me to Sweden. One of the most severe challenges that I encounter is related to my mobility. I am not allowed to move beyond the Swedish borders to travel or attend international events. I am a poet and am regularly invited to international conferences and meetings in other countries. Therefore, this is a serious hurdle, but thanks to the Internet and Google, the world has shrunk and is at our fingertips anyway. So, my legal status prevents me from traveling and holds me as a hostage in an open prison in Sweden. I have a fake resident permit and need to ask the authorities to extend it once a year. They renewed it and have also promised not to deport me to Turkey, as they know the consequences for me. Nevertheless, I have always lived with the fear of being deported. I handed in my documents to a friend to keep them safe in case of my deportation, and I also asked the Swedish authorities in 2009 to give me a document testifying that I would not be accepted as a refugee in Sweden if they rejected my asylum claim. I wanted to

118   V. DAG

voluntarily leave Sweden for another European country, the Kurdistan region of Iraq, or the mountains. I realized that my life was not bearable and needed to be changed. I even escaped to Germany, but the German authorities found out, by following my fingerprints, that I had applied for asylum in Sweden. The German home office ensured to grant me asylum status when the Swedish authorities did not request my deportation in connection with Dublin regulation. However, the Swedish authorities requested my repatriation from Germany and promised to accept my asylum. As soon as I arrived in Sweden, they provided me with a fake resident's permit that made me feel like I had been fooled. It was not fair how they treated me, which aggravated my living conditions and mental health.

It is hard to claim that our lives as refugees in Sweden are as smooth as we wish. Our lives are rather unpredictable and uncertain, although Swedish democracy sounds wonderful and is certainly presented as a unique model from afar. However, I have never had any feeling or experience that this narrative and perception of Swedish democracy and welfare are realistic. I have only witnessed fake democracy in Sweden. For example, to obtain the chance to talk to a judge, I have submitted at least ten applications, but I have never been offered the chance to discuss the reasons for my asylum case in a normal court process. The authorities always send a member of staff to ask me questions, write out my statement, and then leave. This only happens once per year. The authorities then send me a letter and tell me of their decision, which they make behind the scenes. I am forced to accept this. I am over 60 now and can imagine living for another 20 years. I have lived this way for 17 years, and I might live for another 17 years in the same way, but I do not know what would happen! Nevertheless, I carry on my work, read, and write.

Some people turn these obstacles into strengths, and the conditions become a lesson and an experience that strengthens them. Similarly, I have developed my lifestyle under these liminal conditions and continue to educate myself. I also tell myself that the Europeans and Swedes did not send me a letter of invitation to come seek asylum in their countries. I came voluntarily to this country, but I have to either leave it in an illegal way or wait and see what happens. During this time, I have continued to write and pursue my career. I make efforts to thwart the negative implications of the lack of a resident permit. Nevertheless, when I had an appropriate resident permit, I could have at least learned the Swedish language and found a job in an academic field according to my qualifications. The asylum status would have provided me with asylum rights, including housing opportunities. These rights would have enabled me to rent a proper flat too. Since I do not possess asylum rights, I do not have access to welfare benefits and structures, and this affects my mental state and life.

I am neither deported nor recognized as a refugee!
    —Deza—France

I am an undocumented asylum seeker. I have applied for asylum many times, but the authorities have rejected my applications, arguing that there is nothing that connects me with France. I told them last time that I agree that there is nothing connecting me with France. Even if I am tied up with a chain to stay in France, I would not remain here if I had one milligram of belief that I would not be harmed and have a normal and safe life in Kurdistan. Being undocumented means that we are not allowed to legally work and cannot easily find employment. It causes problems and psychological pressure when we clandestinely work at the construction site or when we are seen by the police on a train. I told the judge during my court process that being here has not changed a lot for me because I had to escape from the police and hide in Turkey, as I do here. I have been living under these conditions in France for 11 years. I am also not allowed to travel to my homeland; my father passed away, but I could travel to attend his funeral. Many of my relatives passed away, but I could not attend their funerals. Since I lack legal documents, I am not allowed to rent a flat. I have to live in basements, which are also not documented. These flats are illegal because they come without tenancy agreements. The landlords do not inform the authorities that they are renting their flats to avoid paying tax. What the landlords receive from us is extra income. There are thousands of such flats in Paris that are not registered, and 95percent of residents are undocumented immigrants who do not possess resident permits.

Once, the police caught me driving a car and took away my driving license, which I had from Turkey. They told me that I was not allowed to drive with my Turkish driving license. I know of many people who drive with such licenses; it was my bad luck that the police caught me. I had to go to prison for 18 days, which was more severe than the prison in Turkey, where I spent two and a half months. In Turkey, being in prison was understandable because we were engaged in a struggle for freedom for our homeland, but I am in prison in France because I did not have the correct documents. I am still undocumented and exist without legal documents, so I am nothing. I do not have a state, culture, or language. We are told that this is the life we have to accept, whether we like it or not. Being undocumented or not having an ID card indicates that we are criminals and guilty. This is the procedure in a country that calls itself democratic. I think it is not possible that this county is democratic. The French state and its democracy oppose each other. The state is an instrument of colonialism and exploitation, while democracy means freedom and common will. Accordingly, some countries are harsh, while others are softer in their policies of oppression. I do not believe that there is a democratic country at all. If a country like France had democracy and freedom, life would be totally different, but you see how bad it is.

I have been living here for 11 years, even though I would never voluntarily stay in France for a day. I am neither deported nor recognized as a refugee. We do not have proper health insurance, nor even the lowest form of insurance that would enable us to get basic treatment to survive. We possess some sort of health insurance, but not all hospitals in France accept it. This basic insurance, called AME (state medical aid), is comparable with the Turkish green card, which is issued to farmers and the poorest people in Turkey and Kurdistan. With this card, we neither die nor live but receive some breath. This insurance in France exists for people like us who are not illegal. I cannot imagine having survived without the Kurdish community here.

> *...I had not seen any doctors for four years because I am illegal!*
> —Shehriban—Sweden

I am an undocumented asylum seeker. With other Kurdish refugees, I live in Stockholm like a hostage, and every day I fear arrest. When I see police officers, I start worrying since they might ask me for my ID card and find out that I am an undocumented asylum seeker. I constantly worry about being arrested during a routine check. Sometimes, friends tell me to be more careful and avoid crowds. This anxiety causes extreme stress that permanently dominates my life. Accordingly, there is no difference between my life in Kurdistan and in Sweden, as I faced similar anxiety and worries in both places. Moreover, we are excluded from basic public services here. For example, once I was heavily sick for two weeks and did not dare to see a doctor or go to the hospital as I did not have my resident permit. I worried that I would be arrested and deported. Nevertheless, friends advised me to visit a doctor, and I went with a friend who tried to ensure my safety. He stayed at a distance and observed whether I was safe.

4 ASYLUM PROCESSES AND CHALLENGES: "WE NEITHER DIE NOR LIVE... 121

I told the doctor that I had not seen any doctors for four years because I am illegal. He normally sees patients who do not have a resident permit. He said that the government has introduced a rule for all undocumented immigrants to be examined and treated regardless of their resident permit status. Nevertheless, I cannot behave like a normal citizen. This situation indicates injustice, making me feel inferior, helpless, aggrieved, oppressed, and unprotected. I am telling you this since I have endured all these tragic experiences. Perhaps I would not have told you about these experiences if I had not encountered them. I think it is difficult to understand these experiences if someone has not gone through them. Consequently, I am always distressed and unhappy. However, I feel comfortable when I am amongst my own people at the Kurdish House, which is a nest of such pain and suffering since everyone who goes there is racked with similar pain, misery, and problems. Most Kurdish refugees visiting Kurdish Houses in Europe are traumatized and wounded. They are not normal people, as they have experienced war and victimhood. Therefore, we understand each other's problems when we meet at Kurdish Houses in European countries.

As asylum seekers, we are legally deprived of all our rights.
—Argesh—Germany

As asylum seekers, we are legally deprived of all our rights. My attorney informed me that I would not be able to move into an apartment and begin employment. In Germany, I have no legal status and therefore no rights. I would love to get a driver's license, but I've been advised that it's impossible for me to do so at this time. I do not have any rights, including the right to rent a council flat or the right to travel outside of the city in which I currently dwell. I have no choice but to remain confined behind these walls for a period of time. I recently visited the Berlin immigration office to renew my residence permit. I received only a three-month resident permit. I have informed the relevant authorities that, due to my status, I am unable to get employment or a rental apartment. However, I was informed that we are required to embrace whatever the government provides. We must wait until we are reunited with our children if the authorities decide that we are allowed to stay in Germany. If the German authorities decide to deport us to Iraq, we must accept the decision and return home. Our asylum cases are uncertain, and it could be three or four years before they are concluded. During this period, there will be major

122 V. DAG

challenges in the lives of our children. They have already suffered mentally and physically since they were abandoned and cannot be treated by a qualified doctor. This is having an increasingly negative impact on our lives in Germany. While we are in German class, we are unable to concentrate on our lessons because our thoughts are constantly going back to Kurdistan and the concerns, we have for our children there. As a result, we fail to comprehend the subject that is being taught. Our children are 7 years old, 11 years old, and 13 years old, respectively. I have developed a mental disorder as a result of the amount of worry I have over them. My wife has also been severely psychologically impacted by the predicament of our children, who phone twice a day to speak with their mother. I have to take her to the doctor often for treatment of her mental health. My family has completely fallen apart, and we have been scattered all over the world.

...because of my uncertain status, I am totally paralyzed.
—Alan—Sweden

I submitted my asylum application four years ago, and authorities have interviewed me regarding my claim; however, I am still awaiting a decision and am still an asylum seeker. I have asked the authorities several times whether they have made a decision; they have informed me that it has not been made yet. I told the Swedish authorities that I escaped from Turkey because of my Kurdish and political identity. I have many family members who have been living for many years in Sweden. I would not have escaped to Sweden as an asylum seeker for a little freedom; I could have emigrated to Sweden through marriage and the associated family reunion procedure. However, I escaped to Sweden because I believed that it was a democratic country and could defend my individual freedom and rights. This is the reason why I am now in Sweden and have claimed asylum. However, the authorities have a negative attitude towards my asylum case. I think the Turkish state provided them with a file accusing me of crimes and terrorism. Based on these documents and the fake facts that the Turkish authorities prepared about me associating with the PKK and submitted to the Swedish authorities, my asylum process is continuing as the Swedish authorities do not want to make a decision. During my interviews with the Swedish authorities, I was asked what I thought about the PKK and the HDP. I responded that the HDP is an official and legal party in Turkey, while the PKK is an armed movement. However, we share some commonalities in our agendas. The PKK demands the recognition of the Kurdish language, self-determination, and human rights and uses armed methods to achieve these objectives, while we (the HDP) demand the same aims through legal means. Our claims and those of the PKK intersect, but I want to achieve these objectives not through violence but rather via political means, which are my natural rights. This is why I am considered a "terrorist."

I have the impression that the Swedish authorities harbor suspicions against me and mistrust me. This affects my life very much. Moreover, when I go to a bar or somewhere else and my ID is checked, I am not allowed to enter these places because of my status. I feel like a second-class individual. In my homeland, I was oppressed and discriminated against by the Turkish state, and I again feel excluded and discriminated against in Sweden. Nothing has changed in my life. This situation evokes a feeling of inferiority and has led my psychological state to deteriorate. It means I am nothing and do not exist officially. I think my future is uncertain, as I do not know whether I will be able to stay in this country, escape to another country, or be deported to Turkey. I cannot settle in this country properly. For example, I am single and might be interested in marrying and setting up a business. However, because of my uncertain status, I am totally paralyzed. I have been living in Sweden for almost four years, but I cannot officially have my own flat and register it. I always have to stay somewhere else. I feel bored and unmotivated to manage my life in this country. I cannot learn the language, and this uncertainty eliminates all my motivation. I do not want to socialize and make efforts to get closer to Swedish society, as it has given me the feeling that I am not a complete human being. I'm aware of this feeling when I go to a bar or a restaurant. When they find out that I do not have an ID, they refuse to say hello to me the following time. They ask for my identity and assess my personality according to my legal status, which does not exist.

CHAPTER 5

Toward Integration: "We Cannot Achieve Integration Without Struggle"

The process of integrating Kurdish-Yezidi refugees into receiving cultures entails a variety of obstacles and policies. However, the role of the diaspora in the process of integrating refugees into host societies should not be underestimated. Some of these problems consist of the failures of authorities to respond to the needs of refugees and their difficulties in understanding bureaucratic challenges in the integration and settlement process. However, the self-established Kurdish-Yezidi refugee organizations play a crucial role in assisting Kurdish-Yezidi refugees in overcoming hurdles and obstructions that they face.

The first set of challenges is related to the authorities' neglected approaches and policies regarding newly arrived refugees in the processes of integration and settlement, which require a variety of interventions and support services. These services range from the provision of fundamental necessities such as housing and a means of subsistence to the instruction of a language and the attainment of qualifications for employment market. Additionally, the social and cultural requirements are not less relevant for refugees to acquire adequate perspectives and orient themselves in new host societies. Likewise, many refugees are traumatized individuals who have been subjected to violence, torture, imprisonment, and societal disruption. Within this context, Kurdish-Yezidi refugees confront numerous challenges, for example, in Italy and France, due to the underdeveloped local and national integration policies allowing refugees to settle and build a foothold. One of these challenges is that refugees are not offered welfare

© The Author(s), under exclusive license to Springer Nature Switzerland AG 2024
V. Dag, *Voices of the Disenfranchized*, Mobility & Politics, https://doi.org/10.1007/978-3-031-46809-4_5

125

benefits, which would help them with accommodation, the local language, and job training while also allowing them to set up their lives. Since refugees perceive their circumstances to be neglected, they turn to transnational spaces to live clandestinely with institutionalized cultural, social, and structural discrimination. The Kurdish-Yezidi refugees in Sweden, Austria, Germany, and Denmark do not gain better experiences regarding their neglected situation, albeit to varying degrees and in various fields. While Kurdish-Yezidi refugees in Sweden, Germany, and Austria lack authorities' understanding of their traumatized circumstances rooted in their homelands and thus face pressure in the integration process to adjust to employment demands, Kurdish-Yezidi refugees in Denmark are relocated to Bornholm, an island, where they face unstable procedures in resident permit and settlement processes and their family reunion is ignored. Most decisions regarding the extension of refugee resident status are discretionary, and these assessments frequently neglect the mental health and life prospects of refugees.

The negligible situation of refugees is frequently discussed regarding the difficulties that they face in navigating the bureaucratic processes involved in their integration. Most Kurdish-Yezidi refugees originate from failed states such as Syria and Iraq, where they had no prior experience with functioning statehood, institutional decision-making, hierarchical structures, or control mechanisms. Their experiences with authoritarian rulers or corrupt and nepotistic systems in their home countries influence how they perceive states. Most Kurdish-Yezidi people lived in a conflictual relationship with the state regimes they escaped from, concealing often significant mistrust in official authorities. However, in the new hosting environments, the refugees in question run into a great deal of bureaucracy in the receiving countries, confronting institutionalized decision-making and an overwhelming amount of paperwork. These new conditions are both overwhelming for newly arrived refugees and less understandable when they deal with the social and structural obstacles they face when they go to officials to receive advice on how to deal with a large amount of paperwork and how to fill out forms written in a language that is highly administrative in nature. While refugees are subjected to a tremendous amount of stress resulting from bureaucratic procedures and a lack of understanding and experience with bureaucracy, authorities fail to take this cultural context into account. The Kurdish-Yezidi refugees also suffer from initial trauma and victimization as a result of the oppressive treatment they received from the authorities. Ignoring their mental state and the social environments in which they find themselves frequently leads to neglect, which can have increasingly negative consequences. As a result, these refugees feel alienated and frequently fail to focus on improving their lives in the integration process.

Kurdish-Yezidi refugees frequently fail to effectively complete their settlement process due to the restrictive procedures employed by authorities and their particular settings, which are tied to their experiences in their home countries as well as ongoing political events addressed in the second and third chapters of this book. Negligence and bureaucratic burden on the part of authorities, as well as the consequences of these policies, frequently result in various forms of social isolation among refugees, leading to mental illness and disorientation. Thus, the refugees are unable to participate in social life or obtain access to social settings in the countries that have taken them in. Many refugees form social bonds with their ethnic and religious diaspora communities. They adhere to social structures and end up in homeland-oriented ghettos. These circumstances have an adverse impact on the integration and settlement processes of refugees, instead of favoring them. While refugees frequently find themselves abandoned, helpless, and marginalized in a clandestine or "black world," the institutional structures of the diasporas operate to mitigate these problems to a limited extent. The leaders of immigrant and diaspora organizations highlight their assistance possibilities and offerings for refugees. They possess first-hand knowledge of the refugee context, access to refugees' social and transnational networks, the ability to communicate with refugees' multiple language dialects, the capacity to provide refugees with cultural and social services, an understanding of the legal, political, and structural settings, and information regarding the refugees' matters in host states, as well as knowledge and expertise in dealing with refugees' everyday problems. Furthermore, forerunners from diaspora structures have acquired knowledge of the local language and are familiar with ways to connect with key players in host states. These self-organized structures can be of great help to host societies in fulfilling an important role in connecting recently arrived refugees with cultural and social structures in receiving states if authorities recognize and promote them. Thus, these establishments are able to step up and fill the gap left by the authorities. In this chapter, ordinary Kurdish-Yezidi refugees highlight multiple obstacles impeding their settlement process, while leaders of diaspora structures present the refugees' challenges and how they strive to resolve the refugees' everyday problems in the adjustment and settlement processes.

128   V. DAG

Negligence

They would not have used drugs if they had lived normal lives....
    —Dana—Italy

I have a resident permit, but it is completely useless until the authorities provide us with housing assistance, educate us about our rights and effective life management ways, and connect us with employers and Italian citizens. For instance, despite my illness, I've been searching for work for a while, but I've had no success. I have significant experience working in the catering industry and am proficient in the preparation of a variety of dishes, including pizza and other foods, but I have been unable to secure any employment possibilities. So, I went to the Commune (social welfare benefit service authority) twice to request the help I needed to integrate myself in the job market, but they turned me down each time since I did not have an address. Yes, I live in an apartment with six or seven other peers because we're lacking funds. Since I failed to provide an address, the authorities will be unable to contact me. Therefore, we face many challenges in Italy, but we do not receive any assistance or financial aid to help us deal with these challenges or our daily lives. However, we are able to participate in language classes provided by a charitable organization but not by the Commune. This non-profit organization occasionally assists us by providing language lessons. As a result, I only have a basic understanding of the Italian language.

In general, the Italian authorities do not offer any assistance or resources to us, but rather violate our rights. I am a refugee who has been living in this country for ten years. It is essential for the European Union to exert control over the policies that the Italian government has adopted towards refugees since living conditions in Italy are extremely precarious. Everywhere you look, there are asylum seekers and refugees from Syria, Somalia, and Iraq who live in parks and on the streets. These individuals are completely reliant on the assistance provided by the EU. Normally, refugees who come to Europe from countries with no legal systems obtain justice and rights, but in Italy, they learn how to perform criminal activities. Many of my friends turn to using drugs as an alternative way of coping with the loneliness and depression they feel. They would not have used drugs if they had lived normal lives and had their own homes. However, these criminal activities will decline, and people will refrain from using drugs if the government supports refugees and offers us resources to

5 TOWARD INTEGRATION: "WE CANNOT ACHIEVE INTEGRATION... 129

secure apartments, learn the language, or find employment. Many people in Italy underwent training to engage in criminal activities. Many of the refugees I know are addicted to drugs and struggle with a variety of issues as a direct result of their precarious living situations. I am granted political asylum, hold a five-year resident permit, and desire to work in Germany and Norway; yet the authorities of both countries prevent me from taking employment. I have friends in Finland, Germany, Norway, and Sweden, so if authorities allow me to work in other European states, I'll find five jobs there tomorrow. I will take any job and will not focus on one type of job because working in every area to survive is far better than sitting and sleeping in a park from morning to evening with no purpose. Alternatively, I can also open shops, run them, and return government funds if I am granted loans. I would hire four of my friends who are refugees, all of whom would present no problem. We would operate within the law and pay all of our taxes. We would be in a better position to take advantage of opportunities and rent our apartments. If this is not the case, then the government is to blame for all of these problems since it ignores our needs and does not offer any kind of welfare services. Currently, we refugees have a very difficult time surviving in Italy due to the conditions here.

They leave us to perish gradually.
—Kosret—Denmark

Apart from me, all of the Kurdish refugees have resolved their concerns and are settled. My concern centers on the process of reuniting with my family, which is significant for us Kurds and the rest of the world. It's not normal to be separated from family members. I merely want to be with my wife again and do not ask for money or an apartment to live in because I am obviously not destitute. I am the father of four children, two of whom reside with me in this country while the other two are raised by their mother in Germany. I brought along both of my girls, who are 12 and 13 years old, respectively. They have extended an invitation to their mother, but unfortunately, their application has also been turned down. I have approached prominent politicians, but they have not shown any interest in helping me. I've written three letters to Danish TV to protest about my predicament in an effort to prevail in my case. I have not yet received a response, which is disappointing. Additionally, I engaged a lawyer to argue my case against the Danish government, but my application was denied. I have attempted on three separate occasions to get reunited with my family,

130   V. DAG

but the Danish government has been adamant that we cannot move together. Prior to attempting to reunite with my family, I was not informed of the legal requirements. If the authorities reject our request for a reunion, they must expel us from Denmark. However, they neither permit us to live with my family in this country nor compel us to leave. They leave us to perish gradually. When I first came to this country, I did not have any gray hairs at all. Right now, I look like an old man. Look at me, how do I look? Every day, I find myself in a state of confusion. Can you imagine what it would sound like if your family was not there with you? I thought that if we arrived in a democratic country, it would welcome us with open arms. Our family should not be divided by it. In the event that they make the decision to deport refugees, I should be the first one to be sent away.

> *...These refugees are provided with spoiled food and are neglected!*
> —Kendal-Sweden

The Turkish government has opened its borders to "threaten" Europe with 3 million refugees, and the Swedish government has agreed to accept many asylum seekers from Turkey over the last five or six years. In some ways, the Turkish government was successful in putting pressure on the Europeans by using refugees as a bargaining chip. During this period, Sweden and other European nations maintained an open door policy towards new asylum seekers. However, the arrival of the refugees in Sweden sparked a debate over the asylum system. Sweden was unable to accept asylum seekers in the same manner as in the past, but it was also unable to deny them shelter. The government made the decision to alter its policies and reception procedures, which were changed to a tender-based system. The use of this system has resulted in the rise of numerous cooperatives and enterprises. This has led to the commodification and commercialization of the integration policy. The cooperatives were created to accommodate the refugee families while providing them with the care that they require. The government pays these cooperatives for these services on behalf of each individual refugee, leaving their families in the hands of these commercial enterprises. The management and operations of these cooperatives result in many shortcomings. Some cooperatives, for example, have taken in numerous families with children and adults, but they do not provide them with basic supplies and food, fail to manage their paperwork, and fall short of resolving their difficulties. In other words, these enterprises mistreat the refugees. It has also been extensively reported in the media that substantial sums of money have been granted to these enterprises to spend on refugees.

Each day, the government pays a sizable sum to these businesses for each refugee, but these refugees are provided with spoiled food and are neglected. As a result, the quality of the integration process deteriorates while a few of these businesses make a significant amount of profit, and the government avoids taking responsibility for this situation. These businesses receive their funding from the government, but they engage subcontractors to carry out the work for them. They are unconcerned with how the subcontractors handle and support the integration of refugees. Both Swedish society and refugees are impacted by this negligence. During the past five to six years in Sweden, the refugees that were produced as a result of the assaults carried out by IS in Iraq and Syria as well as by conflicts in Sudan, Somalia, and Afghanistan have built mafia-like gangsters of criminals and mobsters in every suburb due to the lack of institutional control and information provided by the government, which did not pay attention to these cases. Every week, two or three people are killed here because the government has lost control, leaving refugee governance to the mercy of the refugees themselves and private corporations. The majority of these refugees have fled violent conflicts; some of them have even committed murder or spent time in prison, something the government chooses to disregard. They returned to their children and families after collaborating with IS. They live among us in Sweden and continue to follow their traditional ways of life. There is currently a significant public debate over how to control these individuals. This is the result of failing integration and asylum policies.

Our money benefits them under the table but they complain over the table....
—Erdelan—Italy

Living conditions in Italy do not resemble those in other European countries in relation to the social welfare benefit system. As refugees, we do not have access to any support from welfare benefits promoting our integration. Therefore, it is very hard to manage our lives in Italy, even if we take on hard work. The living conditions in Italy are not only harsh for us Kurdish refugees but also for Italian citizens. This becomes even more complicated due to political organizations in the Italian state, which is even worse than Turkey, especially in relation to their gangsters and mafia groups. The Italian state was part of Gladio, whose roots are deeply

132 V. DAG

embedded in the current organization. We are now in 2019, but the Italian state is dominated by gangsters and mafia groups. For example, Berlusconi is the largest gang leader. The Lega Party from Sicilia and Napoli (to which Salvini belongs) consists of small mafia-like groups. It is a fascist party of criminal gangs. Fascism is not only limited to Italy but to the whole of Europe and affects people's attitudes towards us. However, it is very strong in Italy, where the tradition of fascism is well known. Greed for power amongst Italians is covert but becomes immediate when they find an opportunity. For example, the right-wing and fascist parties do not achieve more than 20 percent of votes in Italy, but these parties received around 35 percent of votes. The reason why these parties achieve such high votes is because they use the subject of refugees.

These fascist parties criticize refugees, but they benefit from them when they receive a high number of votes. For example, Italy is the number one beneficiary in the EU, receiving more money for refugees than other countries because of the Dublin Treaty and because of its spatial location, which is on the main refugee route. So, Italy benefits a lot from refugee money, but Italians are resentful of refugees. If Germany complains about refugees and demands a tough asylum policy, we might understand because Germany has a generous welfare benefit system, and refugees might abuse this system by not working and living only off welfare benefits. I am critical of such refugees' approach because they become lazy when they rely only on welfare benefits. This is also against our political vision and life philosophy. So, I could understand the German objection to refugees and when they want to introduce a new system to create an obstacle to reducing the number of refugees. All these demands are understandable. However, this is not the case in Italy because the Italians do not pay a penny to refugees. I have been living here for five years as a political refugee, but I have not received a penny during my stay because Italy does not pay me anything in terms of welfare, yet Italians receive my money from the EU for themselves every month. It is not only about my money, which the Italians keep for themselves, but that they take money from all refugees. I think the Italians receive millions of euros every month. Our money benefits them under the table, but they complain over the table about refugees. This policy is similar to that of Erdogan.

I think the Italians do not want to close the refugee routes because they benefit from this policy, but they also complain that there isn't employment in Italy and that the country is becoming dirty, all because of refugees. They also mention that refugees steal and commit criminal activities.

5 TOWARD INTEGRATION: "WE CANNOT ACHIEVE INTEGRATION... 133

This creates legitimacy for the Italian government's abuse of and discrimination against refugees, who face many difficulties and challenges, mainly in Rome (the largest city in Italy). Over the last two years, Salvini has become more powerful, creating a domino effect. If he says something, it has an impact on citizens, cops, and fascist groups. For example, two years ago, you would never hear anyone say that refugees are bad because the Italian people felt ashamed and would not dare to say it directly and overtly, although many people were still xenophobic. This racism was hidden. Now, Italians have started using violence against refugees. After Salvini became a minister, the attitude of cops changed. In the past, they asked us for our ID cards and residence permits and searched us in a nice way, but now they show us directly that they are hostile to us. They do not tell us this in language but through their eyes and behavior, indicating we are not desired. Therefore, it has been very difficult to be a refugee for the past two years. In this sense, we escaped from Turkey and became refugees in Italy, but we should not accept Turkish conditions—those that pushed us to escape to seek asylum—in Italy. Nevertheless, the worst and most subjugated living conditions for refugees in Europe are in Italy. This discrimination also applies to employment conditions. Normally, Italians work eight hours and receive a minimum of €1300 or €1400. However, refugees barely receive employment, and if they do, they are refugees from Afghanistan, North or South Kurdistan, working back in the kitchen and doing the worst, hardest, and dirtiest jobs. Normally, refugees are supposed to work with papers and need to have social and health insurance, but employers ask refugees to work without legal documents in order to pay them less money and exploit them more.

There are around 60 or 80 Kurdish families in Grosseto, where my brother lives and works in agriculture. They start at 4 a.m. early in the morning and work until 4 p.m. in the afternoon. The work is very hard because these Kurdish refugee employees work in the sun, dirt, dust, and around chemicals that are used for crops and grapes. They work more than ten hours but receive €50 per day. It is not possible for refugees to lead a normal life with this money. We cannot compare the miserable lives of refugees in Italy with those of refugees in other European countries. There is blatant discrimination and injustice in Italy. All Kurdish refugees living in Italy are helpless, while other refugees who have prospects do not stay in Italy and move to other European countries. Italy is not like other European countries where they can easily open kebab shops and run them successfully. Thousands of people have opened kebab shops in Italy, but

134 V. DAG

they have not been successful. They went bankrupt, closed their shops, and left for other countries.

BUREAUCRATIC BURDEN

Our lives consist entirely of bureaucracy and arbitrary decisions....
—Rodan—Austria

The government provided me with welfare benefits and offered me German lessons to assist me in settling in this country so that I could satisfy my commitments. However, they require 3000 documents and forms to be filled out, signed, photocopied, and delivered to the authorities. Our lives consist entirely of bureaucracy and arbitrary decisions, and the authorities are driving us insane with all the paperwork and bureaucracy that they require of us. Thousands of papers were requested by the authorities. When we have a scheduled appointment for the next day, they do not allow us to sleep because there are documents to be completed. They are European, and we cannot be like them in having to deal with the obstacles posed by bureaucracy and paperwork. Because we lacked a functioning state and system in Syria, we were not accustomed to complying with bureaucratic requirements. We did not have a mailbox in Syria since we never received letters, and we did not take the government seriously, but they did not take us seriously either. As a result, they did not bother to send us any letters either. We mutually disregarded one another. However, we went completely insane as a result of the mountain of paperwork that the Austrian authorities demanded from us. They have threatened to cut off the benefits that we rely on if we do not turn in our papers on time. I was forced to flee my country and now rely on the government's welfare assistance. Apart from that, nobody will help me survive here. My father farmed in Rojava for a living and had several hectares of land that yielded many thousands of metric tons of wheat and corn. We could have sold it for a substantial profit and used the funds to pay for my wedding and purchase a car. I was not a refugee, and I did not plead for government assistance. I cannot imagine living in Syria and relying on government benefits.

Authorities such as the job center hampered my integration....
—Alwan—Germany

Authorities such as the job center hampered my integration and prevented me from carrying out my intentions. They provided me with some money but required me to follow their instructions. I had to comply with their requirements because I was dependent on them. For instance, I found a room in a shared flat, and I was excited to live there because I was taking a German class and needed to interact with Germans to advance my German language abilities. However, the authorities at the job center informed me that they would decide how and where I had to live and that they had control over my life. I made it clear to them, though, that I am in charge of my own fate and that they should support me since I make an effort to live a life of integrity. They have been the source of a great deal of difficulty for me. Although I intended to further my education, they insisted that I begin an apprenticeship instead. By instructing me on what to do, they effectively shut down any further opportunities for my development. They did not want me to follow my own interests or pursue what I was passionate about. However, I met many people who aided me in gaining new perspectives and opening my eyes. After doing some research, I learned about a variety of options and possibilities. My self-awareness allowed me to resist the imposed approach of the authorities. A significant number of refugees are forced to contend with these obstacles. Many people believe that whatever the job center tells them is correct since this government institution has power and represents the state.

I believe that the requirements the job center places on refugees are an attempt to prevent them from voluntarily integrating. They have the misconception that we do not comprehend their regulations and procedures and that we are not aware of our rights. So, these authorities assume we will accept their word as truth when they tell us that something is right when it is actually wrong. Although we cannot claim that the entire job center follows this policy, certain staff members have unfavorable opinions of us. They additionally threatened to reduce my allowances or welfare benefits if I refused to conform to their requests. These perspectives have an impact on both my perception and the quality of my social relationships since they make life significantly more challenging, despite the fact that there are ways in which we can handle the challenges of daily life more effectively. In my opinion, many refugees would regard this strategy as the main factor in their decision to leave this country. Even if they are unable to travel to a different state and return there, they will not be considered a member of this society. This policy is not only unjust but also generates a great deal of problems. Nevertheless, this approach has inspired me to better myself and encouraged me to convey to the authorities that I am a free person who appreciates the freedom I have in Germany. This has been one of the things that motivates me to live intentionally and advance. Every country, like Germany, proclaims to be free, but we are not free if

136   V. DAG

we live there as refugees. We must put in a great deal of effort and put up some resistance in order to preserve our freedom, as many of the authorities do not want us to be free. Furthermore, the authorities are unconcerned with the traumatic events we have gone through in our native countries. They never inquired about the struggles we had to overcome on our journey to this country. They are just concerned with us being capable of speaking the language as quickly as possible so that we may begin contributing to Germany's economy and helping the country in different capacities.

> *There are a great number of obstacles that stand in the way of our integration!*
> —Kuvan—Sweden

There are a great number of obstacles that stand in the way of our integration and community cohesion. One of the significant obstacles we find it tough to overcome is language. Before making our way to Sweden, we took refuge in Turkey. There, we were able to communicate with one another without difficulty because we were neighbors and spoke each other's language. We could understand Turkish and Arabic spoken by others. Nevertheless, we are currently in Sweden, where nobody speaks any language that we can understand. The second issue is that Swedish society and European societies in general do not resemble our society because these societies are highly reserved. It is extremely challenging for outsiders to carve out a place for themselves and gain acceptance within these societies. We Kurds are everywhere and have no boundaries. For instance, we never shy away from disclosing things like our ages or wages. The third issue is one that concerns people's ability to find work. In Kurdistan, we are free to switch jobs at any time and take on new responsibilities without being subject to any prerequisites or other constraints. However, we are not able to completely abandon our current position in Sweden to begin a fresh endeavor. There are fewer options available to us, and the processes involved in finding work are challenging. We are expected to bring in the relevant qualifications and experience, in addition to being invited to interviews and being required to have Swedish language skills. Even if we have specific certificates for the degrees we earned in our native countries, the Swedish authorities might not recognize these degrees until we receive the education necessary to obtain the degrees they demand. As a result, they might provide us with the position for which we are qualified. They do not have faith in our own official qualifications that come from our

5 TOWARD INTEGRATION: "WE CANNOT ACHIEVE INTEGRATION... 137

home country. The struggle that refugees go through is directly attributable to this obstacle.

Unsettledness

We live in deplorable conditions....
　　—Osman—France (2)

We live in deplorable conditions in France since we cannot present the authorities with the required address when we seek asylum. We Kurds have experienced anguish and pain since the beginning of our history. The anguish and distress that we have been going through back in our homeland have followed us here, where they have manifested themselves on a new scale and in an entirely new set of circumstances, but we have also been subjected to ongoing discrimination and repression. This is both the truth and one of our main problems. The second challenge that we confront in France is connected to the language, and it is something that occurs on a continuous basis. We are unable to articulate ourselves in a general sense and are unable to make claims for our rights, which exist for all refugees. Even if some of the refugees are aware of their rights, the majority of them cannot assert these rights. For instance, I have been lawfully employed for the last year and pay taxes to the appropriate authorities. Therefore, I have the right to request council housing from the government, but I am unable to apply for a flat because I cannot speak French.

Generally speaking, I am unable to assert my rights to receive what I am entitled to because of my lack of language, inability to explain myself, and/or mental distress. My inability to get my benefits is mostly attributable to the language barrier. Therefore, we are unaware of the justice and rights to which we, as refugees, are entitled in this country. I believe that all Kurdish refugees are confronted with the same challenges. Therefore, whether we have asylum rights or not is, in my opinion, less significant. We are unable to exercise all of our rights, even though we have a resident permit and an ID card, because we are unable to communicate in the local language. The advantages of a resident permit and rights to asylum are undermined by the lack of language. Although I now have a residence permit, I am still confronted with many of the same challenges that I had before I obtained asylum status. The only advantage of possessing a residence permit is that it allows our Kurdish employers to formally hire us at

138 V. DAG

the construction site, as the majority of Kurds work in the construction sector. The residence permit enables us to work lawfully in this sense. The shortage of Kurdish translators and the inability of Kurdish refugees to articulate themselves is the third challenge that we face. Housing is the fourth pressing challenge, as many people seeking refuge are currently without a place to call home. There are no refugee camps in France where asylum seekers may be housed. They face very significant obstacles, and I have personal experience with the challenges that asylum seekers face.

...the conditions of my life became much more challenging!
—Dadyar—Sweden

My residence permit arrived in the mail only a short while ago. The asylum status, however, has little impact on my life and is of no significance. As soon as I was granted asylum rights, the conditions of my life became much more challenging. I then returned my refugee identification card, passport, and bank card to the authorities, as I have never been so miserable since receiving these documents. I claimed my asylum seeker ID card, which I obtained upon arrival when I applied for refuge. With this ID card, I had a comfortable place to stay and could at least sleep in the refugee camp. Yet, I currently have the status of refugee, but I no longer have permission to reside in the refugee camp; instead, I sleep on the streets. I asserted that it would be preferable for me to continue living in this camp as an asylum seeker than to be homeless as a refugee. I still do not have a flat where I could provide my address for registration. I shift my residence from one place to another on a permanent basis. I have not received any language, translation, or paperwork assistance since moving to Stockholm because I don't have an address to register at or an apartment to live in. My visit to the Swedish school will be approved by the government, so I can study Swedish. However, I do not feel prepared to start school until I rent a flat and am able to gradually develop my system and organize my life. Due to my homelessness, I am unable to bring my fiancée to Sweden to reunite with her. The first prerequisite for reuniting with my fiancé in Sweden is to rent my flat, which the authorities refuse to provide but require as a precondition. I am currently homeless even though I am sleeping in a hotel as a temporary accommodation until the end of the month, but I do not know where I should go for a permanent place to live. After moving out of the hotel, I will collect my belongings and then find myself in the position of being homeless once more. I am

5 TOWARD INTEGRATION: "WE CANNOT ACHIEVE INTEGRATION... 139

searching for a one-bedroom apartment or even a shared room. Landlords in our social environment exploit us and are to blame for the injustices we endure. For instance, the only people I could rely on in Sweden were my two closest friends. One of these friends invited me to stay at his house when I was homeless because he wanted to rent me a room. He requested that I pay him 5000 Swedish krona. I offered him an installment payment plan in which I would pay 3000 Swedish Krona now and the remainder in a month, but he declined. I did not move into his apartment and instead left. He let me down even though I assumed he was one of my closest friends.

In terms of employment, I have met many patriotic Kurdish long-established refugees at the Kurdish association. They made the offer to hire me as one of their employees. I accepted their offers, but they have always been a hassle by pressuring me to work long hours for little income. When they asked me to work for 15 hours, I worked for the full period that they requested. However, they failed to compensate me for my labor, and I was under a lot of pressure there. Since I've been living in Sweden, I believe that certain individuals have taken advantage of my situation and caused me significant harm. I protested about their practices at the Kurdish Association, and I used abusive language, but my companions were furious with me and scolded me for my expression. Some of the individuals who are abusing me work for the Kurdish organization. The problem began precisely there when our own people started exploiting those who were countrymen. I've made the decision to return to Turkey. I'm only waiting for my government paycheck. As soon as I arrive in Turkey, I'll be placed in prison, but at least I'll have a place to stay and food to eat. My basic needs will be met in prison, and I will be content if my family visits once a month. In this country, I have never once witnessed anything resembling freedom. After being subjected to all this maltreatment in this country at the hands of our friends and the government, I believe that maybe it will be even better to sit in prison in Turkey.

> *...a wide variety of concerns that the refugees bring to our advice center!*
> —Jiwan—Germany

There are a wide variety of concerns that the refugees bring to our advice center. They come to us with concerns regarding both their arrivals and their settlements in the new land. These include the translations of the letters and documents they receive from the government but are unable to

140   V. DAG

read and comprehend. We assist them in presenting their asylum applications to the courts. The reunification of separated family members is one of the most significant challenges. We also provide them with advice regarding the employment opportunities for which they are searching. There are also many challenges with their settling because they are uncertain whether they will stay in Germany or be repatriated. They seek our advice as they struggle with bureaucratic challenges while searching for schools for their children. Many immigrants over the age of 50 who have endured difficult experiences must learn the language and take their children to the doctors and schools while living in Berlin. They are facing an extremely challenging situation. We also provide translation services for refugees who need to visit hospitals.

We help them during the process of looking for apartments. Berlin's housing market is distinct from that of the rest of Europe. The most significant issue is the current severe lack of housing opportunities. Some individuals pay €7000 or €8000 to acquire a two-bedroom flat illegally. The government places many families in hotels, but the owners pressure these refugees to stay at their second, more expensive hotels. The government does not construct new homes but does have a few council apartments. For instance, one of these individuals who came to us for help was a woman who was accompanied by two of her children. She and the children stay in a hotel. Her rent is covered by the government with a monthly payment of €2000. This woman's application will be denied by the government because her maximum monthly rent is only €650 if she finds a property that costs €700. It is pretty strange. Therefore, there are pre-established immigrants who take advantage of the housing crisis and have organized mafia-like groups. If there was a Kurdish mafia, they would have benefited from the housing shortage as well. The housing mafia controls an apartment but will divide it into ten cramped rooms and force refugees to live there. Otherwise, they will continue to be homeless. The housing situation is catastrophic, and the housing mafia is in charge of these few apartments. If the mafia receives €10,000 from each family, they will have €200,000 each month. As these criminal organizations use fabricated documents, housing fraud is an endless problem. For instance, they fabricate false European passports using the information from tenants' records to rent apartments from landlords who frequently do not rent to immigrants. These landlords discover the fraud after six months and notify the authorities. The result is that the tenants have to move out, are subject to a fine, and occasionally even go to prison. The victims are refugees who cannot

5 TOWARD INTEGRATION: "WE CANNOT ACHIEVE INTEGRATION... 141

speak the local language and must borrow a substantial sum of cash to avoid living in refugee camps.

We receive between 25 and 28 advice seekers every day, which is a substantial number. We frequently assist refugees with their multiple concerns; consequently, we occasionally find ourselves without time for an appropriate lunch. I worked as a lawyer in Syria for a large number of these individuals, who are now refugees in Berlin. Many of my friends also fled to Germany, and I feel compelled to help them resolve their problems. Additionally, we help them find their place within German society. A significant number of refugees carry on in Berlin with the same habits they had in their original countries. They use, for instance, public transportation without purchasing a valid ticket. I warn them that using transportation without purchasing a ticket is illegal and may end up putting them in prison if they are caught. Being a fare evader can also have an impact on their asylum cases or the extension of their resident permits. There are some refugees who have a history of abusing or physically assaulting their wives. I warn them about the repercussions of their behavior, which could result in the Youth Welfare Association taking their children away. I strive to enlighten and educate them on how life works in Berlin.

This discriminatory policy and approach from the authorities give refugees a feeling of humiliation....
—Shevger—Austria

The authorities have a very negative attitude towards us refugees. This negative attitude is expressed through bureaucratic issues, such as paperwork and applications that are intentionally delayed for three or four months. They let us keep going back and forth without a plausible reason. When we apply for welfare benefits and living costs, they delay our applications to discourage us from making such applications. They also delay applicants' asylum processes for many years to prevent new refugee waves from escaping to Austria. They do not want us to stay in this country and encourage us to leave Austria and go back to our homeland, where we will not survive because of the civil war. This was also the reason that we left our homeland, which was peaceful before the outbreak of conflict. However, European, and other powerful countries caused this war in our homeland, so we were forced to leave. This discriminatory policy and approach from the authorities give refugees a feeling of humiliation that they cannot stand anymore. This discriminatory approach happens not

142   V. DAG

only once or twice, but very often. Many refugees cannot bear this policy and decide to return to their homeland despite the fact that violent conflict is going on.

I have witnessed many refugees returning to their homeland, and the authorities are happy about these refugees' decision. In this way, they discourage new waves of asylum seekers from immigrating to Austria. Many asylum seekers escape to this country, but they neither speak the language nor have any knowledge of the system. Refugees are required to rent their flats, but how can they rent flats if they are aliens in this country? There are some Arabic and Turkish long-term migrant gangsters who offer refugees flats for a high bribe, amounting to €5000 and more. They receive these flats from landlords and rent them to refugees, who borrow this money to avoid being homeless. Sometimes, the landlords do not wish to rent their flats to refugees. In the end, the refugees neither receive the promised flats nor see the bribe money that they paid to these gangsters (who speak the German language well and are familiar with the laws of this country) again. They prepare a tenancy agreement, which looks correct, and refugees sign it, although they do not understand it. However, these tenancy agreements are fake. They can easily get away with their crimes. The authorities are aware of these practices but are ignorant and ask refugees to find their own flats. I think the state is responsible for these practices, as they do not manage the appropriate accommodations for refugees. If the state grants asylum rights to refugees, it is also responsible for their accommodation.

SOCIAL ISOLATION

We also have children who are raised in isolation!
—Bermal—Denmark

The housing situation and the natural environment of the island are the two most pressing concerns for us right now. We are assigned to and confined to this island, so we are unable to leave where we are currently placed. We live in a flat in poor condition and are unable to leave since moving to another flat would require a large sum of funds that we cannot afford. We have registered for a council flat for more than two years, but we have not yet received one. Even when we receive a new flat, the time it takes to move into the new one is relatively short. We also have children who are raised in isolation. They do not have somebody with whom our children may nurture a sense of connection. When our children see other

5 TOWARD INTEGRATION: "WE CANNOT ACHIEVE INTEGRATION... 143

children being picked up by their parents and grandparents, they often ask us why they are not collected by their grandparents or if we do not have any other relatives. My children also want their grandparents to come and pick them up. However, we are pleased to make new Kurdish friends on this island. We experience a sense of emotional release when we are reunited with them. We, along with our children, had always wished that we would receive the chance to meet both sides of our parents as well as their grandparents. In addition, we are not free to leave the island whenever we choose because the moment, we leave is very dependent on the ferry and its schedule. This island has prevented us from maintaining our social connections and has had a negative impact on our social life. Furthermore, we are unable to leave this island because we are required to remain here for a period of five years in accordance with the regulations governing our asylum claim. Otherwise, we would have to find work elsewhere and would not be eligible for government assistance. We have family members who live in different areas of the country, but we are unable to visit them since the journey is too far, and we are unable to travel there and back on the same day due to the schedule of the ferry service.

When we are all together, our psychological well-being improves....
—Delal—Austria

We have ten Kurdish families here, so we do not require Kurdish structures. Our family, as well as the families of my daughters, sons, and sons-in-law, live together. We are a large family, and we spend more time together, so we can keep our bond strong and continue to communicate as we did back in our own place. Due to our constant connectivity, we never see or engage with other people. When we are all together, our psychological well-being improves, and we are able to put our issues out of our minds. However, we never stop missing our hometown, which we will never forget. We were forced to leave our homeland due to conflicts and violence, but we always talk about these memories of our childhoods, villages, and lifestyles with our children and the elderly people in our community. In Vienna, these memories never leave our thoughts or our lives. We maintain our sense of community through these interactions. We talk with one another and want to know about one another's well-being when we run into one another on the street or at a market. We live in our neighborhood as if we were still in our homeland, with all our traditions and cultural practices. In addition, we share information with one another in

144   V. DAG

Kurdish regarding the political situation in our homeland, the legal system in Austria, and the cultural norms of European countries in general. We can keep this information in our heads and understanding it if it is presented to us in Kurdish. We provide for one another and listen to one another's concerns and suggestions within our circle of family. We do not, therefore, require the Kurdish associations or authorities. Additionally, we take part in festivities like Newroz and Memorial days. We also attend demonstrations in solidarity with our homeland when we are notified about associated events.

> *We were dispatched to this island to live in isolation!*
> —Dara—Denmark

Our isolation is the greatest hardship on this island. We could have attended two to three weddings per week when we were in Kurdistan. Whereas we do not have many of these kinds of relationships where we currently live, we are fortunate to have numerous relatives there. We were dispatched to this island to live in isolation. I have relatives in Germany and other places in Denmark, but I am unable to visit them because we have limited access to this island that is encircled by water. We cannot leave the island whenever we wish since we must adhere to the ferry schedule. We need to schedule our trip two months ahead of time for this season. However, we do not know whether we will have time or how our schedule will change because we cannot forecast. It's possible that I'll have time, but my wife will not, or that she'll have time but I will not. Either way, neither of us will have time. Second, I have no idea what will happen to us tomorrow. Some of our friends might be able to go to another city if they are not accepted here, but we are not animals that constantly change locations. Our thoughts are always focused on this problem. Every time we wake up, the first thing that goes through our minds is what would happen if the Danish authorities require that we leave the country the next day. It would be extremely difficult for us and our families. We are concerned about the effects that this will have on our children and other family members. There is a great deal of unpredictability, which causes us a great deal of concern. We have been granted residence permits for a period of two years, but we are unsure of what will happen after that. For one or two years, we are always given resident permits with instructions to be prepared to return. We can settle and put our lives in focus if we are granted citizenship after four years or indefinite resident permits.

Otherwise, we exist in a state of liminality. We want to have certainty before our children grow to the age where they become acclimated to living in this country. They educate themselves in the local language and modify their behavior to fit in with the local population. They leave their own culture behind and lose their original language as well.

Struggle for Integration

If the association's fundamental services are discontinued, Kurdish refugees will suffer more!
—Mirza—Italy

The association serves as a venue for the establishment of trust, the introduction of new people, the delivery of presentations, and the empowerment of members. In my opinion, if the association's fundamental services are discontinued, Kurdish refugees will suffer more. Being alone in Italy is a challenging experience, but the association helps mitigate the negative effects of this loneliness. Even if the refugees and asylum seekers are not permitted to sleep in the building of the organization because of concerns with the authorities, they are still able to remain in the surroundings of the association, which additionally provide an extensive social environment. We are able to construct our own community, thanks to the association. Without the association, none of the Kurdish refugees would know who resided in the various neighborhoods and cities in Italy unless they had close connections or had established contact beforehand. The Kurdish Association, which we may refer to as the hub of solidarity and friendship, helps us meet friends and maintain social cohesion.

The source of collective solidarity is the statelessness of the Kurdish people; this can be regarded as the propelling force behind Kurdish mutual support. This is not something that arises in a country of settlement but rather an aspect that has its origins in the homeland. The Kurdish refugees create space through the association to establish their lives collectively, organize themselves, connect with one another, and develop commitments to fill the gap ignored by authorities. In other words, the Kurdish association is a response to the authorities' failure and absence of service supply. Nonetheless, the authorities intend to shut down this Kurdish association and prevent it from engaging in these activities since its leading members have not signed a lease agreement. The court is going to have to make a decision about this association at this point. As far as we

146   V. DAG

understand, the message that the authorities are trying to convey to us is that we should continue to be homeless and sleep on the streets, ignore what happens to other people, obtain our travel documents as a consequence of our refugee status, and leave the country.

> *They should break down their prejudice towards our association....*
> —Dewran—Germany (2)

We have officially submitted several funding applications to obtain some opportunities for our refugee-related responsibilities, but the authorities did not approve our project. I think their decisions are linked to a negative policy towards our association. This biased approach affects our activities to a limited extent. There is DITIB in Germany, for instance, which cooperates with and works for Turkish fascism. This association has monopolized Islam for its political power and used it for its dirty policy. However, we want to teach people about real Islam. We only want to suggest that the authorities investigate our political, economic, and social activities—what we do and how much we work. If our activities produce a positive and societal impact on humanity, the authorities should also develop a positive approach to our mosque and our activities. So, we can further make a positive contribution to and provide dynamic responses to problems in this society. They will find out how hard we work to provide solutions and answers to the problems of the people who visit our mosque. They should break down their prejudice towards our association and find a way to support our activities. We need government support in every area since there is a large Kurdish community in Berlin that has many problems that need to be solved. We have evidence that 87,000 Kurdish immigrants live in Berlin, but the figure is much higher. These people rely on any kind of support to manage their lives. We cannot only respond to their needs with one small association. If the authorities took a positive approach towards our mosque, we would work more dynamically, have a bigger impact, and make a great contribution to the integration of Kurdish refugees. We would be acting as a bridge for integration between German society and Kurdish immigrants. However, the authorities neglect Kurdish organizations and the integration process of Kurdish refugees. I think that these authorities do not care if we are integrated or not, even though Kurdish refugees are comparatively inclined to integrate smoothly and instantly into German society and show great respect for Germany. It is a fact that Kurdish refugees are not involved in narcotics and criminal activities such as drugs, prostitution, and other dirty stuff. The activities in which the Kurds are involved are campaigns against these dirty activities and for the liberation of our homeland, our language, and our nation. These are human rights that we demand. We only work for our homeland, and this society knows that we are only demanding our freedom. We are not involved in any criminal activities and do not inflict damage, destruction, or threaten German society. We Kurds have ethics, decency, and culture that do not allow us to undertake subversive activities. Therefore, we want the authorities to reconsider their view of our organizations and approach us not only according to their self-reception but rather according to our reality and experience. That is the only demand of the Kurdish organizations; that is the thing that they want to address.

> *We are eager to make the space available to the Kurdish refugees....*
> —Reber—Italy (2)

We provide the Kurdish refugees with attorneys, advice, and translation assistance throughout their asylum proceedings in collaboration with our Italian partner organizations. Our organization provides language classes to Kurdish refugees. We coordinate volunteer Italian teachers who offer language lessons to Kurdish refugees and asylum seekers. A female Italian school teacher devotes her entire day to teaching Kurdish refugees. We supply the infrastructure and place to support her. We, as the association, stress the significance of a Kurdish education and encourage Kurdish refugees to study the language so that they will be able to communicate effectively with Italians in the future when they settle there. We are unable to alter the skills and capabilities of refugees, including their ability to learn and speak the language. However, Italy is the first but not the last destination for many Kurds seeking shelter in Europe. After realizing there are no welfare benefits, housing, or employment opportunities, they do not wish to stay in Italy. They migrate to other European countries where they already have family members and friends to settle down after receiving their documents. A tiny percentage of refugees choose to remain, build their lives in Italy, start businesses, and settle there. A limited number of refugees choose to remain in Italy, establish their lives, launch businesses, and eventually settle there.

We are eager to make the space available to the Kurdish refugees so that they organize themselves, meet one another, engage in conversation with their Italian friends, and plan cultural events. We serve as the voice of the

148 V. DAG

Kurdish people, observe the Kurdish Newroz holiday, and host numerous cultural events, including movie performances. All of the films we show have been outlawed by the Turkish government and are not available in Turkish cinemas. Through film, we convey to Italian audiences the culture and way of life of the Kurds. At the same time, the organization plays a significant role in encouraging Kurdish refugees to steer clear of involvement in criminal activities. The impact of the Kurdish association is significant and prevents many unpleasant things from happening because of how we instruct Kurdish refugees on how to appear, how to behave, how to approach other people, and how to communicate. Our objective is to treat people with dignity. As a result, the Kurdish refugees are attentive when they visit the Kurdish organization. They are aware of this fact because they respect the organization and make certain that their actions are not associated with any criminal activity.

> *Many Kurdish refugees may be at risk of developing mental illnesses if they are cut off from the Kurdish association.*
> —Evraz—Germany

In Germany, I have the impression that I am imprisoned. Our neighbors have complained that we should refrain from creating noise while moving around in our flat. We also should not talk to each other and should not receive visitors. This is the kind of suffocating confinement that permeates every aspect of our everyday lives and serves as the prevailing force. For this reason, I avoid going home and instead spend each day at the Kurdish community center. Many Kurdish refugees may be at risk of developing mental illnesses if they are cut off from the Kurdish association. We make friends at Kurdish associations whose members are knowledgeable about German society and history. They educate us from their experience, and we learn from one another in the process. Additionally, the bulk of us refugees receive welfare payments, for which we submit applications at the job center. As a result, we receive many letters every day, but we cannot understand them because we cannot speak German. I was unable to ask a translator to join me because I had no idea where to find one. It was an extremely difficult and stressful situation. However, I ask friends who work at the Kurdish associations to assist me in completing my paperwork at no charge. Every time I require a translator, I ask them, and they voluntarily accompany me to the authorities to help me resolve my problems and complete my paperwork.

At the Kurdish association, we also receive a variety of services and assistance in resolving conflicts that may arise not only between Kurdish refugees but also within Kurdish refugee families. The friends from the association visit these families' homes and act as mediators to help them work out their differences. A year ago, I, too, suffered from problems. My friends from the organization helped me solve my problems with respect and care. As soon as Kurdish immigrants seek assistance, the Kurdish associations provide all types of assistance to help them settle their problems. The Kurdish Association is similar to our home that we brought from Syria to Berlin. In Arabic, we call it the Kurdish embassy. It is not less than that, but more, since we cannot sit and talk at the embassy like we do at the Kurdish association. There is food, tea, and coffee available, along with everything else that we require. The Kurdish organization also provides various services that aid refugees in settling in Berlin and renting their own apartments. These offerings include cultural events and workshops for refugee children to learn dancing and perform musical instruments such as the tambur. They also provide free lessons in German and Kurdish for anyone interested in learning those languages.

We can also enjoy the Kurdish food and Kurdish atmosphere there!
—Ferman—Germany

When we arrived in Germany, we did not know anything about the social and cultural environment in Berlin. We were not aware of the Kurdish organizations since, for the first time, we were in a large city where we did not know anyone. Our lives were in the hands of the German authorities. Nevertheless, we asked other refugee friends from Rojava about the Kurdish organizations, and they helped us find out that Kurdish organizations operate in Berlin. We found them and started to visit them since we were living in Berlin. I feel happy and comfortable when I am at the Kurdish association since it is the house, community, and organization of the Kurds. We can also enjoy Kurdish food and the Kurdish atmosphere there. So, it is wonderful to be at the Kurdish House in Berlin. We feel relieved when we are at the Kurdish associations since we interact with other Kurdish friends. I know that many people became mentally ill because they were alone and consequently committed suicide because of their social isolation. However, Kurdish activists founded the Kurdish associations, which we visit and where we meet other Kurdish refugees. The Kurdish organizations organize various cultural events, such as

150   V. DAG

Newroz and other Kurdish festivals. We attend these events, where refugees meet each other and become happy when they see other Kurdish refugees. We develop a sense of Kurdish belonging.

Without the Kurdish organization's events, we might lose our minds. We cannot always attend language courses, go on working, and suffer from the stress that the job center creates. This lifestyle is unbearable. Thus, the Kurdish associations help with our issues based on their possibilities, but they are not supported by the authorities, which even accuse the Kurdish bodies of being linked to the PKK. Many activities organized by the Kurdish associations are beneficial for us. The most important aspect is the fact that we maintain our Kurdish identity and avoid being connected with bad or dodgy people. For example, we are not involved in drug-related issues or other criminal activities. The Kurdish associations advise us and raise our consciousness against drug and gambling-related activities. These organizations encourage us to study, work, and develop ourselves. Without them, I could not imagine developing any friendships. Thanks to these associations, I was able to meet my best friends, who helped me settle in Berlin owing to our common identity in relation to Kurdistan and martyrs. Without the struggle for Kurdistan and respect for our martyrs, Kurdish refugees might have been worse than Arabs in terms of their criminal behavior and illegal activities relating to drug trafficking. The Kurdish associations do not wish for this culture among Kurds to take root within the Kurdish refugee community. The associations try to communicate with the Kurds concerned in an attempt to convince them to avoid their unacceptable habits. However, they cannot force these Kurdish refugees to stop their bad habits, as they might complain about the Kurdish initiative to the authorities, who might bother these associations.

> *So, Kurdish refugees view our affiliation as an entry point!*
> —Gulaw—Germany

As the organization for Kurdish refugee parents, we are highly involved in the Berlin community and have strong ties to a wide variety of local and transnational networks. Every Kurdish refugee that arrives in Berlin seeks advice from our organization on a variety of social and homeland-related matters. So, Kurdish refugees view our affiliation as an entry point. The primary concerns that bring them to our organization are the asylum application and court processes, support in hiring lawyers, and providing translators to accompany them to institutions. As soon as they hand in

5 TOWARD INTEGRATION: "WE CANNOT ACHIEVE INTEGRATION... 151

their asylum applications, they make their way to our association, inquire about the best approach to managing their paperwork, and be prepared to undergo the interviews that are associated with their asylum applications. They face numerous challenges, one of which is the search for an apartment, which is a highly important, yet sensitive matter given the fact that it is so hard to find apartments in Berlin. We provide them with directions on where and how to look for apartments. We strive to arrange for a translator to accompany and help them when they go to view an apartment. Refugees come to us for help managing their everyday lives as well as for the registration of their children in daycare centers or schools. We also assist them with filling out their forms and dealing with their paperwork. We offer assistance with welfare benefits at the job center and employment office.

There are also numerous Kurdish-speaking families, which we divide into Kurdish father and mother working groups. We train them on best practices for supporting, educating, and raising their children. Our aim is to grant our Kurdish children the tools they need to compete on an equal basis with German children. The most important cornerstone of this education is their parents. Therefore, it is crucial that the parents of Kurdish children understand the German educational system, how German society functions and operates, as well as their own obligations and rights. As a result, we run a number of projects, such as a service that offers refugee seekers advice. There are only six centers in Berlin, and our service is one of them. The service center is supported by the Berlin government's office for immigration. We have an initiative called "empower yourself" for the Kurdish families that encourages their independence. The Berlin government also supports this endeavor. We offer all of our services in Kurdish and German, as well as other Kurdish dialects, including Kurmancî, Sorani, and Zazaki. Berlin has become a Kurdish metropolis as a result of the arrival of Kurdish refugees from Rojava and their culture and traditions. These developments have created multiple opportunities for Kurdish organizations and associations in Berlin to function and affect their participation in a dynamic and effective manner. Kurds from Rojava speak Kurdish and place a strong emphasis on their Kurdish identity wherever they go, in contrast to the Kurdish refugees from North Kurdistan, who speak little to no Kurdish. Therefore, there is a high demand for Kurdish-speaking educators and pedagogues. We maintain these efforts because we are aware of how education shapes children. Consequently, we employ educators who are sensitive to the education of young children. We thus

152   V. DAG

manage four multilingual educational projects. All of these things take place under the roof of the parent association.

> *...these Kurdish establishments boost my self-esteem as a Kurdish refugee....*
> —Birusk—Austria

Once a week, I visit the Kurdish diaspora associations and participate in their events, such as film screenings, meetings, and entertainment. We eat and drink together while engaging in social interaction. When I am there, I have a positive experience because the Kurdish refugees from the four different regions of Kurdistan get together, share their narratives and perspectives, and build a community that makes me feel at home. I approach them for advice when I need something related to my German language course, housing, or any other concerns, and they are willing to provide me the support that I need. For instance, I requested help with a flat-related problem. They accompanied me to the viewing of the apartment and provided me with information on the requirements imposed by the landlord. The Kurdish organization plays a significant role in helping me manage my life in Austria by resolving my integration-related problems and offering advice. As a young refugee, I am dependent on these advisory services since I do not have any family members who are in a position to assist me on these matters. I respect the members of the Kurdish organization as my brothers and fathers and pay close attention to what they have to say since it is in my best interests. When I did not have my own flat, some Kurdish families that I met at the Kurdish organization invited me to stay at their homes. They supplied me with food for around two to three months while I was looking for my own place to live and gaining a better understanding of the possibilities for the future. Some Kurdish organizations also provide Kurdish language lessons for individuals who have forgotten how to speak Kurdish or for Austrian citizens who want to learn Kurdish. By providing Kurdish language classes, the Kurdish association satisfies the wishes of Austrians who desire to learn the language, while also supporting the resettlement and integration of Kurdish refugees. As a result, these Kurdish establishments boost my self-esteem as a Kurdish refugee, and I would like to contribute to their activities in return.

5 TOWARD INTEGRATION: "WE CANNOT ACHIEVE INTEGRATION... 153

Our association fills the integration void left by the government's failures!
—Nimet—Austria

There are a significant number of Kurdish refugees who are dependent on the necessary help to build a life in this country. Few associations exist that do not have many possibilities to assist all recently arrived refugees. We have made the decision to establish a cultural organization to fill this gap and assist recently arrived refugees in accordance with our abilities. We want to provide our Kurdish refugees with a sense of community, attend to their needs, and assist them in finding their place in the world. Following the formation of our organization, we approached Kurdish refugees and requested their donations to help cover our costs. We also obtained assistance from a Kurdish party in Kurdistan, which enabled us to establish this association in an effort to reconnect and gain the support of the Kurdish refugees in our campaigns. We plan several events for Kurdish refugees. For instance, we were aware that Kurdish immigrants, especially older ones, find it difficult to learn German. Many of them lack basic literacy skills and have never attended school in Syria. These governmental institutions are incapable of comprehending the reality of this situation. For example, when refugees are sent to a language school to study German, their teachers for basic lessons are Germans who fail to understand the participants' questions. Even if the German teachers respond, the immigrants who posed the question may not comprehend their answers. We provide these courses in a unique way. I am one of the teachers who successfully teaches German to refugees since we have studied the language ourselves and initially educate them in their home tongue, Kurdish. Within our organization, we could instruct around 100 Kurdish refugees. For example, there is a Kurdish refugee who is 75 years old and has never taken German courses. The job center also did not offer him German classes due to his age. However, he attended our German lessons and was able to acquire basic German. Furthermore, understanding is critical for overcoming some of the problems that refugees face.

My perception, however, is that authorities do not pay close enough attention to what refugees assert since they view all refugees as the same subjects and hence fail to distinguish between them. As a Kurdish refugee who has lived in this country for a few years, I have experienced first-hand the difficulties that refugees encounter. However, Austrian institutions are uninterested in obtaining insight into these issues and challenges. These refugee organizations view the refugee situation from various angles. We

154   V. DAG

have an in-depth familiarity with the members of our community. We may serve as intermediaries and a link in the chain between the government, non-governmental organizations, refugees, and Kurds in their homeland. In this sense, we have the capacity to be of greater assistance to the authorities in the matter of the integration of Kurdish refugees, but our capabilities are not being fully recognized. Our association fills the integration void left by the government's failures.

In addition, we offer services to aid Kurdish refugees with their paperwork. Authorities frequently send letters and documents to refugees. Refugees can receive free translations of these papers from our association, as well as help filling out their applications. We walk them through the paperwork and procedures of the bureaucracy, as well as provide advice and assistance. When we were unable to provide them with advice due to our lack of understanding, we contacted other institutions and specialists and requested information on behalf of the refugees. In addition, we provide Kurdish refugees with a six-month computer training program that trains them how to use the internet, Microsoft Word, Microsoft Excel, and other software. This association also organizes social events related to Kurdish culture, such as celebrations, festivities, and anniversaries. The celebration of Newroz, funerals, festivities, weddings, and other celebrations fall within this category. We put this organization at their discretion for their funerals or celebrations. We also appoint a committee of wise Kurdish men to intervene in the matters and disputes of concerned refugees to find resolutions. However, we do not become engaged in political confrontations between parties; rather, we organize activities that aid our countrymen in Kurdistan and advocate for Kurdish rights. We wish to increase awareness of the Kurdish cause and aid our people. We teach Kurdish to children and provide them with dance and music instrument classes. Occasionally, we organize evenings of music, storytelling, and entertainment for the Kurdish refugees. This has a positive effect on the mental conditions of Kurdish refugees and contributes to their gradual reintegration into society.

CRIMINALIZATION

> *...the government stopped providing us with any funds!*
> —Ferze—France

Because the government abandons asylum seekers, France is also a challenging country for them. They have to organize their lives on their own

5 TOWARD INTEGRATION: "WE CANNOT ACHIEVE INTEGRATION... 155

without the support of the state. The asylum seekers have to arrange an appointment at the refugee reception center via phone for their asylum application. When they call this center, their call is on hold for hours in order to speak with someone and receive an answer. There are fewer refugee support centers and charities because these institutions receive little money from the government and cannot survive. Therefore, there are not many associations that can provide services to asylum seekers. This difficulty applies to our association too, which cannot deal with asylum seekers' issues when we do not receive grants. There is no financial support for non-state organizations serving refugees. Nevertheless, some refugee associations offer French language courses from time to time. Our association can still function because of the support of the Kurdish diaspora constituencies. We help asylum seekers when we know them or have references. For example, recently, an asylum seeker arrived in France with his daughter and came to our association. We helped them in different ways because they had a reference. However, there are many asylum seekers who we do not know. We only help asylum seekers when we know where they are from and what they are doing in Kurdistan. We could support many asylum seekers if we had an office and resources, but our capacity is limited.

I normally support asylum seekers too, even though I am not in charge of dealing with their issues. I work on communication, public relations, and foreign affairs for the Kurdish association. However, I often stop doing my actual work and deal with the issues of newly arrived refugees. I go with them to the authorities to help with translation and other paperwork. It is very hard for me. We have also opened French language courses for asylum seekers. Many asylum seekers have attended these courses, and we provided them with certificates for their course attendance. This Kurdish association sometimes offers Kurdish language courses and finances itself, as it does not receive any grants from the government. In the past, we received some funds to organize such activities, but the government ceased this financial support. The government has filed several suits against our association in relation to terrorism. This was the reason that the government stopped providing us with any funds. The authorities consider our association to be a PKK center and connect it with terrorism. Consequently, this French approach has an enormous economic and political impact on our activities. This discrimination policy prevents us from applying for and receiving grants for our activities. The political aspect constrains our political and cultural relationships within institutional structures. For example, if we want to cooperate with an institution on

156   V. DAG

some cultural activities, this institution will check the background of our association, do some research on the internet about what kind of association we are, and find out that there are court cases against us. For this reason, they might avoid cooperating with us. Some French institutions, civil society organizations, or individuals might be scared to work with us and keep a distance from our association. However, this association is a crucial place where Kurdish immigrants can get to know each other and interact with each other. In this way, they find employment and accommodation. Thus, this association is a place of solidarity and self-help among Kurds, even though it does not have an established system.

> *...Kurdish associations are criminalized!*
> —Mezdar—Germany (2)

European states do not recognize Kurdish identity. They only recognize the Kurds in connection with the nationalities of the countries we had to leave. If we possess Iraqi nationality, we have to go to the Iraqi embassy. If we want to establish an association, we need to go to their embassy to seek support. This applies to citizens of Turkey as well. They probably do not understand why we Kurdish refugees escaped to Germany. A few years ago, we demanded recognition of Kurdish identity and submitted many original documents. However, the German parliament rejected our request. They did not accept that a Kurdish community exists in Germany. They recognize the Turkish community as consisting of Turkmens, Kurds, Azeris, and Arabs. They connect the Kurds with their countries of origin. The parliament has not acknowledged the Kurdish lobby claiming their cultural and human rights, organizing their people, establishing their associations, and finally creating their community. Thus, European countries are not our supporters.

Since they do not support our cause, they are also very distant from the associations we establish. We have presented to them many associations operating in various fields of expertise. For example, Kurdish organizations were established to serve Kurdish youths to help manage their needs according to the rules and to contribute to their integration, but the authorities remain ignorant. If we look at the government budget they spend on integration and migration-related issues, we can see a big difference in how much is used for all projects and how much is granted to Turkish associations, which get the largest part of these resources. Kurdish associations do not get any money unless they know an MP or have contact with government institutions. The government spends all the money on the projects of Turkish or Iraqi associations and other groups. They grant money according to nationalities. The Kurds are excluded from the available resources since they do not have a lobby. Since the Kurdish identity as a collective community is not recognized, this denial negatively affects the organization and engagement of the Kurdish associations.

We are a large community and actively engaged in political and social activities in the whole of Germany. We are voluntarily engaged and do not receive any funding or salary from any state institutions, apart from some small donations for our projects from non-state institutions. Nevertheless, Kurdish associations are criminalized. This criminalization is not related to the Berlin government but rather refers to politics in Germany and Turkey. The criminalization of Kurdish organizations occurs as a result of the political interests of both states. Turkey is a NATO partner, which has an impact on our lives and activities in Germany too. Our publishing houses and music studies are banned, and our associations and members are criminalized, even though we arrange many social activities here for the benefit of Kurdish refugees. We encourage the integration of Kurdish refugees with their color, culture, language, and diversity. We support refugees' participation in social structures in Germany that enable them to establish their social lives. However, we organize many Kurdistan-related activities that give the authorities an excuse to connect us with the PKK, even though we are a civil society organization. We do not have any military connections with the PKK. However, we adopt Öcalan's ideology and work with it, which also inspired the revolution in Rojava and is implemented there. We do implement this idea in our organizations too. However, this ideology is perceived as a threat since we do not use any state mechanisms. We try to organize Kurdish refugees to make their own decisions, to become aware of their condition, and to take care of themselves. This approach is perceived as a threat since we reject state bodies. Therefore, the authorities have a negative impression of our organizations.

We stick to democratic rights, but we are still criminalized!
—Ruken—Austria

In the past, we have cooperated with local authorities and the city government of Vienna. We also worked on a project for the twin city

158   V. DAG

government of Diyarbakir. Although the Vienna City Government consists of the Socialist Party, they kept their distance from us because of the reports that the Austrian intelligence provided about our association: that we take the line of the PKK. They emphasize that the Kurds are an oppressed group, but they are under the influence of the Turkish government, and they categorize Kurds into good and bad groups. They have a positive attitude towards individual Kurds and groups, but they have a very negative attitude towards our association in particular. They talk to us in a nice way when we hold unofficial meetings but have a negative approach when we are in an official venue. This approach has changed in the last two years. This materialized through a range of prohibitions and the sudden attack by the Austrian police on May 1. The left-wing party also made a negative statement about our organization. I think its new chair does not know anything about the Kurdish people. His statement was an attack against us and served to criminalize the Kurdish community. Politicians' lack of knowledge is also a serious challenge we are facing. At the local level, the politicians have their own networks and factions within the same parties and organizations. These networks have their own political approach towards outsiders and do not represent the party's policies. The previous chair of the left-wing party was a Kurdish friend, and he tried to travel to Kobanî, but he was prevented by the Turkish state. However, the current chair of the left-wing party has a totally different approach. They belong to the same party, but a contradiction emerges because of their own interests, which they can easily abandon. To remove this contradiction, we cannot change anything on our own, but our counterpart has double standards, as they cause problems while we are transparent to them. Whatever we do here, the authorities know that. We exercise our democratic rights through democratic channels that the authorities provide. We stick to democratic rights, but we are still criminalized.

> *...the German authorities are against the Kurdish struggle....*
> —Elwand—Germany

We Kurds live in Germany, but we are connected with our homeland, Kurdistan, where a war and bloodshed are ongoing, and our children and brothers are being killed. Hence, we are mobilized in Germany for our homeland struggle. However, we think that the German authorities are against the Kurdish struggle and have taken many actions against our activities. The Turkish state is fighting against us, but with their political

5 TOWARD INTEGRATION: "WE CANNOT ACHIEVE INTEGRATION... 159

approach and economy, the Germans are helping the Turkish state. This is an obvious policy against the Kurds. We can read this hostility in the actions of the German authorities, who are working against us. They do not want us to live and work freely in Germany with our culture, language, and reality. We perceive the German state's approach as hostile to Kurds. The German government instead opts for the criminalization of Kurdish organizations. Many Kurdish refugees want to visit our association to seek advice and help for their issues, but they stay away from it because they fear the German police and the criminalization policy, which are intimidating. A few months ago, the police raided our association and broke all its doors and windows. These forces do not want Kurdish refugees to create a community and cooperate with non-Kurdish people and young German citizens, who are keen to be present at our association. The police scare them off while criminalizing our association. Therefore, they launch permanent assaults on our associations. If we have demonstrations and marches, the police officers deal with us in a violent way as if our events were banned, although we have permission. Thus, the officers' behavior causes fear amongst our constituencies. Consequently, these governmental authorities are not helpful to our community organizations in integrating Kurdish refugees into the German social, political, and institutional frameworks.

We have also applied for support in order to contribute to the integration of Kurdish refugees according to German laws, but the authorities present adverse reactions, put our association under pressure, curb its activities, and prevent it from producing better work. Our friends always establish contact with the authorities, but they do not allow us to work freely and constructively. Recently, we have told the authorities that we do not need their help, but they should let us do our work freely in peace. We live in Berlin and respect German law, which we have not disrespected. We also have not allowed anyone to disrespect German laws or the German state. However, the authorities are very disrespectful towards the Kurds and Kurdistan. They have often assaulted us because of Kurdish and Kurdistani symbols such as the flag of Kurdistan, Kurdish colors, and other Kurdish symbols. They do not allow us to use these symbols freely or to carry them with us. The authorities also launch assaults against the Kurdish clothes that the Kurds wear in Kurdistan. Many refugees affiliated with this association are reluctant to wear their traditional Kurdish clothes since they fear that the authorities will criminalize them and ban Kurdish clothes. The police have even recently banned the Kurdish V sign, although it is an

160 V. DAG

international symbol and not a Kurdish symbol alone since the Kurds use the V sign more often. Nevertheless, the authorities associated this sign only with the Kurds and the PKK. Therefore, the approach of German authorities is very negative towards us. This attitude indicates animosity towards us. Maybe they do not tell us that they are hostile to us, but their approach is obviously hostile. Maybe there are some German police officers with a Turkish background who are manipulating, misleading, and provoking German police officers against us. This compels us not to carry out our work properly or smoothly. This is also a reason. We have told them that we have never disrespected or violated German laws. We will also not allow that for anyone else. The authorities should also respect our Kurdish people, Kurdistan, and Kurdish symbols. This is our expectation. However, we cannot say that German citizens share the same approach as the German state. We think that German society perceives our struggle differently.

> *I witnessed the discriminatory approach of the authorities!*
> —Yawer—Germany

We have very weak contact with government institutions. We might be in contact with one or two non-governmental associations, such as Rote Hilfe. Apart from these contacts, I have not witnessed any of the governmental institutions indicate recognition of us or show cooperation in responding to the needs of Kurdish refugees. We face many obstacles when we are stateless, and our association is not recognized by the government. Due to our statelessness, it is hard for us to make a claim and find understanding within this society. We are often constrained by the authorities during the organization of our activities and are perceived as suspicious. Therefore, people coming to our association are intimidated. They are told that if they visit our association, their asylum case might not be successful since our institutions have been labeled and marked in relation to homeland affairs. Many people I met told me that they avoid visiting our association until they receive their asylum status. They might only come to visit our association when they have an issue that they need our help solving. Otherwise, they avoid our association in order to have some clarity about their asylum cases. We have also not received any support from governmental institutions for our projects. In the past, I witnessed that some governmental associations asked us and other Kurdish associations to label as terrorists some Kurdish groups that are involved in armed conflict in the homeland. Then they would consider offering us funding. Otherwise, they could not support our activities. All government institutions and authorities assume that we are supporters of the PKK. This can never be accepted. Even when I was working at the Kurdish Institute of Berlin, I witnessed the discriminatory approach of the authorities. If our institutions have accepted such allegations, then we would ask ourselves why we have left our homeland in Kurdistan. We do not accept any Kurdish groups as terrorists, and none of the Kurdish groups have committed terrorism. The Kurdish groups, ranging from leftist to Islamist and nationalist groups, might have made some mistakes, but they have never systematically been involved in any acts of terrorism.

The Kurds are always deemed guilty in their liberation struggle, regardless of what methods they resort to. They have used the most radical methods, but also the most modest and reformist methods that other populations in the world have used for their own freedom and liberation. These methods have been defined as Ghandism or Guavaraism. Kurdish groups have not been successful in applying these methods yet but have been blamed for terrorism and unlawfulness. However, I believe that, as a method for a colonized population such as the Kurds', armed struggle is legitimate and similar to their mother's unspoiled milk. The Kurds have been hungry for five months since they went on hunger strike. We have now had dinner, but it is very embarrassing as thousands of people are on hunger strike in mountains, prisons, Europe, and everywhere else. We sent many letters to the German government about the meaning and message of the hunger strike. One of the letters was also sent by the daughter of a friend who has been on hunger strike. A 17-year-old daughter received a response from the German government saying that she should tell her father to stop the hunger strike and that she has to find another method for his cause. What do they expect us to come up with?

We are fighting, but they label us as terrorists; we demonstrate, but police forces prevent our demonstrations and ban our symbols. As a journalist, I have recently witnessed how the Kurdish demonstrators are even not allowed to raise their fingers as a symbol of solidarity. If we complain about this approach, the authorities come up with the argument that oppressed and poor people ask for help, but not in the way the Kurds do. These politics obviously constrain Kurdish activities. Sometimes, when we meet with authorities or encounter them at our events, they ask us whether the PKK and Kurds are the same. We tell the authorities that we are Kurds and organized with a legal association. We confirm that the PKK is a

162   V. DAG

Kurdish movement representing Kurdish honor. We tell them that if they forced us to express sympathy for the PKK, we would not deny our sympathy towards them, but we are a legal organization that does not have any links to the PKK. We tell the authorities that the PKK is fighting for the Kurdish people, and this is the way we see it, but we do not represent the PKK when we have a meeting with the authorities. If the PKK representatives found out that we were claiming to represent them while meeting certain authorities, they would be very angry with us since we do not have anything to do with their organization. Nevertheless, whatever we undertake and every project we present to the authorities is seen in connection with the PKK. When we submit a project to the authority for refugee issues, they come to check on our association. When they see that we have images of martyrs and Kurdish politicians, they reject our projects.

The whole world is aware of this fact, but the German authorities do not accept it. I think this is due to satisfying the states that have colonized Kurdistan. These states are influential and strong. I am referring especially to the colonizing Turkish state, which is powerful and influential in Europe. It is an important NATO member and plays a key role in politics in the Middle East. Additionally, it is an economically and militarily significant state and a crucial actor for European states. These ruling states in the Middle East determined the fate of the Kurdish people and caused Kurdish statelessness after the World War I. States such as Germany, the United Kingdom, and France have been very close partners with the Turkish state for almost 200 years. Therefore, they will never leave the Turks and hold the hands of the Kurds because of humanity or human rights. They will never prevent the Turkish state from killing Kurdish children, raping Kurdish women, or razing the Kurdish homeland to the ground. They will not sacrifice their business, economic, and military gains for the Kurds. They do not consider the Kurds an important issue.

> *...we are criminalized through the PKK and the label of terrorism!*
> —Ferda—Germany

The Kurds are the second-largest group of immigrants in Germany, but they are still not recognized as having their own identity. In official statistics, immigrants are registered according to their nationalities. Since they do not have their own state, Kurds do not appear in German statistics. Therefore, Kurds are classified as Turks, Arabs, or Persians. They have

5 TOWARD INTEGRATION: "WE CANNOT ACHIEVE INTEGRATION... 163

lived in Berlin for a long time but are still suffering from the policy of denial of their identity. For this reason, we have not been able to develop many projects. The director of the Kurdish parents' association told us that when they founded the association, a representative of the Berlin government was invited. While giving a speech, he stated that he was happy about the opening ceremony of this Turkish association. The association was designated as Turkish. There is a policy of criminalizing the Kurds in Germany. Regardless of the political line and activities of Kurdish associations, we are criminalized through the PKK and the label of terrorism. In the past, all our projects were rejected by the Berlin government, although many Kurdish refugees live in Berlin. Compared with many immigrant groups with other ethnic and religious backgrounds running hundreds of associations, the Kurds have only a few associations, including our association, which is active and interested in contributing to solutions to migrant matters.

We have been engaged in a long-term battle to explain that our association works for the interests of the Kurdish refugees who live in Berlin and Germany, respectively. For example, we want to offer Kurdish in German schools since many Kurdish children have to attend Turkish lessons and welcome classes. Many Kurdish children have learned Arabic in these welcome classes. I met Yezidi children speaking Arabic. I asked myself how a Yezidi could speak Arabic. When I asked them where they learned Arabic, they said in the welcome classes for pupils in public schools. It is problematic, and there is also no pedagogical offer for Kurdish children. Therefore, cooperation did not work well for a long time since trust was missing. However, there is now constructive cooperation at a higher level with the council and the Berlin government. We have successfully managed some projects to build trust. We have demonstrated that we are neither a terrorist association nor something else.

CHAPTER 6

Self-Governance from Below: "Self-Help Services Are Necessary to Mitigate Our Suffering"

The self-governance of Kurdish-Yezidi refugees is deeply rooted in their homeland's social reality, which has its origins in the history of this population prior to the establishment of modern states in the Middle East. The other connected element that drives Kurdish-Yezidi refugees to exercise self-governance in Europe is related to the combination of Kurdish-Yezidi statelessness and the neglected policies in their adjustment processes. Kurdish-Yezidi statelessness denotes the absence of state institutions devoted to equitably promoting and protecting the interests as well as meeting the cultural and social requirements of ethnically and religiously diverse Kurdish-Yezidi citizenries. Despite the civil citizenship rights granted by Middle Eastern and European states, Kurdish-Yezidi people are far from experiencing a sense of belonging to these nations via citizenship rights in either their home countries in the Global South or European countries in the Global North. Their identification with citizenship rights is quite weak since these do not provide the communities in question with equal opportunities to preserve and freely practice their cultural, political, and religious identities. The Kurdish-Yezidi population is mostly denied the right to assert their local autonomy regarding their way of life and embrace their cultural and ethnic identities. Nevertheless, the extended refugee and diaspora components exercise various forms of self-governance in their new environments in European receiving states (Dag 2023). Self-governing models of the Kurdish-Yezidi community include refugee and diaspora actors in receiving cities, self-built joint initiatives and

© The Author(s), under exclusive license to Springer Nature
Switzerland AG 2024
V. Dag, *Voices of the Disenfranchized*, Mobility & Politics,
https://doi.org/10.1007/978-3-031-46809-4_6

committees, and alternative management mechanisms. These self-formed establishments aim to accomplish spiritual and practical objectives ranging from identity construction, a sense of belonging, and engagement in cultural practices to the self-establishment of autonomous communities, building agency for self-regulation of bureaucratic, economic, and social challenges. The Kurdish-Yezidi refugees are able to continue living their traditional way of life, thanks to the self-governing models that they have developed. This way of life is influenced by the social structures that exist among Kurdish tribes and Yezidi castes in Kurdistan. Even if the aforementioned structures have been increasingly weakened as a result of external interference from controlling states and displacement, the Kurdish-Yezidi population at home and abroad has been able to maintain its traditions of self-governance.

As laid out in the introduction and the second chapter, the Kurdish-Yezidi people are minoritized in their homeland, and they share a long history of persecution, displacement, and genocide as a result. The cultural and social environments of these people have been impacted, and they have been subjected to a variety of sufferings as a result of the cataclysmic events that have befallen them. These experiences have pushed these people to reduce their dependency on governmental institutions for services while strengthening their will and capacity for self-management. Therefore, these communities have struggled to preserve their self-governing intra-tribe and intra-cast structures inspired by their oral traditions, ancestral memories, everyday practices from their homeland, and political and social circumstances, as well as narratives that are passed down by refugees in new environments abroad. They come together to form their community, within which they organize themselves and build agency to exercise self-governance by utilizing their formal and informal structures consisting of associations, joint initiatives, and committees to address refugee problems and offer them self-services. These services include resolving intra-community disputes without the aid of official state institutions, promoting peace and well-being, and providing information on orientation in settlement processes, including employment, housing, family reunions, bureaucracy, and general paperwork. The Kurdish-Yezidi organizations also take steps to prevent the assimilation of their refugee constituents and to sustain their connections to their homeland brethren. Last but not least, the self-built structures that are homeland-oriented also involve the Kurdish-Yezidi refugees in the cultural, humanitarian, and political affairs of their homeland through donations to charitable

6 SELF-GOVERNANCE FROM BELOW: "SELF-HELP SERVICES ARE... 167

organizations, participation in protests to increase awareness, and involvement in cultural festivals to maintain the community cohesion of the Kurdish-Yezidi diaspora community.

Despite the presence of multiple Kurdish-Yezidi establishments and their provision of vital services, their practices toward refugees and their relationships with them are not harmonious. While these establishments may associate their service provisions with ideological and political conditions and loyalty requirements because they frequently act along the ideological lines of political actors in the homeland, individual refugees use these establishments in an instrumental way to obtain ideal and material support for the resolution of their issues or advice and then disappear without being available for these organizations. In other words, the relationship between institutional structures and Kurdish-Yezidi refugees is occasionally based on a "tit for tat" approach and is susceptible to criticism from both sides. Kurdish-Yezidi refugees and representatives of diaspora organizations in Europe describe their own experiences with concerns regarding identity formation, community cohesion, self-governing models, and homeland-related cultural and social affairs at the local and transnational levels in their own words and discuss their critical perspectives within the context of these challenges.

IDENTITY RE-CONSTRUCTION

...aware of my Kurdish identity, but also feel a sense of belonging to Sweden!
—Mirhat—Sweden

The residence permit does not only offer us language and employment opportunities and new prospects for life in Sweden but also evokes a feeling that we are a part of Swedish society. I am aware of my Kurdish identity but also feel a sense of belonging to Sweden and want to dedicate my life to this country. I neither feel a sense of temporality in Sweden nor intend to return to my homeland after a while. However, I am also confronted with the difficulty that we have been divided in two. One part is located in the homeland, and the other part is in this country. We have our parents in our homeland, and we have our kids and our own families in this country. We cannot leave this country and go back to my homeland since I have responsibility for the future of my own family too. If I stay in Sweden, I am leaving behind my parents and the family who raised me. If I cannot look after my parents or forget them, I also forget my homeland

and do not value my ancestry and roots. I might go back at some point, but I must accomplish something for this country and for myself. I am not in Sweden to sit at home all day and waste my time. We can also obtain citizenship, which enhances our commitment to Swedish society. I would like to become a Swedish citizen, but I appreciate my Kurdish identity as well. I will also make sure that my children hold on to their Kurdish identity. They should never forget who they are and should keep their identity and ancestry when they are among various people in Sweden. My Kurdish identity also motivates me to prioritize the employment of Kurdish refugees, but I am also rational and run a restaurant. I need employees whose ethnic background is not relevant, and I am also not racist in choosing workers according to their ethnic background. I know that the Turks are racist and do not like us, Kurds. However, I would be racist like the Turks if I also hated them and did not employ people based on their Turkish background. If we are hostile to them in someone else's country, then there would be no difference between us and them in terms of the hostility that they feel towards us in Turkey. We should show them that we have tolerance, are not like them, and will not become racist.

> *...if someone rejects my Yezidi identity, I will also deny his identity....*
> —Sipan—Germany

You know, even if I knew that I would starve in Berlin, I would never go to any Kurdish associations due to their Islamic approaches. I have just heard that Yezidi associations exist in Berlin, but this is not true, as these associations are all Islamic and work for Kurdistan and Barzani. They are not members of the Yezidi community and do not work for me. I do not want to go see them because of the political and religious beliefs they have. I recently met a Kurdish refugee at Alexanderplatz who invited me to the Kurdish association and offered me his help. I told him that I am a Yezidi refugee and not Kurdish. He then said immediately that we do not know each other, I guess because of my Yezidi identification. I told him my frustration and feelings of humiliation when he did not recognize my Yezidi identity. If this approach exists, how can I visit Kurdish associations? I would have accepted his invitation if he had not rejected my Yezidi identity. Nevertheless, I would visit every Kurdish association that recognized my Yezidi identity, but if someone rejects my Yezidi identity, I will also deny his identity and his religious affiliation. I will respond to him in the way in which he treats me and avoid establishing contact with these

6 SELF-GOVERNANCE FROM BELOW: "SELF-HELP SERVICES ARE... 169

people. I do not have any problems with Kurds but rather with Muslim Kurds since they inflict harm on Yezidis.

The Kurdish association imposes Kurdish identity on us Yezidis. For example, when I visit a Kurdish association and ask the Kurdish refugees to help me write a letter concerning my asylum case and send it to court, they identify me as a Kurdish Yezidi, even though I do not want to be identified as a Kurdish-Yezidi refugee but rather as a Yezidi refugee. We have the feeling that the Kurdish identity is imposed on us, but we do not like it. If I meet a Kurd, he will first ask whether I am Kurdish, but I am not Kurdish but rather Yezidi. They then say that we do not know each other. I am not against the Kurds, but I expect recognition for my own identity regardless of my Yezidi, Jewish, or Christian background. Hopefully, I will never need to ask for support from any Kurdish associations. I do not have any links to them. I have only Yezidi friends, mainly from Shengal. When I meet my Yezidi friends, we always start to talk about our Yezidi pain and matters in Shengal. Since we are always occupied by homeland affairs, we cannot improve ourselves and undertake activities. We realize that we do not have any rights in either Germany or our homeland and suffer from Yezidi statelessness.

...my Kurdish identity in order to realize myself, be myself, and free myself....
—Serhildan—France

I experience socialization and gain my identity through my participation in social life. As the Kurds are dispersed and fragmented, it is necessary to raise awareness of my Kurdish identity. I define and introduce my Kurdish identity to realize myself, be myself, and free myself, as well as give meaning to it, and ensure my existence. Therefore, I am an ideal human being who wants the Kurds to experience their national identity in a rightful and pure way and is concerned with their freedom. I am an activist participating in civil disobedience within the democratic framework, struggling for and defending the values that Kurdistani society has constituted, wherever these values are under threat, attacked, or denied. I speak out, explain the Kurdish issue, and expose repressive policies towards Kurds according to the opportunities I am given and to my ability. If any activities take place, I dynamically attend these too. I defend the Kurdish identity everywhere and believe Kurds urgently need to become a collective community, both in Europe and in Kurdistan. Sociologically and

170 V. DAG

historically, Kurdish identity, the issue of its recognition, and the politics of international power go back to the situation in the Middle East. It is well known that British policies played a crucial role in dividing up the Middle East and constructing the current political map. This situation continues to this day.

French politics also played an important role in the division of the Middle East and Kurdistan, especially during the Lausanne Treaty. Nevertheless, the Kurds have managed to defend their identity but have not yet achieved recognition according to international law. They are currently not in a position to develop this collective national process to respond to and solve education, health, and economic issues. If the Kurds claim more rights for their Kurdish national identity and the advancement of their living standards, they will come across oppression and persecution. Within this context, the IS attacks and international politics are making great efforts to dehumanize the Kurdish population in Kurdistan. Unfortunately, the Turkish state plays a leading role in the realization of this policy. Thus, despite having gained some opportunities, the Kurdish people are kept in exile on their own geographic soil and homeland. At the same time, less politicized Kurdish individuals and immigrants who have been forced to leave their homeland—not only for European countries but also the US (United States) as well as countries in the far and near East—lead exiled lives.

Community Creation

...I am very satisfied with the self-services of the Kurdish refugees....
—Ako—Sweden

When we were granted asylum rights and needed to leave the refugee camps, the authorities did not look after us anymore. We were on our own to find employment, a flat, and a way to establish our new life. They only paid us some money that barely sufficed for our daily needs. I decided to move to another city and lived with my cousin for eight months. He was very generous in accommodating me. I then moved to Lund and met Kurdish refugees from the Turkish part of Kurdistan. What they have done for me in Sweden—maybe even my brother would not have helped me to the same extent! Their assistance was unforgettable. They provided me with employment, managed my paperwork, and translated my documents. A friend from Mardin was closer to me than my brother. He was a refugee

6 SELF-GOVERNANCE FROM BELOW: "SELF-HELP SERVICES ARE... 171

too, but he is now a citizen. He handed me money and met all of my needs. He allowed me to live with him in his flat and said that I should feel like the owner of the flat too and behave freely. He was very generous and considered me a family member. However, we both needed to leave his flat to make room for a Kurdish family, who had difficulty finding and renting a flat. He showed his solidarity with this family and stayed outside too. It was difficult for both of us. We thought that we were single men and could even sleep on the streets, but this was not possible for a family. We both had to find a temporary place, and we did not know what would happen to us. I am staying with a friend, but I do not feel comfortable as the landlord is putting pressure on us. Thus, the main problem is renting a proper flat, which is difficult to find.

I have changed flats eight times to date, moving in and out of new flats. I needed to register for a flat with the council, but I had to wait my turn because the flats are allocated according to a points system. However, the authorities removed me from the waiting list because they said that I came to Sweden voluntarily and had applied for asylum. The government did not invite me via UNCHR, and the flats are reserved for those refugees that are invited. I am now on the list of the private estate agency and have to wait my turn. Generally, Kurdish refugees help each other and show their solidarity in relation to the provision of resources, opportunities, and knowledge. If they could not help, they would ask other friends to help as much as they could. I could not force them to find a flat for me, although they need a flat too. In general, I am very satisfied with the self-service of the Kurdish refugees in Lund. They are down and out but live together, support each other, and treat each other well. They love their Kurdish identity and serve it according to their possibilities. Some make donations, while others use their time to attend demonstrations and homeland-related activities. Unemployed refugees cannot make donations every time but attend all demonstrations, events, and meetings related to homeland affairs. I am always present at these events, as for me, Kurds and Kurdistan are above being Muslims.

> *...common feelings of belonging to the Kurdish community!*
> —Memu—Germany (2)

We have established an initiative consisting of four members. I am one of them. If we hear that a new Kurdish family is arriving in Landshut, we go and see them and ask what they need. We also send our children with

172   V. DAG

them to the authorities that deal with refugee-related issues. We arrange for our friends to see newly arrived families and accompany them to the job center or other authorities to translate and fill out their forms. We sometimes help them with money, according to our own means. If they are granted asylum, they pay this money back to us. We collect, for example, a few hundred euros and hand them over, telling them to take this money until they establish their lives. If their situation improves, they will pay this money back. We incorporate the newly arrived families into our communities and encourage them to take responsibility for other newly arrived families. They understand our organizational pattern and are motivated to join our community in helping those families that need our support. They feel relieved if we help them. We recommend certain schools, share our experience with them, and offer help with how to register their children. The reason why we organize ourselves is related to the fact that we are alone. Kurdish refugees share common feelings of belonging to the Kurdish community. This motivates us to feel committed to each other. If we are, for example, on the bus and hear someone speaking Kurdish, we immediately approach them. We ask them how they are and whether they are newcomers, and we show our solidarity by offering our help if they need anything we can do for them. We encourage each other to maintain our culture of solidarity, as being in exile or in a foreign country is hard. We do not confine our solidarity to Kurdish refugees but also support Arabic-speaking refugees. We ask them if they need any help we can offer. We do not have any problems with their Arabic background, and they are also refugees, as we are. We consider them human beings because we are in a foreign country and in exile.

We also support each other and have close family contacts....
   —Ibrahim—Italy

We are lucky to live in this town with other Kurdish refugee families and refugee workers because we look after each other, visit each other, and exchange advice on our problems. We also support each other and have close family contacts, like in the homeland. It is very important to stick together, especially somewhere like Italy. In other European countries, it is easy to meet some relatives or friends, but this is difficult in Italy, where the number of Kurdish immigrants is very low. However, all of us Kurdish families live in a small town very close to each other. A Kurdish friend also has a café bar in this town, where we see each other every day. We always meet at his bar when we are off. Our wives are not working but stay at home and deal with the household. When they have managed their housework, they visit each other at someone's house or meet in a park to drink tea. So, they do not have a very strong longing for the homeland because they interact with each other very often. We work on the wine farms. Our employers are generally Kurdish refugees. We are thankful to them for employing us, and it means we can look after our families, but they also become rich thanks to our labor. We provide each other with mutual support. However, the conditions of our employment are very hard, and I complain about them. We work hard in the fields in the sun. It is very cold in the winter and very hot in the summer, and we struggle with our hard conditions, which are normally not bearable. I am not happy with these conditions and requirements. Normally, I would not work when I was not compelled to. For example, the Kurdish employers are appointed to take care of a field, but they ask for little money. Accordingly, the Kurdish employers hire us refugee employees and force us to quickly finish each field within two days, although this work would normally be finished in a week. They really exploit us, and I am not happy with this form of employment. Maybe they must force us to work hard to avoid suffering a loss since they ask the owners of the fields for little money. Nevertheless, we work under hard conditions and carry out difficult work, but we do not get a wage for our labor in return. If we worked in this sector in a country like Germany, our daily wage would be €100 and more, but in Italy we receive a maximum of €64. We work eight hours every day in the fields without taking into account the time we spend on the way and our break. We are paid for 8 hours, but it takes us 12 hours from when we leave home because we have to work in different fields, which might be 80 km away from where we live. In general, our conditions are very hard, and the payment is very low. We are under mental pressure because of these employment conditions. For this reason, many friends cannot stand them and move to other European countries, but they cannot take root there and come back here, while some other friends are successful and manage their lives in other countries. Whether we stay here or move to another country, it is a bad fate to be a stateless refugee who always has a very difficult life. We are cut off from our indigenous homeland, landscape, and compatriots. Some of our values are gradually getting lost. We are disconnected from these values. Nevertheless, we try to maintain our cultural values within the community, but this community maintenance cannot always be taken for granted because we sometimes become estranged from those values. I do not wish to be a refugee for anyone.

> *...we are motivated to maintain and foster our Kurdish culture, identity, and community!*
> —Zehra—Austria

Since we are not linked to any political party, we appreciate our Kurdish language and advance it. Because of our distance from political parties, we can come together and make progress in our culture and lives. Some friends might be affiliated with various political parties, but we leave the politics of these parties behind as soon as we are sitting here together. In the past, when we were disconnected and isolated, we kept our pain within ourselves and suppressed our feelings, which led to distress and distraction. However, now we meet up, discuss our issues, and share our pain and troubles with each other, enhancing our solidarity regardless of our gender. It is important for us that we are aware of our issues and are ready for each other. In Europe, refugees are in search of work or studies and might get lost. However, under these conditions, we stick together through the Kurdish Institute and see how we can support, protect, and advance each other. Moreover, I have been able to improve my Kurdish language and restore my roots. I tried to mix with Austrian youth organizations, but it was impossible to understand each other. It is smooth and easy for me to be among the Kurdish youths because of our understanding, despite our different social classes in terms of our experience and background, habits, and culture. I and other fellow Kurds are far away from our families and homeland, but we pay more attention to our mutual matters and take care of each other. We left our homeland, but we are motivated to maintain and foster our Kurdish culture, identity, and community. Since I joined this initiative, I have started to read more Kurdish books and meet Kurdish authors. I attach more importance to Kurdish culture now. It is crucial for us to come here because these gatherings bring us closer so that we do not forget our culture, language, and identity. These gatherings empower me to talk among elderly people too and to gain self-esteem and confidence. We do not hide or keep our thoughts to ourselves, but rather share our opinions with each other.

6 SELF-GOVERNANCE FROM BELOW: "SELF-HELP SERVICES ARE... 175

We cannot live without a social and collective life and a social community....
—Serbest—Sweden

The Kurdish structures are crucial in providing societal space for individual human beings as social entities. Without a social and collective life, as well as the social community that our associations facilitate, we cannot survive. A community with its culture and structures is very important for dispersed people like us, Kurdish refugees. As human beings, we Kurdish refugees always rely on our own community and organizations. If we are distant from our collective community and organizations, we may suffer psychological problems. We live in exile and face many social, cultural, and psychological issues. For example, couples get divorced, their children are involved in criminal activities, and many families have lost control over their children. In the end, these families dissolve since they cannot cope with these overwhelming issues. They regret that they did not contact the Kurdish associations beforehand. In contrast, those refugees who stick to Kurdish culture and are associated with these institutional structures have no experience of these problems. They manage their lives in an autonomous way and deal with social and economic problems, as well as employment and housing, because these associations are at their service and bring them together. These structures empower them to manage their lives and deal with serious issues. They do not ask the Swedish authorities to help solve their issues; instead, they come to the Kurdish associations and seek advice and support to solve their problems. They are satisfied and happy and do not need recourse to state authorities. In other words, our collective bodies are engaged in solving various problems and preventing additional problems. Thus, those refugees who are linked to the Kurdish organizations are less frequently confronted with these problems, while isolated Kurdish refugees encounter more problems because they have situated themselves outside these organizations.

SELF-GOVERNANCE

...common will of the population....
—Awaz—France

In the past, the services of Kurdish associations provided to newly arrived refugees included primary language courses, translation, and employment and housing-related activities, but the issues facing Kurdish

176   V. DAG

refugees have currently changed. Kurdish children grow up, and the issues and troubles of Kurdish families increase, especially when they seek to maintain their identity and security within other migrant communities and to resist the effect of degeneracy that the state produces to cause the dissolution and separation of Kurdish families. Furthermore, these issues include conflict between women and children, couples' divorces, kidnapping of partners, threatening one another, confiscating property, employing each other without payment, etc. Kurdish refugees avoid looking for solutions via government institutions since most of these issues are undocumented and unlawful. They do not have a lawful basis. For example, employers hire asylum seekers very cheaply without documents and often do not pay their remuneration. All of these are different problems. To manage these issues, we have formed justice committees that deal with them. These committees consist of eight or nine members, who every day receive a few requests from Kurdish immigrants hoping to solve their problems. Those families that accept the authority, legitimacy, and principles of the Kurdish associations utilize the services of committees. These members divide the tasks amongst themselves and visit the people in dispute at their homes, call them on the phone, invite them to the Kurdish associations, and meet them separately to convince them. They broker between disputed families to solve most of their issues and conflicts. Some issues are too complicated and cannot be solved. This situation bothers the committee members, who insist on solving these problems. These committees do not have strict rules like those that the state courts impose without discussion or question. Our decisions are discussable, touchable, and criticizable. Any side of the conflict might be reluctant to accept the committee's decisions when they are unhappy with them. This position causes trouble for the committee members too and leads to an unpleasant culture. We cannot claim that these services are sufficient and respond to all issues because we come across many extreme cases that cause a lot of trouble.

Another essential benefit of the Kurdish organizations is their success in keeping Kurdish refugees clean and unassimilated under their roofs. Instead, these entities facilitate the Kurdish refugees in maintaining their commitment to the Kurdish homeland and culture and developing a stance within the framework of Kurdish principles and rules to avoid engaging in misconduct, bad habits, and criminal activities. It is true that there are Kurdish refugees who are involved in criminal activities. These are some individuals with negative practices pursuing individual interests, but this misconduct does not take place within the organized Kurdish community. For this reason, it is not wrong to say that the organized, collective social Kurdish forces in general can be judged to be mostly clean and pure people. Through many activities, the Kurdish organizations make efforts to change those refugees with bad conduct and to create a better future for their children. However, we can discuss whether these activities are sufficient. Whenever these organizations undertake positive deeds, we regard them as beneficial for the Kurdish population. For example, these associations organize many cultural activities, which include dancing courses, music groups, and large assemblies with 70 or 80 people. They offer a dynamic basis for services and activities that contribute to the organization of Kurdish refugees and enable them to defend themselves and develop a political approach. This is the way in which the common will of the population, which remains immune from bad habits and activities, occurs.

The Kurdish associations are engaged in aiding the homeland and political campaigns for elections, and they motivate people for these kinds of mobilization. Our friends collect donations for those affected by natural and political crises. For example, there was flooding in East Kurdistan, and the friends launched a campaign to help them. Moreover, the Kurdish associations responded to the difficulties in Kobanî, Afrin, and other parts of Rojava through practical and economic activities. Additionally, these structures organized Kurdish individuals in France to donate and help the many Kurdish civilians who have become destitute and face hardship because of the war in North Kurdistan. Therefore, the role of these associations in the Kurdish community should not be undermined. However, there are also some friends who cause problems and complain about these associations, claiming to be neglected, ignored, or unfairly treated. But this struggle is not for the benefit of an individual but for collective interests. Whatever happened or should happen concerns us all, and we experience the same issues and responsibilities. It is very important that individuals take a stance towards this collective and social reality. There is a dynamic struggle in the homeland: the Kurds are resisting with their will and belief against the dark forces and states that cause darkness in their homeland.

We contribute to reconciling refugees in dispute and solving their problems....
—Udan—Sweden

178   V. DAG

We contribute to reconciling refugees in dispute and solving their problems, which relate to their lives and businesses in Sweden. They have fewer homeland-related issues for which they seek advice. I have been a member of the peace and reconciliation committee for three years. We have received requests to solve interesting and complex disputes. The conflicting refugees previously went to the Swedish authorities to solve their disputes since their cases were complicated, but without success. The authorities asked those involved whether they would accept asking our reconciliation and peace committee for help finding a solution to their disputes. One side accepted, while the other side was initially hesitant but, in the end, accepted too. We solved their dispute, which was about business interests and deception. They had been involved in business without signing official documents but based on hearsay. The authorities could not have solved this issue for lack of evidence, so they decided to send them to our association as they worried about failing to find a solution to this dispute since both sides might have used violence. The authorities sent us a letter to confirm that they could not solve this case and to ask for our help. So, our committee was able to do a great job. Both sides were not even Kurdish; they were from Turkey. Immigrants seeking advice and asking us to intervene are not only Kurds but also Iranians and other people. We also sometimes look at cases from Kurdistan. We had one from Belgium. We might go to these places, but it is very rare, as we have our networks in these countries.

We provide each other with self-help....
  —Sertan—Italy

The government has never offered us any economic resources as part of welfare benefits or spiritual support. Whatever we have created in this village is the outcome of our own power, strength, and self-organization. We have mobilized our social ties and social capital. For example, if we come to a new place, we ask pre-established friends to help us find accommodation or employment. If we lacked money, they would pay for us and complete the price of an item we bought. They also host us at their homes. For example, there are many friends who have accommodated many families at their homes for a few months until issues were settled and solved. In this sense, we continue to socialize and consolidate our social relationships. We provide each other with self-help and do not receive any support services from the government. Our statelessness has been the driving force behind our self-power, strength, and governance because we Kurds have never had any direct ties with states, neither in Kurdistan in Turkey nor in other parts of Kurdistan. The Kurds have always solved their own problems in their villages, mountains, or regions. They have never relied on any state bodies. These practices continue in this village in Italy too; although these patterns of self-governance are modern, they carry on in the same way as in the past. People seek the relevant help and solutions to their problems on their own.

We arrived in this town as individual refugees because we relied on employment and jobs, as well as essential documents to work, in order to stand on our feet. We picked up our families and reunited with them as soon as we settled here. With the arrival of our families, new needs and requirements emerged as we became a social community. For example, young refugees marry, and we need to arrange their weddings; the kids are born, and they need to be circumcised; some refugees are religious, and then they might need prayer rooms. There are also women's and youth issues that arise all the time since we settled here. The Kurds have different religions, and they are not only Muslims. Our children are born and grow up here. Some of them arrive here with their parents while they are still children. These offspring need to remember who they are and where they are from. We need to tell them about their Kurdish identity and run traditional Kurdish cuisine and Kurdish musical instrument courses in a common space that we call the Kurdish association. We also need to educate them in their native language. They can also learn their traditions and customs because we are a community that cannot be separated from each other. It does not matter what we do; we cannot be cut off from each other. This development means that we have completed the first phase, namely arrival, as we have formed a social space and become a family. We are now in the second phase of the consolidation in that we are becoming a community that meets its needs concerning belief, tradition, and mores, as well as culture and social life. Therefore, we live mainly together and have a large number of populations within a limited geography.

They find human warmth in the Kurdish organization!
  —Filya—France

As soon as many asylum seekers arrive in Paris, they come straight to the Kurdish associations because they consider them their home in a foreign country. There are also some mothers who are very old; they leave their home and come on their own to the associations, which they regard as the community's home. They live in their homes between four walls, like in a prison in a foreign country, and do not speak the language. They take the road to the Kurdish associations because they know where to find their community and people. They feel spiritually strong and pleasant and can open up to other people when they are at the Kurdish associations. They find human warmth in the Kurdish organization. We all share a common pain, a common homeland, and a common culture. We are all aware of the fact that we are those people who celebrate their national identity. We cannot say that everyone is a patriot because we cannot measure patriotism, and everyone has a different understanding of patriotism. I mean, people coming to our association attach importance to their Kurdish identity, but they are still lacking something of it, and they try to complete their Kurdish identification when they are at the House of Kurds. They feel this spiritual emptiness in relation to their Kurdish identity, but they find the way to fill this empty space at the Kurdish associations. In this sense, the Kurdish association is also the house of our culture and tradition, as well as of Kurdish identification.

Through Kurdish associations, many newly arrived refugees have stayed at our places for many days. A while ago, some families stayed at my home too because the Kurdish associations asked me. There was also a Kurdish family from the Kurdistan region of Iraq. The woman was pregnant, and the family had stayed on the streets for many days. They were on their way to the UK, and as you know, the Kurds from South Kurdistan prefer to apply for asylum in the UK. This woman gave birth in the hospital but had to leave. She did not have a place to stay. They stayed for a week at my house. Their friends booked train tickets for them to travel from one city to another. Similarly, a few days ago, our friends from the House of Kurds called me and explained that they had met a Kurdish family at the train station who needed to travel to another city. They needed a train ticket but did not have any money. The friends wanted to book their train tickets, but their bank cards did not work. They asked me for my bank card details, which I shared with them. In the end, they did not use my bank card, as their bank card worked. In general, we are Kurds, and if another Kurd seeks shelter, we will make efforts to meet their needs and look after them. It is our humanitarian responsibility to take care of Kurdish asylum seekers in need. My heart does not accept me saying that I will not help another human being.

6 SELF-GOVERNANCE FROM BELOW: "SELF-HELP SERVICES ARE... 181

...this association offered me the culture, habits, and customs of my ancestry....
—Felemez—Austria

When I entered the House of the Kurds, I met many Kurdish friends and did not feel that I was an outsider because this association offered me the culture, habits, and customs of my ancestry as well as friendship, solidarity, and respect. Within this association, I was able to attend Kurdish dancing classes, speak my Kurdish language, see my colors, and experience my culture. I could see all the Kurdish values, symbols, images, philosophy, and attributes of my Kurdish history and identity, for which I lived and was struggling in Kurdistan. The homeland and its narratives are our priorities in conversation, and these cannot be forgotten. The homeland is always present in our lives. When I look at any images or symbols at the Kurdish association, I immediately think of the homeland, Kurdish culture, tradition, and way of life. When I speak the Kurdish language, I can breathe and feel mentally relieved from mental pressure. This gives me the feeling that I am at home in Kurdistan. I was very happy to be at this association and see all these attributes. Gradually, I became closer to friends within this association and met many youths, women, and families from Rojava, whom I asked for their life experiences, cities of origin in Rojava, and stories of their refugee journey. Rojava encompasses a long territory, and I met many Kurdish refugees from Afrin, Kobanî, Al-Darbasiyah, Amude, and Qamishli at this association and built friendships with them, becoming part of the Kurdish community. I attended many meetings and became involved in the activities of different committees initiated by this association. I became an executive member of it, and now I am an executive member of the Kurdish Assembly of Vienna. We also make great efforts to be successful in our activities, and we rely on the Kurdish community in Vienna, our will, and our friends. Many Kurdish youths and children in Austria are involved in criminal and drug-related activities. With the football and social events, we try to prevent youths from participating in these activities and encourage them to play football, to approach the Kurdish community, and to interact with other Kurdish refugee groups as well as Kurdish families and friends. The criminal activities do not fit us Kurds and Rojava, as we became refugees in this country for a cause. We do not want the Kurdish refugees to damage the good reputation of the Kurds. We introduce ourselves as Kurds from Rojava to Austrians and other immigrant groups.

182   V. DAG

...our association acts as bridge....
—Kardux—Germany

We opened an association in order to respond to the needs of the Kurdish refugees in Berlin and help them. We try to help refugees as much as we can. For example, a Kurdish refugee recently passed away in the hospital. For the transportation of his body, we arranged financial resources and dealt with the bureaucratic process. Since the government refused to pay for the transportation of his body, we were committed to arranging the necessary resources to transport it to Kurdistan. This is one of the issues that the Kurdish organizations oversee. In this regard, we also help refugees respond to multiple issues such as housing, language, employment, and other social problems. For example, Kurdish businessmen were looking for employees and asked us. At the same time, some refugees were searching for employment. We put them in contact so that both their needs were met. Thus, our association acts as a bridge between newly arrived Kurdish refugees and long-term immigrants to fill the needs of refugee groups. If we do not reach out to the Kurdish refugees, they will stay on the streets and become involved in criminal activities, such as drug trafficking. Criminal groups without principles and ethics could abuse Kurdish refugees who are unaware of these groups and cooperate with them. However, if Kurdish refugees join our association, we attempt to educate them in various fields relating to their lives in Berlin and Kurdistan, introduce them to the Kurdish struggle, and promote their understanding. We keep them closer to the Kurdish struggle and Kurdistan. The living conditions in Germany are appalling for newly arriving refugees, who can easily become lost on these streets.

...the associations connect Kurds who were disconnected....
—Xezal—France

The House of the Kurds is the place where we Kurdish families gather, exchange our experiences, share the same politics and ideologies, and come together around many other common values. We have many Kurdish families in Paris that do not normally want to see each other as they are in dispute, but when they visit the Kurdish associations, they leave these negative feelings outside and create a cohesive family. Kurdish families involved in disputes visit the Kurdish associations and seek advice on solving their problems within the Kurdish community, as we speak the same language and have similar backgrounds. So, we can understand one another better and know how to solve our own disputes. The words of our community centers are respected and taken seriously. These practices have taken place in France and many other countries. These centers can efficiently solve the problems of Kurdish immigrants, and there are many examples, including my own. In this sense, the Kurdish organizations shoulder responsibility for solutions to different issues affecting the Kurdish refugee, asylum seeker, and immigrant communities in other European countries and in France.

A few days ago, for example, we received a phone call in the middle of the night from friends at the Kurdish associations. They told us that several Kurdish asylum seekers from South Kurdistan need a place to sleep as they were homeless. We agreed to host them, and they came to our place and slept overnight. When the friends called in the middle of the night, we were almost asleep, but we were fine with the request. We never question these requests and accept these people because the associations ask us to host them. There were also eight Kurdish athletes from Germany who came to Paris to attend some Kurdish events. Again, the organization asked us whether we could host them. I said yes and accommodated them for a few days. We do not only host asylum seekers but also Kurdish groups from other European countries who come to Paris on holiday or for meetings. The House of Kurds allocates them to Kurdish families.

Through the coordination of the Kurdish associations, the dispersed Kurds in Europe come together. In other words, the associations connect Kurds who were disconnected and become a kind of bridge. The reason that we do not question the backgrounds of the Kurdish asylum seekers and refugees whom we host immediately is because the Kurdish associations send them to us. Therefore, we trust them and believe that they are clean. The Kurdish refugees in the social environment of the Kurdish organizations are trustworthy and respectful. We also have children who might misbehave towards these guests. However, we educate them on how to behave when we have guests via the Kurdish associations. We make our children aware of the discipline required of Kurdish associations. Our children recognize their boundaries and know the way in which they act. Thanks to the discipline and culture of the Kurdish associations, our children are respectful. We live in these foreign countries and cannot be the same as we are at home in Kurdistan.

184   V. DAG

Intra-community Affairs

...they use the pain and weakness of the undocumented immigrants....
  —Demhat—France

Many Kurdish employers hire undocumented migrants and asylum seekers for 10 or 15 days and exploit them. These employers know the consequences for the undocumented asylum seekers who conduct illegal work and are arrested by the authorities. Therefore, they use the pain and weakness of the undocumented immigrants, for whom it is very hard to seek rights and justice. They have good intentions about working without papers, as they rely on Kurdish patriotism and think that the employers will not cheat them. The employers introduce themselves to the Kurdish asylum seekers as a part of the Kurdish community, even though these discriminatory employers do not appear in the social environment of Kurdish associations as they are right-wing groups and undertake bad deeds. So, I have often been cheated, even though I have legally worked for some employers too. I have worked on a construction site, but I did not receive my payment from my Kurdish employers for many years and did not have any resources to obtain it. I could not go to court because I did not have a contract or evidence. In some cases, I complained about them, but the authorities could not find these employers because they had changed their names or had a new label. So, I could not even receive my money through the authorities. French law cannot solve these problems either, or the government is not in a position to undertake a commitment to prevent these practices.

Employing someone but not paying them exists only within immigrant communities, and these groups of immigrants are from Turkey, whether they are Turkish or Kurdish. There are tricksters in every community. They constantly change their fronts and claim that they are Kurds today, but tomorrow they become Turks. They change their political front constantly, becoming right-wing or left-wing according to their interests. For these interests, they are involved in any unethical activities. They are always greedy and covetous, even though they are rich. If these people possess the whole world, they still desire more. If these employers had a shred of patriotism or a democratic attitude, they would accept their mistake and pay the Kurdish asylum seekers their money. They would not exploit their vulnerable people. So, we face extreme discrimination even though we have legal documents. It is not only about the exploitation of undocumented asylum seekers but also of documented immigrants. However, the Kurdish associations can solve the problems of undocumented asylum seekers by urging employers to stop exploiting them and start paying them. The Kurdish associations can communicate with these discriminatory employers in a civilized way and convince them to pay our wages, but they cannot act as police to arrest them. Otherwise, these employers might report them to the authorities and complain about the associations.

> *It is problematic when we discriminate against each other....*
> —Keyo—Italy

It is problematic when we discriminate against each other and come up with prejudices. When we were in Turkish cities, the Turks were racist towards us and discriminated against us because of our Kurdish identity, regardless of our city of origin. However, long-term Kurdish refugees here have prejudices against us in relation to our city of origin. For example, refugees from Bingol have particular characteristics, while those from Urfa or Diyarbakir are accused of having different attributes. I attended my asylum interview in court, and my translator was a Kurdish female friend. She asked me for my city of origin, and I told her, but she accused me of using Turkish words when I speak Kurdish. She threatened to tell the judge that I speak Turkish. It is not my fault because the Turks imposed an assimilation policy on us. We do not speak the Turkish language voluntarily, but it is nice that we speak Turkish as another language, though we do not identify ourselves as Turks. We also have some problems that are related to our dialectics. We cannot express ourselves in an appropriate way. Some Kurdish translators working at the courts do not translate our statements when we use Turkish words, but it is not our fault when we do not speak Kurdish properly. In this sense, the Kurdish translators do not help us in court, rather, they cause problems in relation to the language when we have our asylum interview. Half of the Kurdish dialect from Urfa is Turkish, but it is not our fault. I heard many Kurdish words for the first time in my life in Italy. If we had been in possession of opportunities to speak our Kurdish language freely and had our own schools and our own state, we would not have been in this situation and had these troubles anyway.

186   V. DAG

...the refugees are tired of talking permanently about politics.
—Havin—Sweden (2)

I was born in Sweden and have been involved in Kurdish organizations for 15 or 16 years. I have started to attend dance classes. I am part of the youth wing of the Kurdish association. We organize predominantly cultural activities such as dancing, language, and music events in order to contribute to the integration of refugees from Kurdistan into Swedish society and enable them to learn the Swedish language. We promote Kurdish culture as well. Some refugees come to attend dancing classes, while others learn to play musical instruments. When our activities end, we hang out together with all participant refugees to get to know each other more in person. We socialize and become close friends. We do not talk about politics because we are not interested in it. Instead, we talk about cultural activities and attend Kurdish festivities and parties. I think the refugees are tired of talking permanently about politics. When they come here, they want to dance, sing, laugh, and have fun. We give them the feeling that they are included in our groups, and we are not exclusive towards them. We do not give them any feeling of being excluded because of their political positions or opinions. They are sad when they talk about their tough experiences in the homeland since they are traumatized. We can imagine what kind of experience they had, but we do not ask them about it since they might not feel secure. We invite them to come join us, and we are honest with them when we do not talk about the war in Syria. We just focus on our activities and give them the feeling that they are part of us. Some refugees do not know their birthdays, but we remind them and take them out. We just give them the feeling that they are part of us. We also help them with orientation for their education in Sweden. So, we focus on positive and good experiences and plans and encourage them to move on.

I think we Kurds in Sweden are more culture-oriented than the Kurds in Berlin or Germany, who are politicized. We talk more about Kurdish and Swedish issues, hang out with Swedish friends, and go to the cinema, for instance, while the Kurds in Berlin are engaged only in Kurdish matters and politics. They do not mingle with Germans, as they are more political than the Kurds in Sweden. Maybe this reality is associated with their parents, who are political activists. They know each other and have a close community, while we were born and grew up without talking about politics in our families. We discussed cultural issues and focused on other

6 SELF-GOVERNANCE FROM BELOW: "SELF-HELP SERVICES ARE... 187

social activities. We learn more about Kurdish history than political affairs, to which we do not pay attention. I am Kurdish because of the Kurdish culture, but I am disinterested in Kurdish politics. However, we do not ignore these developments but discuss them with our parents.

We are tired of political discussions, which occupy our lives permanently. We want to show that we have more than solely political discussions; we also have cultural values and attributes such as Kurdish dances and language that are very important too. We grow up with the culture, not necessarily with politics. In Sweden, as well as in Germany, the politics divide the Kurds into antagonistic factions. We do not want to be part of these factions but rather to focus on the culture that brings us, Kurds from different parts of Kurdistan, together. If we had been involved in political disputes, we would have failed to create the unity that we have created in Sweden. We would have been baffled by the various factions from each part of Kurdistan. Nevertheless, our individual members attend the demonstrations (which we do not organize) in solidarity with Kurdistan. For example, I have attended demonstrations against the Turkish invasion in Afrin to show my solidarity with the Kurds. When Kobanî was under siege, with two other members of our groups, we collected donations, organized a fund-raising event, and donated our revenues. We went to Kobanî and purchased essentials and clothes for domestically dispersed refugees. It was in 2016. I dedicated my school project to Kobanî and organized a large event. We went to Duhok, a city close to Rojava. We bought a large amount of school materials, such as pencils, books, and toys, for refugees from Rojava.

We are exploited by pre-established Kurdish refugee employers....
   —Berxwedan—France

We are exploited by pre-established Kurdish refugee employers, which we can designate as modern slavery. The employers earn millions of euros but do not pay us what we are entitled to because we do not have our legal documents and arrived here a few years after them. For example, if our remuneration amounts to €10, they pay us €2.5. I think they condescend to bad deeds, which do not only refer to robberies or drugs but also to violations of rights and justice. We always claim rights and justice, but we do not seem to have rights and justice ourselves. This applies to me too. We are Kurds, and none of us have rights or justice, but we demand them. It is true that the absence of rights and justice in our case refers to the way

188   V. DAG

in which we were brutally, unfairly, and unjustly treated. Nevertheless, it is wrong to resort to the same unjust treatment that we have experienced. If those refugees who arrived here before us have experienced these practices, they should not implement them towards those refugees arriving after them. However, we Kurds have a strange mindset when the long-term refugees who have faced negative practices and discrimination in France expect us, the newly arrived asylum seekers, to undergo the same path and process too, like a military system. Our employers and people with opportunities deploy this system permanently in an extreme way. We reflected on this system after three or four years of encountering hardship. We asked ourselves questions about how they behaved in the past and how they behave now. With time, some changes occur without our realizing them immediately. I think we made some sacrifices to realize this situation. Without sacrifice, we cannot realize what is happening, but we make this sacrifice, which becomes painful to us. In this sense, we deal with each other. This occurs to us because the basis of our relationship is not solid.

> *...our people introduced their own system to exploit vulnerable refugees....*
> —Mertal—Italy

I have been living for a year in these parks around us and on the streets, and I am often hungry. This situation continues, although we are trying to resist these conditions. I consider our conditions to be torture that we experience in vain. We do not receive any support services in Italy, and life is very harsh here. I went to Switzerland for six months to work with a friend, but we could not agree on terms. I gained experience with refugees there too. People working there received 5000 or 6000 Swiss francs per month, while he paid me 1500 Swiss francs, although I was working as a pizza chef. I baked at least 100 pizzas for him every day. He was a Turkish shopkeeper and offered me a job, as the Kurdish employers did not. However, he hit me too, but I am used to this. He did not pay me any money, not even my 1500 Swiss francs. I did not want to have an argument with him because I did not have my documents. I worried that he would connect me with a serious crime and report me to the authorities, as I was in Switzerland illegally. I was silent, although I wanted to slaughter him. I am a Kurd, and we do not easily accept injustice, but this refugee status suppresses me. Nevertheless, I left him the money because I could

6 SELF-GOVERNANCE FROM BELOW: "SELF-HELP SERVICES ARE... 189

not speak the language there either. In the end, before I left his shop, he said that the Turks hate the Kurds, and the Kurds hate the Kurds. When he used this expression, I asked him why he had helped me, and he responded that God wished to help me. He deceived me, although I thought that he was an honest person, and therefore, he helped me.

I also had a similar experience at the hands of my brother and his Kurdish wife in Finland, where I lived for four years and worked for them without any payment. My brother and his wife promised me they would help reunite my children and family with me in Finland. They told me to work for them for five years without any payment, but they would pay my rent and expenses until I received my residence permits and indefinite leave to remain. This was how our people introduced their own system to exploit vulnerable refugees until they received indefinite leave to remain. However, I worked for five years for my brother, but he did not give me my money, broke his promise to bring my children and family, and on top of all this, I was punished (crying).

Recently, I went to a kebab shop in Rome and negotiated with its Kurdish owner, but we did not come to terms. I had the impression that he would mistreat me, as my previous employers did. In the end, I told him that I could not work. He followed me by yelling behind me that I was going to end up living on the streets, which is what we and I deserve. I turned back to him and said that I would not work for him even if I had to collect bread from bins and eat and sleep on the streets. I said that I was not committed to working for him because he did not pay me what I deserve. I said to him that I will be able to eat three times a day when I work at his kebab shop, but I prefer to eat twice a day or once every two days, as it is better for me. He cursed me, but I ignored him and left. Our people have been absorbed in this system and have grasped some opportunities, but they are extremely exploitative and have lost their humanity and Kurdish identity. They have a name that is Kurdish, but they have nothing to do with Kurdish values or content. This is the outcome of Turkish colonial politics towards us, in which the Turkish state penetrates our DNA and destroys us from the inside. Therefore, I do not want anyone to leave their homeland and collapse abroad. A piece of dry bread and an onion in the homeland are a thousand times better than the meat, kebabs, lives, and languages of European societies.

190   V. DAG

...interests and agendas of their parties over homeland tragedy!
—Mazin—Sweden

The main issue that we encounter is that we are disconnected. Why do we not connect with each other when we claim to feel responsible for our homeland? I think the reason is the approach of some Kurdish activists in Sweden, who prioritize the interests and agendas of their parties over homeland tragedy. For instance, I went to Copenhagen to attend a protest event for solidarity with Kurdistan, but when I was at the demonstration, organizers used the symbols of particular parties and shouted slogans pointing out these party interests. We were mobilized to raise our voices to create visibility for the homeland struggle, but these protest and solidarity activities turned into solidarity with some political parties in the homeland. We have made many mistakes that have led to many Kurdish refugees moving away from our actual Kurdish cause. This cannot help with addressing our issues and claims. I have also decided to keep a distance from all these political groups, as they are concerned about their interests and agendas. This discourages me from participating in political events and communities. I was unhappy with this situation and criticized the leading Kurdish activists, who ignored my criticism, so I decided to give up the idea of associations, connections, and collective activities.

However, if a Kurdish refugee arrives here and needs my help, I will provide him with accommodation and food and book his ticket to wherever he wants to travel. I have helped many Kurdish refugees since I am patriotic and love my Kurdish homeland and my people. If I hear or receive a phone call saying that a Kurdish refugee is arriving in Copenhagen, I will go and pick him up. However, I want to stay away from political groups that are more concerned with their parties than with their homeland. We have an expression emphasizing that people in trouble do not have friends. I am aware of this fact. I have been living in Malmo for a while, but I have not seen long-term established refugees helping newly arrived refugees. I know many individual Kurdish shopkeepers who employ newly arrived refugees but exploit them and do not pay them. In this sense, there is less solidarity than long-term established refugees show with newly arrived refugees in Sweden. They mistreat them and blame them for not working hard enough. I think it is easy to say that we Kurds love each other and are there for each other, but when it comes to reality, these attitudes might change. When I was in Kurdistan, I was an activist

6 SELF-GOVERNANCE FROM BELOW: "SELF-HELP SERVICES ARE... 191

and engaged in the Kurdish struggle in every country, but when I needed help, my request was ignored. When I was in the homeland, I was also religious and went to mosques to pray. However, I have left politics and religion behind since I have been in this country. I have less of a headache here.

CRITICAL EXPRESSIONS

...most Kurdish associations...strongly under the influence of political parties from the homeland!
—Armanc—Austria

The association is a social place where many people come together based on similar views, interests, values, and statelessness in our Kurdish case. These interests and goals encourage people to find each other under a common roof. However, most Kurdish associations that have been established for 20 or 30 years are affiliated with political and ideological parties or strongly under the influence of political parties from the homeland. When these parties and movements did not improve themselves and the activists and politicians engaged in these parties in the homeland came to Europe, they controlled the Kurdish diaspora communities as if they were their owners, mayors, and fathers. However, the main problem with these people is the extent to which they have not advanced themselves or their children. They have failed to create opportunities for the new generation and prevented the improvement of Kurdish communities in general. They have a grip on power within the Kurdish community in Kurdistan, like a chicken sitting on eggs, by controlling the Kurdish organizations. They consider the Kurdish community their own capital. However, they do not have the power in the diaspora that they had in the homeland. The rules and economic structures of the community have changed, and these people do not have this influence and power anymore.

Individualism is more evolved, and the collective life that we had in Kurdistan does not exist in the diaspora anymore. When we met elderly Kurdish people in Kurdistan, we respected them and did not say that they were wrong or had lied. However, in the diaspora, when they speak to us and are not correct, a youth could easily accuse them of lying. The traditional respect does not exist anymore, as it did in the homeland. These elderly people cannot behave in the way they did there. This changed, especially when we Kurdish academics and students from Rojava arrived in

192   V. DAG

Austria and became refugees after the civil conflict and the Syrian revolution in 2011. We criticize them for changing their attitudes in order to collaborate and find our places within these organizations, which they use as coffee shops. They meet up at an association and speak either Turkish or Kurdish among old people. We expected them to provide services for the Kurdish community in cultural, social, and linguistic areas and to enable communication among and between the Kurdish refugees and Austrian society. We realize that their organizations do not play their role within either their own community or between their community and the host society. They are reserved and narrow-minded. This is a mistake: they close themselves off to Kurdish youths, change, alternatives, and new ideas. They are also not integrated into Austrian society in any way. Their activities do not respond to our needs and wishes. I have the impression that these diasporic groups and the homeland are disconnected and that their developments in the diaspora are moving in different directions. They have a conservative mindset because they are away from their homeland, even though they maintain their culture and identity. So, I am not hostile to these people and do not accuse them of being bad people. On the contrary, they are patriotic, as they have worked hard for their community and participated in the Kurdish struggle. I do not disrespect them when I criticize them. However, respect is one thing, and activism is something else. I want them to work in a professional way and to stop preventing young university graduates who could play a crucial role in transforming our society and act as a bridge between the Kurdish community and Austrian society.

> *...the Kurdish associations...lead to Kurdish fragmentation and factionalism!*
> —Xebat—Germany

There are several Kurdish groups in Berlin that strive to organize cultural and social activities for Kurdish refugees in order to bridge the gap between their lives abroad and their homeland. These Kurdish groups could have organized cultural and artistic events such as Newroz, traditional festivals, and anniversary days to unite Kurdish refugees while meeting their fundamental needs. They could develop a strong community while maintaining links between the refugees and their home countries by engaging in these activities. However, the Kurdish associations do not function as intended in practice; rather, they lead to Kurdish

6 SELF-GOVERNANCE FROM BELOW: "SELF-HELP SERVICES ARE... 193

fragmentation and factionalism. They contribute to troubling conduct, gossiping, and mutual discrediting. The main reason is that the Kurdish parties do not work on a solution to the political and ideological problems that impact Kurdish refugees abroad. So, they do not make efforts to organize Kurdish refugees abroad but actually cause their fragmentation, like in the homeland. They do not consider the complex situation of the Kurdish community but would even claim that they work in its interests. These parties do not understand that we live outside Kurdistan and that they have to be more careful and sensitive. Instead of building up unity and collective representation towards the German government, they are far from this position and have a subversive approach. This means that they do not attempt to solve the problems of Kurdish refugees but rather deal with each other. They do not pay attention to these important deeds or the interests of the Kurdish refugees. This is an unfortunate fact.

I have not witnessed these associations providing any services for the integration of Kurdish refugees. I work with four associations, including the German-Kurdish umbrella organization, but there are no Kurdish associations that help with integration. They do not advise the refugees about the housing crisis or where they could find flats or attend language classes. Some associations organize German classes on the weekend since they receive money from the government, but these are insufficient. Thus, the Kurdish organizations do not have proper projects for the integration and management of refugees' lives in Berlin. As individual refugees, we help the Kurdish associations continue to exist and undertake some work. We help them, but they do not provide us with any support. The assistance that we provide them is related to their activities in organizing conferences and cultural events. We join the Kurdish organizations, become their members, and rekindle their dynamics. Some of these organizations have existed for 10 to 15 years, but Kurdish individuals have less interest in working in or with them. Therefore, these organizations become rather meaningless when refugees are less inclined to join them and remain weak and marginal. They also do not organize meaningful activities for the homeland. That is the reality of the Kurdish organizations in Berlin.

> *...Kurdish associations neglect the newly arrived asylum seekers....*
> —Serpehat—France

Kurdish associations neglect the newly arrived asylum seekers and make little effort to help them obtain asylum status. For example, despite my

194   V. DAG

own personal sacrifice, pain, and engagement in the Kurdish struggle and that of my family, or the heroism in my home city of Botan, where thousands of martyrs shed their blood, this association did not pay attention to my case and neglected my request for some help with the provision of shelter in a refugee camp, my application for asylum, and the establishment of a new life in this country. I still do not have an address, which I will need very soon when I go to court. When I submit my application to OPFRA in a few days, I am required to provide them with an electricity or water bill confirming my residency and address. It requires us to provide them with the address where we stay. The House of Kurds could not even help me with an address, although I have asked friends several times. They said that they would deal with my request, but I have not heard from them, although I have been living here for a month. Moreover, I asked the House of the Kurds whether they could help translate my documents from Turkish into French, but they told me that they do not have a translator but recommended a Kurdish patriot at the association, who asked for much more money than the translation bureau. This individual introduced herself as a Kurdish patriot, but she uses her service as a sort of business. Despite my lack of financial options, I had to pay €400 to a bureau for its French translation of my documents and files of my case when I was persecuted and put in prison in Turkey. Instead of these commercial practices, the Kurdish associations in France could organize ten Kurdish translators who could deal with the paperwork of the Kurdish asylum seekers. These services could have an extremely positive impact on Kurdish asylum seekers. Unfortunately, this arrangement does not exist, and it is the failure of the Kurdish associations. I have not received any support from them yet and have suffered from the failure of the Kurdish associations. Hopefully, their inability and unresponsiveness will not affect another newly arrived asylum seeker who escaped from the homeland because of their engagement in political activities and subsequent oppression and discrimination.

They left the Kurdish house and never made their way to it again.
   —Felat—Austria

I arrived in Vienna alone three years ago, and my family reunited with me. When I arrived here, I did not have a flat and was homeless. I was told that there is a Kurdish House and that all the Kurdish refugees, who know each other, are there. I was very happy that we had a Kurdish House in Vienna that served newly arrived refugees. I went to the association,

6 SELF-GOVERNANCE FROM BELOW: "SELF-HELP SERVICES ARE...   195

exchanged phone numbers, and gained confidence that the Kurdish association existed here. I was happy to bring my family to the association and that we had a Kurdish House, which represents our homeland and brings the homeland to us. I needed to register my children at school but did not know how or where to do so. I brought them to the Kurdish House and asked whether anybody could help me or give some advice, but I was told that there was nobody available who could help. Although the association has been operating for 20 years, there was nobody to help me. I went very often to the association, sat down, and had a cup of tea, but nobody spoke to me. I was told that there were Turkish comrades who spoke only Turkish. They had been living in this country for 30 or 40 years. I tried to explain my issue, but they started talking to me in Turkish. I could not speak Turkish or German but expected to speak to someone who could speak Kurdish with me in order for us to understand each other—someone who would come with me to translate to register my children at school. However, they speak only Turkish and stick together. We visit the Kurdish association because we are all Kurds and say good morning (*roj bash*) to a few people present; they respond in Turkish, welcome (*Hoşgeldiniz*); I repeat it by saying *Hoşgeldiniz* too since this is the only word I know. I want to watch Ronahi TV to follow the news in the homeland, but they turn on the Turkish channels and watch Turkish TV. I do not understand anything. If I am interested in watching Turkish TV, I can do that at home. My newly arrived fellow Kurdish refugees do not speak German as they just arrived, and they need support in managing their lives in this new country. I came here three, four, and five times, but nothing changed. My friends came here a few times too, but they were always disappointed. They left the Kurdish House and never made their way to it again.

The Kurdish refugees avoid the Kurdish House and break off contact. There are essential issues that need to be solved. I need the help of the association, but they do not serve us in solving our issues. I do not visit the Kurdish House anymore like before, but only one or two times a month when a friend calls me to say that he is going there. I just go to the Kurdish House to meet my friend, with whom I arrange a time. I will not come to the association if I have not arranged a meeting. During my presence at a Kurdish association, if my children call me and ask where I am, when I say that I am at the Kurdish House, they join me there too. They ask their neighbors to join them too, and many people are there in the end. Otherwise, the association is always empty, and we cannot see many

196   V. DAG

people apart from a few Turkish-speaking individuals. In general, this association is the Kurdish House and should be open to everyone. All the refugees arriving here need everything for their new lives, including flats, employment, and language skills. However, the association cannot respond to their needs and issues. When the refugees are here, they cannot communicate with activists at the Kurdish House because of the language barriers. They speak Kurdish with activists who are mainly from North Kurdistan, but they respond in Turkish. The Kurdish refugees are ignored and cannot make themselves understood. They come here two or three times, but they realize that they are ignored and neglected, so they stop coming. It is also difficult for us to change these organizations since we have only been here for three or four years.

> *These kinds of Kurdish refugees are not welcome.*
> —Alin—Austria

In Kurdish society, parents' approach is crucial for children and their main source of knowledge of life. But these parents are complicit in assimilation. They do not teach their children about patriotism, Kurdish values and spirit, or their roots in the homeland. They say that they live in Europe now and have to adapt to the European lifestyle, but they are Kurds and not Europeans. They have principles to sustain and cannot live like Europeans since the Kurds do not have their own nation state like European states. It is also wrong when they compare their children with those of their European neighbors and the way they think and live. When we visit them at their houses, they keep their children away. This is a profound mistake. Unfortunately, we fall short of responding to these issues. We had some projects to try to convince every Kurdish family that they should not abandon their children and must maintain their identification with Kurdistan. Members of this association communicate with Kurdish families and raise their awareness about these issues. We urge them to visit this Kurdish association and ask for Kurdish language and culture classes. However, there are also many Kurdish refugees who do not want to be connected to their homeland, for which many Kurdish activists sacrifice their lives. In Kurdistan, we do not have an education in our Kurdish language and culture. We see these people in Europe who do not want to serve their homeland but share a sense of belonging to it. They come to our association only when they face integration-related matters such as

6 SELF-GOVERNANCE FROM BELOW: "SELF-HELP SERVICES ARE... 197

language and flat issues. We help them solve these problems according to our means. However, many refugees approach us for their personal interests—to exploit us—but not for their patriotism. They might disappear as soon as they have their issues resolved in relation to their integration matters. They change their phone number and disappear in order to break contact with us. Maybe 10 out of 100 newly arrived refugees are patriotic and worry about their homeland. The rest of them are in foreign countries and are learning the foreign language. They do not care about their Kurdish identity but want to establish their lives here. These kinds of Kurdish refugees are not welcome. They should not visit our association when they are only seeking help.

Kurdish organizations are isolated and exclusive!
—Hisyar—Sweden

These associations fail to reach out to Kurdish refugees as they do not make efforts to find us newly arrived refugees, who do not know the associations exist at all since there is no information available about them. On our arrival, we did not even know if Kurds existed in Sweden. All the Kurdish associations are under the influence of the political parties from Kurdistan, while many refugees from Rojava in particular are not pro-particular political groups. Thus, it is not true that the associations are politically independent. When we ask the activists to whom their associations belong, they claim that the Kurdish associations belong to all Kurds. This claim is only true in rhetoric, not in reality.

I joined the Kurdish associations when I found out that they exist and operate in Stockholm. I used to be very active last year and was always present, but I was ignored and neglected. As I did not understand anything given that the Turkish language is the spoken language within many Kurdish associations, I felt like I was among strangers. From listening to them, I finally learned a bit of Turkish. I often critiqued their language of communication and demanded that they speak Kurdish. For my criticism, I was also criticized, but my criticism was partially successful since Turkish was spoken less. It was very helpful. Some friends conceded that they had spoken much more Turkish before. I think that most people engaged in this association are old people, and it is difficult to find young people amongst them. All these people have been involved with the institutional bodies for more than ten years. Therefore, it is hard to meet newly arrived refugee activists who come to take on responsibility for the large work-load. We only meet long-term and old Kurds who dominate these organizations. Therefore, Kurdish organizations are isolated and exclusive. They do not organize any activities related to refugees. Once, I suggested they arrange some integration-related activities. They accepted but asked me to initiate them. However, I faced many problems at their hands when I came up with an agenda and many projects. Suddenly, I turned out to be a bad person! These members elected some individuals and created a committee for the management of Kurdish culture, art, and language. This was initiated six or seven times, but without success. I wanted to invite musicians to teach a Saz course and other cultural activities, which I wanted to be free from party politics. But financial problems, the government's ignorance towards our activities, and the approach of our friends prevented me from offering these courses. Our friends wanted me to organize these activities under the names and flags of the Kurdish associations perceived as affiliated with political parties. They wanted to create space for those refugees who follow their political lines, but not space for those refugees who stick to their Kurdish identity but are critical of political parties. Yet, because it is dominated by the political and ideological agendas of political parties, the association cannot be outward-facing and remains restrictive. The people involved in these organizations are restricted to their friends and family members. They offer space to people they already know and who are part of their organizations anyway. This approach resembles family-like relationships. They will be meaningless and marginal if they demand loyalty to a political party.

I believe it is crucial to eliminate this relationship, which is dominated by political groups. In the past, we might have accepted the thoughts and agendas of the PKK but criticized some individuals that dominated its bodies. These individuals have created their own environment within the Kurdish community and are very exclusive towards other people who represent a critical approach but are not embedded or integrated within these political networks. This approach is very divisive and disconnecting. It is difficult to change these organizations and people in one or two years. In order to change these structures, an organized group should act, but such a group does not exist. If we try to kick out pre-established refugees, they will also leave, and the association would not exist anymore. It is a very tricky issue.

6 SELF-GOVERNANCE FROM BELOW: "SELF-HELP SERVICES ARE... 199

Incompetent and unskilled leadership dominates Kurdish organizations!
—Mezdar—Germany (2)

The Kurdish refugees in Germany are not from the same country, city, or village but rather from various countries and cities. They did not know each other before their immigration, were not friends, and have different cultures, but they are forced to find one another in Europe through their collective organizations, which play a crucial role in offering these refugees a roof under which they come together despite their different backgrounds. The creation of a social space and a cultural community is the responsibility of the Kurdish associations, which bring Kurdish immigrants together and make them neighbors and friends who autonomously support each other. This leads to good relationships and cohesion among the Kurdish refugees, which creates a flourishing community. Based on these good relationships, they organize and steer their community to succeed in solving their issues and overcoming their homeland's contradictions.

In Berlin, when I and my friend created a good relationship under the roof of an association, we could reflect this on homeland issues and surmount the political and cultural contradictions that our ancestors failed to solve. These good relationships have implications for the homeland cause too. We can also create a stable community with good relationships and tackle many problems. However, I must be critical of the leaders and forerunners acting within the Kurdish organizations, who are less capable of working in a suitable capacity to respond to refugees' needs and to fulfill their functions. Incompetent and unskilled leadership dominates Kurdish organizations. Therefore, we need individuals with relevant skills to operate them in the right way. Our community unfortunately consists of peasants who are from villages and small towns in Kurdistan. Some Kurds might have worked as seasonal employees for a while in large cities and then escaped to Europe. However, our mindset when we operate is like that of peasants. I think this is not the reason, but it is the reality of our society. With this mindset and knowledge, Kurds have arrived in Europe and established institutions. However, competent Kurds to manage and run these institutions are rare. We do not have many people in exile in Europe with suitable skills engaged in the field of institutions. Additionally, we should consider the disunity of Kurdish society and the dispersion of the Kurds as a result of conflicts and the activities of our enemies. They were forced to leave their towns, flee to European countries, and apply for asylum. These refugees are not professionals and are not able to form and run an association. Nevertheless, they established associations in order to organize and unify Kurdish refugees, even though they might unintentionally be contributing to the disunity, disorganization, and dispersion of the Kurdish community through their mistakes and lack of professionalism, appropriate skills, and leadership. Additionally, it is worth mentioning that I do not see any associations as representing me for two reasons. They have either been established for the interests of a particular part of Kurdistan or for those of individuals. These bodies have not gone beyond the borders drawn across our homeland. We call them Iraqi Kurds', Syrian Kurds', or Iranian Kurds' associations. Therefore, when they represent only one color (which is not the Kurdistani color), I am not happy and do not feel represented by them. They might be classified in relation to a particular part of Kurdistan. If I do not feel represented and cannot express myself because of their narrow orientation, this is the mistake of the management committees.

These organizations and their management committees could bring all refugees together if they were colorful, inclusive, and open-minded, and if they represented different segments of Kurdish society. Otherwise, these committees and their narrow-minded individuals scatter the Kurdish refugees and contribute to their marginalization. Refugees leave the associations if management committees are narrow-minded, regardless of their belonging to a particular part of Kurdistan. Secondly, individuals should waive ownership over the associations, which are not the property of one family or tribe. For example, I know some Arabic associations that have been dominated by specific individuals for more than 20 years. For instance, the head of the Arabic-German friendship association has been in charge for 22 years. These kinds of people have even overtaken the dictators dominating Kurdish parties since they remain in power even though their charters do not allow them to stay so long. These are European charters, which instruct on how long someone can serve and determine the period. But this head of the association for 22 years does not allow someone else to replace him. If someone oversees an organization and does not even allow his son to succeed him, then he is a dictator. I think the institution should seek the recognition of the community, not vice versa. In order to overcome these challenges, I have to tell you that, in truth, if we do not have a state, we cannot establish strong and powerful institutions since we need more support, which only a state can offer. Maybe we have some political parties that support these associations, but they are dividing our community. The domination of political parties with

6 SELF-GOVERNANCE FROM BELOW: "SELF-HELP SERVICES ARE... 201

contradictory agendas, combined with the absence of a Kurdish state, is destroying our community.

...many Kurdish refugees from Rojava are at odds with the association.
—Mendal—Austria

The association has not provided support to any refugees, whether from South Kurdistan or Rojava. Since the association neglects to provide services, many Kurdish refugees from Rojava are at odds with the association. They had just arrived here but did not know anything about life in Austria. However, the Kurdish immigrants from North Kurdistan have been living here for many years and have had more opportunities to help newly arrived refugees, who sought advice on many issues related to life in Austria. Unfortunately, these friends were not helpful, and the Kurdish refugees felt ignored and neglected. For example, we have a Kurdish football team playing in the Austrian league; they are quite successful too. This team asks for our spiritual support, to be present, and to mobilize the Kurdish constituency during matches, but the association ignores their requests and does not provide any support. We cannot mobilize the Kurdish masses because they have lost their faith in this association. We cannot win their trust because of these problems. So, we are not innocent. Consequently, the association has lost its credibility and become weak.

Another reason for which many refugees from Rojava do not visit the association and avoid it is related to events in the homeland. The Turkish invasion of Afrin has increasingly affected the approach of Kurdish refugees, who keep their distance from the Kurdish association and focus on their own individual jobs. The loss of Afrin alienates them, as they do not desire a Kurdistan without Afrin. Since Afrin is lost, they have cut contact with the association. Another group of Kurdish refugees told us that they are affiliated with a rival Kurdish political party. They say that they are independent or related to some political Kurdish parties, but I think they make such statements in order to avoid cooperating with us. There is also the common approach that Kurdish refugees are polarized because of the politics and agendas of Kurdish parties. This attitude—that everyone is associated with a political party—prevailed in the homeland too. There are rival associations that use Kurdish names, but the contents of their policies do not relate to Kurdish identity at all. They do not represent anything affiliated with Kurdish attributes. They are not patriotic and cannot respond to the problems of those Kurdish refugees who are patriotic.

There are many artists and writers among them, but they do not attend our activities. They want to enjoy their comfortable lives and run away from the burden of the homeland. We had a meeting with them about cooperation, but they have disappeared.

Patriotism is very weak here, and everyone focuses on his or her own interests. Most Kurdish refugees who have escaped to Europe are not patriotic. They wanted to leave for Europe a long time ago, but they did not have any opportunities to do so. However, because of the violent conflicts (such as in Shengal, Kobanî, and Afrin), they have an excuse to leave. They use the Kurdish name in order to receive asylum rights. Finally, some Kurdish refugees from Rojava complained that everyone speaks Turkish at this association, and they cannot understand this language and communicate with other people here. Many of these people speak Zazaki, but we cannot understand that, so it is compulsory to speak Turkish. I sometimes criticize our friends when they speak Turkish at meetings, as the refugees from Rojava do not understand and want to leave. The discussion at meetings is translated sometimes, but 30 minutes are compiled into 2 minutes. During meetings, refugees from Rojava fall asleep. We do not have a teacher providing Kurdish lessons, and the multiple languages are a problem. However, if there were lots of us, we could speak Kurdish, and they would have to learn it. We criticize the approach of people at the Kurdish association at our meetings, but everything stays the same. They do not take it seriously, although we constantly address the issue of Kurdish refugees feeling isolated when they come here as they cannot establish contact with other friends. But our Turkish-speaking friends from North Kurdistan are disinterested. I understand a bit of Turkish and can communicate with them about many issues, including the election in Turkey. But because of the dominance of Turkish-speaking friends, the Kurdish House cannot respond to the needs of the newly arrived Kurdish refugees. If some friends spoke Kurdish, they might establish good relationships and could be helpful in relation to translation, but they would not be able to respond to all the issues that the Kurdish refugees from Rojava have.

As a part of the Kurdish association, we want the Kurdish refugees to maintain their dignity, commitment, and identity even though we are abroad. We have a comfortable life in Europe, but our people are suffering and living in pain in their homeland. We should undertake activities in support of our people in Kurdistan, organize ourselves here, and be ready for a return to the homeland. If they do not want to return but stay in Europe, they should serve for the liberation of our people and always be engaged. If we are organized and maintain our identity, we will earn considerable respect too. If we are dispersed and disorganized, we will not have any value. We are refugees, anyway, who do not have any value and are worthless. We should organize ourselves based on our Kurdish identity, regardless of affiliation with any political parties or groups.

REFERENCE

Dag, V. 2023. The Implications of Turkish Interventions in Rojava for US and EU Foreign Policies. *The Commentaries* 3 (1): 51–69.

CHAPTER 7

Exile: "I Have Not Dreamed of Being Here Since I Still Live There"

The majority of Kurdish-Yezidi refugees, especially those from Syria and Turkey, live in protracted exile as a result of forced migration due to persecution, imprisonment, and execution in their home countries. These conditions, which led to their exile, continue to deteriorate, and fail to offer the prospect of a return to their homeland. Simultaneously, settlement and subsequent integration in new environments in receiving societies include various obstacles, as outlined above, which force many refugees into limbo. Many Kurdish-Yezidi refugees encounter social isolation, failure to experience their socially rooted reality in receiving states, and detachment from their families and other members of their homeland's social milieu. As a consequence, many refugees addressed the experience of being uprooted and of loss. However, to maintain as much of a connection as possible with their origins, they strengthen the ties that bind them to their traditional homeland through transnational mobilization.

It is not uncommon for Kurdish-Yezidi refugees to be pushed into exile, and its roots can be traced back to the period when the Ottoman rulers deported Kurdish-Yezidi intellectuals and chieftains to remote places away from their home countries. Since the establishment of the Turkish state in 1923, Turkish governments have adhered to a policy of expelling Kurds into forced exile. This policy was initially instituted by the Turkish leader, Mustafa Kemal, and has been perpetuated by his successors. Many tribes were exiled to Anatolia after the Kurdish uprisings of 1925 and 1938 were crushed (McDowall 2005). There, the exiled Kurds

© The Author(s), under exclusive license to Springer Nature Switzerland AG 2024
V. Dag, *Voices of the Disenfranchized*, Mobility & Politics, https://doi.org/10.1007/978-3-031-46809-4_7

205

established roots while preserving their culture and language. The Kurds of Iran, Iraq, and Syria endured similar exiles to the metropolitan regions of those nations and then to Europe. The banished Kurdish-Yezidi refugees are barred from returning to their native countries and are obliged to live in the countries that they fled to. While living in exile situations, for instance in Sweden, Germany, France, and other European nations, they have the identical experiences of uprooting and loss. However, the younger generations have partly succeeded in establishing their lives and finding limited acceptance in receiving societies.

Despite the fact that many Kurdish-Yezidi refugees' uprooting can be characterized by their alienation from their culture, roots, and traditions as well as their inability to embrace new roots in receiving states, their loss implies that they are out of touch with the social environments that they left behind. They experience the erasure of their cultural existence and traditional way of life, which may be translated into their identity, belonging, and community life in their home countries. They also fail to recover their origins, social contacts, and social world in their home countries. Their uprooting becomes a long-lasting state of cultural and social loss since they are no longer physically connected to their social environment in Kurdistan, live apart from it, and are unable to recover through putting down new roots. The impact of their uprooting and loss manifests itself in mental and emotional disorders as well as estrangement from their cultural and social reality and identity. However, a significant number of Kurdish-Yezidi refugees are actively engaged in a struggle to mitigate the repercussions of their protracted exile. They maintain an ongoing and day-to-day connection to the homeland and take part in a variety of activities related to the political affairs of the homeland. They perform cultural festivals, raise awareness of political and social events, and sustain the sense of community that is impacted by the struggle for the homeland. They also make donations for their fellow compatriots under various conditions.

While at the same time mitigating the negative effects of protracted exile, the Kurdish-Yezidi refugees embrace their homeland as an existential basis for their lives, which can be viewed as a double-edged sword. On the one hand, it serves as a glue that binds different and distant refugees and encourages their identification and community building. It also acts as a source for their memories, thereby enabling them to demonstrate their commitment to their compatriots. On the other hand, the refugees carry the burden of their homeland with them. It becomes pervasive in the daily lives of refugees and distracts them from their daily responsibilities. A significant number of refugees are plagued by feelings of guilt and live their lives in perpetual tension with their social environments. They set aside the necessities of daily life in host states and devote themselves to the struggle that their Kurdish-Yezidi compatriots conduct against the oppressive regimes that rule their ancestral homeland. In other words, these refugees are mobilized in a variety of institutionalized and non-institutionalized settings.

The Kurdish-Yezidi refugees, as addressed above, organize several cultural events such as festivals, concerts, and exhibitions to strengthen their sense of identity, promote the legitimacy of their cultural, ethnic, and religious existence, and garner support for their cultural claims. Kurdish-Yezidi refugee employers, employees, and businesses make donations for their compatriots in home countries enduring political oppression by governing state authorities or suffering from natural tragedies such as earthquakes, flooding, and pandemics. They intend to alleviate the burdensome conditions of their compatriots through their donations and assistance from afar. Furthermore, Kurdish-Yezidi refugees are involved in political initiatives to increase public awareness of the plight of their brethren in the homeland among the local populations. The Kurdish-Yezidi-populated regions of Turkey, Iraq, Iran, and Syria have been the scene of constant warfare between various Kurdish factions, including fratricide (Brakûji), uprisings against oppressions of ruling regimes, and interventions of external American, European, and Russian powers in Iraq and Syria. The Kurdish-Yezidi refugees, who are themselves products of these conflicts, seek, from afar, to improve the political status of their compatriots so that they can live in peace. Last but not least, a sizeable number of Kurdish-Yezidi refugees have been successfully incorporated into the political and social structures of the host countries. They are members of political parties and members of parliament, journalists, intellectuals, academics, and activists who are attempting to promote the Kurdish-Yezidi cause within the venues that are institutionalized. For instance, the engagement of Amineh Kakabaveh, a former Kurdish-Swedish Member of Parliament, was evident in delaying and ultimately preventing Sweden's bid for membership in NATO. Similarly, Kurdish-Yezidi journalist Düzen Tekkal plays a dynamic role in bringing the German public's attention to the atrocities committed by IS against the Kurdish-Yezidi population in Iraq's Kurdistan Region. In their own words, Kurdish-Yezidi refugees recount their exile situations, their relationship with their home countries, and the rationale for their homeland activism.

208 V. DAG

UPROOTEDNESS

I have not dreamt of being here because I still live there....
  —Arya—France

I left my adulthood, my friendships, my family, and my memories in the homeland. I can never feel a sense of belonging here because I cannot form the genuine friendships that I established in my homeland. I cannot enjoy the taste of these friendships. I realize that I have become antisocial in France. I have seen friends whom I know from Turkey. They said that the happy, social, and witty Arya from Turkey has faded away, and instead they see a stagnant, calm, reserved, and asocial Arya. I am still there spiritually, and I do not remember that I had a dream of myself being here. In my dreams, I always see myself either in Diyarbakir or with my family at their home in Istanbul, but I have not dreamt of being here because I still live there in the hope of returning there. I have a bad feeling when I am not able to return. I think everyone here is somehow alone, spiritually isolated, and living without hope. There is nobody here making mutual efforts to transform the loneliness and hopelessness of others. Everyone keeps their problems and troubles to themselves. There is a song by Aram Tigran called *Penaber* (I am a refugee). This explains exile and the dilemma of refugees very well. This song influences me very much, and I listen to it every day, as I feel myself within this song since I am a refugee. Life is very hard, and being cut off from the homeland itself is a very burdensome process. Once, I wrote to one of my friends that being in exile away from the homeland is like being a tree. When it is pulled out by its roots, these roots start gradually drying out, and its leaves drop down, followed by its branches becoming dry, and finally, the tree starts slowly dying. As an individual, I feel like a tree because I was uprooted, and my roots are drying out, affecting my branches too, which have become dry.

It has been 11 years since I left my homeland and have lived here, but I do not feel a sense of belonging to this society. One of my sides is always empty; the other side is longing; and another side is sad and melancholic. It does not matter how well we speak a new language; we do not speak the same language as people because they have different views and perspectives on life than we do. Naturally, we do not laugh at their jokes and humor, and they do not laugh at ours. We feel on a permanent basis that we are refugees and immigrants. Some people do not feel the consequences of being in exile because they escape for economic reasons. They are happy to live here because they have better economic conditions. However, I have not seen or met any Kurdish refugees who were forced to escape for the same reason as me but feel happy here. Europe means freedom for those immigrants who emigrated here for money; refugees like me, struggling for their freedom, were and are free in their thoughts anyway. But I am restless and cannot stay at my place for long. I cannot breathe in Paris and feel depressed. Therefore, at the first opportunity, when I have a holiday, I travel to visit my friends in another European country. I have friends everywhere in Europe with whom I was engaged in political activities in Turkey. I can breathe with them and enjoy the feeling of the homeland, and they do the same with me because they are, like me, not allowed to travel to Turkey and so live in Europe as refugees too.

Our presence is like a fruit tree that has been ripped out of its native soil....
   —Serdan—Italy

I thought it was much better to die on my homeland's soil than to be confronted with many serious troubles on foreign soils. Our presence is like a fruit tree that has been ripped out of its native soil in Kurdistan and planted in Italy, but this tree is not fruitful and tasty in Italy as it belongs to Kurdistan. We were cut off from our roots and came to Italy. It does not matter how happy we are here; it is not comparable with the way in which we were happy in Kurdistan. We will never be fully happy, and something is always missing in our lives. We are always aware that we are lacking something or have a weakness in our lives. I lived in Turkey and suffered from Turkish fascism and oppression, which were hard, but leading a life in Italy as a refugee is much harsher than my life under the Turkish fascist system. I am from Botan and experienced hardship with my family, who suffered from Turkish oppression, but I did not realize what it meant to suffer until I went into exile and became a refugee. In Turkey, I could die once, while in Italy, we are permanently fluctuating between death and life. We cannot live the way we want and be ourselves. We cannot live like European citizens, but we cannot remain like Kurds either. In Turkey, as Kurds, we were always forced to live like Turks, while in Italy we are forced to be like Europeans. We are forced to integrate, but we cannot be ourselves. We are always living with this psychology, and I imagine that we and our friends can never have a happy life. We are like a tree that was uprooted and pulled up by force from our homeland, so we will never be fruitful and efficient. We will never produce the fruit that

210   V. DAG

Europeans expect from us. I have a homeland, but it has been colonized by fascist Turks, Arabs, and Persians.

Love for my homeland is always inside me, and I will carry it because I do not want to go to Turkish schools every day and shout that my existence shall be dedicated to Turkish existence. I should dedicate my existence to Kurdish existence. Our homeland will always remain inside us as love and utopia, but it will materialize when Kurdistan is created. I am optimistic that we will win against our enemies. Because of our statelessness, we cannot live in accordance with our mores, experience our culture, or speak our language. There remains a deficiency and a void in our lives. A while ago, I talked to a gypsy in Rome. During our conversation, he told me that I am a gypsy too, and when I asked why, he said that they call all stateless people "gypsies." I was shocked. Most likely, gypsies do not have their own homeland and do not worry about it. However, I never had this feeling because I have always believed that Kurdistan will be carved out and have always lived with this hope and belief. When I utter the word Kurdistan, my hair stands on end. I escaped from the cruelty of the fascist Turkish state to the Kurdistan region of Iraq because I was told that there was a Kurdistan. When I saw the flag of Kurdistan, once again, my hair stood on end. However, I faced troubles in the Kurdistan region of Iraq too because I was accused of being a spy for the PKK, so the authorities refused to grant me a residence permit. Wherever we go, we miss Kurdistan because we want to live with our mores, costumes, language, and culture. We do not want to live under the flag of other people and countries, but rather under our own, and we want to experience our own language and religion.

BEING LOST

...Being a refugee means losing our adolescence and youth, our homeland, our family, and our culture.
—Ilhan—Italy

If I had known that it was so hard to be a refugee, facing tough conditions, I would not have wanted to be a refugee but rather die in my homeland. Being a refugee means losing our adolescence and youth, our homeland, our family, and our culture. Having considered all these factors, being a refugee means losing my life. I did not count my time as a refugee for 20 years, indicating the discontinuity of my life. I am like a

7 EXILE: "I HAVE NOT DREAMED OF BEING HERE SINCE I STILL LIVE THERE" 211

hostage, permanently kept in prison. Many of our Kurdish people are like me: abandoned. We stay outside, sleeping on the streets, and cannot find food or drink. This policy of abandonment inflicts unlimited suffering on us refugees. I have not been allowed to return to my homeland for 14 years. I live in a kind of prison, as these states want to take our spirit and hold us hostage abroad. They keep us, our knowledge, and our freedom hostage. I now live in Europe, but I am not free because I am banned from traveling to other countries. My family lives in Germany, has German citizenship, and my daughter studies and works there, but I am not allowed to easily travel to Germany to see her. This is the way in which we are stripped of our freedom.

Being a refugee evokes the pain of the homeland. I did not realize the meaning of a homeland, but I reflected on this meaning when I escaped to Italy. I have had many dreams for my entire life, which I wanted to realize in my village in Kurdistan, where all my friends, family, and relatives live and where my roots are planted. I can only continue my life when I go back to my roots. I was born in Kurdistan and spent my childhood and adulthood in Kurdistan, but I left all my dreams in Kurdistan. So, when I do not experience this life in Kurdistan, my current life is very superficial and retrogressive. I do not want to include my experience of being a refugee in my dreams and life in Kurdistan, which is not a free country and where we do not have opportunities to work. I am a refugee, and I am always thinking about my native homeland and about living there. My life is like a film, but half of the film has been cut off. I am curious to watch it. There are many uncertainties in my future life because of my refugee status, which is my problem. Since our future is uncertain, we always think backward. I think we are 95 percent in Kurdistan and 5 percent in Italy. Our souls and thoughts are in the homeland. We are connected to the very development taking place there.

> *…. I escaped to Austria after the Syrian civil war as I lost everything!*
> —Koban—Austria (2)

Being alone and away from my family members is one of the main and most serious challenges that I face. I suffer every day since I live particularly far away from my mother. We are 13 siblings, and all of my siblings are married, have children and families, and live in Kurdistan. Only one of my sisters lives abroad, like me. I worry a lot about them because they have many children and live in Kobanî, a city close to the Turkish border.

212 V. DAG

They are permanently under Turkish attacks. Therefore, they are often forced to leave their homes. It makes me sad to hear of these incidents. They have an uncertain life as they became refugees once they left Kobanî and could be refugees for the second time. This situation affects me here very much, and I do not have any power to change their conditions. I worry a lot about them. I am very keen to resume my studies, which were interrupted when the civil war broke out and the regime forces started to arrest us and take us to the military. However, it is impossible to study now as I must work to support my family in the homeland. I call them and always ask what they need and how I can help. I have applied for two jobs, and I am waiting for their responses. It is uncertain, and I do not know how my life will proceed here. I just must wait, and I do not have any idea what could happen tomorrow. I am still lost and do not have any orientation in this country. I would like to return immediately to my beautiful homeland, where conditions and opportunities were available to me before the civil war. I opened an advice office and guided people. However, I escaped to Austria after the Syrian civil war, as I had lost everything. Europe was always on my list to visit, as I have some relatives who visited the homeland, but I would not have escaped to Austria if Kobanî had not been under IS attacks, which caused us to seek refuge in Turkey. When we returned to Kobanî after six months, we had a tough time as it was razed to the ground. It took people a long time to rebuild the city.

> *We do not distinguish between our dreams, memories, and reality.*
> —Zerdest—Italy

We have faced much suffering, but our grandchildren might see the freedom of Kurdistan. Sometimes, when we come together with our friends, we talk about our suffering and misery, which is extreme, but we laugh because we think about our nice days ten years ago, though we do not know whether our days were real or dreams. These days just pass. We do not distinguish between our dreams, memories, and reality. Sometimes it is difficult to express our painful experiences in Italy. It is not just about sleeping outside; we have had other difficulties too. Once, while we were sleeping, there was flooding that swept over everything, and we were submerged in water. Water flooded our shoes, clothes, and everything else, including one of our female friends. We escaped from the water on a bridge. With friends, I also slept in the snow once. We have experienced many such events and do not know which to narrate. We had to accept

7 EXILE: "I HAVE NOT DREAMED OF BEING HERE SINCE I STILL LIVE THERE" 213

these conditions because we did not have other alternatives. Our friends had long, black hair, but they do not have any hair anymore because of our dreadful experiences. We lit a fire and sat around it for months. When the cops found out what had happened, we told them that we were warming ourselves and that we were Kurdish refugees in our camp. We told them to arrest us and take us away in order to have a warm place to stay, but they did not.

In Kurdistan, we had some relatives or friends who looked after us when we were in urgent situations. Our neighbors offered us a plate of food and asked whether we were fine, but here there is nothing. Nobody cares about us, and everyone tries to screw something out of each other. A Kurdish asylum seeker committed suicide in front of people because he could not bear these conditions. He took his life to liberate himself from his miserable conditions. There was another friend who had an accident and passed away. His family was in Italy to take his body, but the government asked for €35,000 in order to hand his body to his family. His family could not receive his body because they did not have the money to pay the government. His relatives were living under harsh conditions here. We escaped to these countries, but we cannot even rescue our bodies and have to pay a lot of money. It is difficult to die because our families cannot receive our corpses. If someone wants to die, he must jump into a river, leave himself to the mercy of the water, and see where his body comes out. We left our homeland six or seven years ago, but we keep living every day under brutal conditions in Italy. We will continue to live in this inhuman way with our bags, which are our homes. Our bags contain some clothes and socks, and we feel like queens when we find a place to take a shower. We cannot do anything because we are powerless and do not have any opportunities. We are absorbed in this way of living and cannot get out of it anymore. What is good here is that we have not turned mad, did not steal, and were not involved in any criminal or bad activities. Instead, we have been living with dignity and honor. This is our situation.

HOMELAND CONNECTION

We cannot adapt to the lifestyle here because it does not fit us and is not ours!
   —Xece—Austria

Austria is beautiful, but it cannot be my homeland, where I interact in my mother tongue freely and with confidence and relief when I express myself. I cannot speak two words here and am restricted in my feelings and thoughts. We will never belong to the Austrians, even if we lived here for 100 years, but on their part, they will also not recognize us as belonging either. I have Austrian neighbors, but we do not say hi to each other. We do not know each other and cannot interact in our language and lifestyle. I go to the language school where many immigrants go to learn German, but we do not understand each other. This means that I am still a foreigner, and whatever we do does not change anything. In contrast, when we Kurds speak the same language, we can breathe in a way that lets us communicate. We do not have any problems understanding and exchanging our experiences. This is due to the fact that we belong to the same community and space. I feel fine when I am here among my Kurdish people, but it is different when I am in my homeland and can speak my language with my friends, neighbors, and the whole community. I am comfortable and have a sense of belonging. It is beautiful to be in my homeland; it is more beautiful than Austria, which is not my homeland. There were Arabs in my homeland too, but we could not get along with them, and we were always involved in conflicts because we wanted to speak in our own language, which belongs to me. Speaking Kurdish is not only about communication and understanding; I also know how to behave, exchange, respect, sit, and stand in my language. So, our language is beautiful, and we are confident when we speak with our community. Based on our language and culture, we behave here as we do in our homeland, with our own habits. We cannot adapt to the lifestyle here because it does not fit us and is not ours.

> *...my body is here, but my soul is in the homeland!*
> —Osman—France (2)

I have written down my feelings about being a refugee. It has two meanings for me. The first meaning is a silent death, and the second meaning is capitulation. A silent death means that nobody here hears our voice or our cry or listens to us if we cry for help. My physical body is here, but my soul and spirit are in the place where I was born and raised. I translate every inch of the homeland where I grew up into songs and poems. I live there, sleep there, think there, and cry there. Being here means a silent death because I cry but nobody hears me, and my voice does not come out. Nobody understands me or loves me here. The second meaning is capitulation, depending on our conditions. Nobody wants to leave his

7 EXILE: "I HAVE NOT DREAMED OF BEING HERE SINCE I STILL LIVE THERE" 215

homeland, be away from his soil, and lead a life as a refugee. However, if he accepts leaving his homeland, he makes a concession to his values of love, commitment, belief, and philosophy of life. Silent death and capitulation are based on my life experience here. When you ask me, "Why don't I return to my homeland?" This is permanently in my mind because my body is here, but my soul is in the homeland. My dreams, visions, tears, and life are there. When I look at you here, I feel at home. My body and physical form are looking at you, but my soul is in the homeland. However, I cannot return because there are many political problems there. I cannot live in North Kurdistan because of its problems; Rojava and East Kurdistan have many problems too. South Kurdistan is even worse as it has been colonized. It has been turned into a city of Turks and does not have anything to do with the Kurds, so Kurds do not want to live there anymore.

...Our eyes and ears are permanently on news from the homeland....
—Dengdar—Germany (2)

Our eyes and ears are permanently on news from the homeland, which affects us accordingly. Our homeland is constantly under enemy threat, especially from Turks. The interests of many countries in the world are not concerned with the situation in Syria, especially the Kurds. This means that oppressed people always suffer and face negative consequences due to the interests of these states. Collective communities such as Kurds face these troubles, have lost their territories to colonizers, and face demographic changes. For example, their villages and cities are renamed, and their history distorted. The resources under and on the ground in Rojava are stolen by the enemy and sold abroad. They have not left anything. They have also destroyed our humanity, conscience, and compassion. They commit constant genocide against our people. However, our population resists this oppression permanently and relies on their fight in Rojava. They live in tents and always put up resistance. As children, elders, wives, and husbands, they live constantly under destitute conditions. Their eyes and attention are permanently on their homes, villages, and cities, as well as their land, gardens, and property.

Humanity and conscience do not exist. What is left in our homeland are the interests of states that are prevailing and that do not care about humanity at all. What is left for oppressed people is their resistance until the last day of their lives, when they regain their soil and homes and come back to their garden, people, community, and villages. This is people's only life and honor, which we stick to. So, it does not matter that we are living in Europe; our minds and hearts are connected with our homeland. This situation is the source of the greatest pain. So, we forget our own worries and problems and think permanently about the pain of our brethren in the homeland. Consequently, the situation in, and our connections with, the homeland do not allow us to meet the integration-related requirements since they are always distracting us. What is going on in the homeland slows down our development and integration. So, we do not learn the German language quickly. If we do not speak German, it is difficult to find employment. This is also a point of sadness. The German authorities constantly force us to work, but they do not ask or care what happened to me, my people, or my homeland, which lives in pain. They stick only to their own laws and try to implement them without regard for our background. They prioritize their own system. They tell us that we are refugees but have to work and act according to the system and rules. I have tried several times to tell the authorities about my situation in the homeland, but I was always told to forget it. But we can never forget that. My situation is not independent from the conditions of the war in Syria, which affect us all. Nevertheless, we are encouraged to forget this and to focus on our new lives in Germany. We make efforts to help our homeland as much as we can, and we will continue to do so without limits. We know well that this country will not be our own country and homeland because it is far from our culture, social life, and everything else. The Germans stay away from us and do not want to share their homeland and property with us. We live on our own and are very isolated. The only opportunities and common life we have are if we meet the Kurdish community in Germany.

> *...our lives depend on what is happening on our homeland!*
> —Herdem—Sweden

We live in this country, but our lives depend on what is happening in our homeland. Every positive or negative event in Kurdistan affects our lives in Sweden. We are like sick people who stand alone, becoming tired as a result of so many thoughts about our home, homeland, mother, and siblings in Kurdistan. We feel bored and experience anguish. Accordingly, we have a Kurdish expression that says that people who live away from their homeland are also far away from their hearts. It is a different feeling to hug and smell our relatives and to be amongst them than talking to

7 EXILE: "I HAVE NOT DREAMED OF BEING HERE SINCE I STILL LIVE THERE" 217

them on the phone. Sometimes, they celebrate their happiness following a successful event in their homeland, and we are not part of these events. It is awkward for us to be away from these events. It creates a feeling of grief. We accept these conditions as we live in exile far from our homeland. People in exile are barely happy and have difficult lives. However, we do not complain about our conditions in Sweden, even though we miss our family members and our homeland. We are also not allowed to travel to Kurdistan to see them for five years, according to Swedish asylum rights. This causes many difficulties. I think a political decision should be made to grant us permission to travel. My father, for example, passed away, but I was not allowed to attend his funeral. It was very sorrowful. My mother is very old now, and I want to see her, but I am not permitted to travel to Kurdistan until we receive our citizenship in five years. I am not even sure whether I will be allowed to travel to my homeland in my lifetime. Who knows what the future will bring us during this time? However, we Kurdish families have established strong connections amongst ourselves abroad. We do not differentiate between Kurds from different cities in Rojava or parts of Kurdistan. We see each other and jump for each other if there is an event. We do not have any serious problems that we ask each other about, but we see each other if there is a celebration or a funeral. We help each other in times of crisis. For instance, I had an accident, and my leg was broken. I do not have any relatives here, but my Kurdish friends helped me a lot. They never left my home for a month and always came to see if I needed anything. My Kurdish neighbors and friends did not let me down or feel my pain. It was an important event for me, and it made me very happy that my fellow Kurds looked after me and filled the place of my family. We also recently celebrated Newroz together with Kurds from four parts of Kurdistan. We danced and interacted with each other, and we were all very happy.

> *...we cannot separate mothers from their children, we also cannot separate ourselves from our homeland....*
> —Alaz—Germany

Our homeland situation affects our lives abroad since we are tied to our homeland. The most dynamic impact of the homeland on us is related to violent conflicts and negative events that take place every day. These developments strain our activities and lives in Germany since we cannot focus

218 V. DAG

on our studies and work. If peace prevails in Kurdistan and we receive good news, we will remain happy and peaceful in Germany, as we know that our families and relatives living in the homeland are safe. In this sense, the homeland exerts a great impact on our lives abroad. To put it differently, we will have peace, happiness, and prosperity abroad when our families and people enjoy peace, happiness, and prosperity in the homeland. We cannot separate our lives and fate in Berlin from those of our people in Kurdistan, even though we have left our homeland. As we cannot separate mothers from their children, we also cannot separate ourselves from our homeland, as people and territory are linked to each other. This is the reality I have witnessed. Every individual has the right to be and should be recognized in connection with his nation and homeland, where he feels happier and gains recognition. The authorities in Germany need to acknowledge the reality that the homeland has a large impact on our integration in Berlin. Nevertheless, I recognize my reality, have self-knowledge, and do not care about how other people see me.

Our homeland is the place of our ancestry, where we feel connected....
   —Cekdar—France

Our homeland is the place of our ancestry, where we feel connected, and our mind is permanently there. We were born there and opened our eyes for the first time there. Therefore, the homeland means everything that makes up my existence. We want to go and visit, but we are not allowed to travel there. This is a lack that exists permanently in our lives. We call each other sometimes on the phone, but it is not sufficient, and we long permanently for the homeland. Our homeland is in Turkey, despite the fact that we dislike Turkey, but this is a reality. We are the actual owners of Turkey, as we were there before the Turks, but we are now outsiders there. The Turks do not accept us, but we escaped to France, where we are not recognized either. We suffer a lot from being refugees, even if we have our papers and legal documents. The difficulties that we face are not only related to starvation and our legal papers, which we can somehow manage, but rather to our statelessness. We are abandoned and do not have any protectors. In this sense, material resources do not satisfy our needs, and what makes us suffer is that we have many enemies but not a single supporter or state. We are all stateless and suffer permanently, even if the world belongs to us. I wish that I were now in my homeland and in Turkey. I did not want to leave my homeland, but I was obliged to do so because

7 EXILE: "I HAVE NOT DREAMED OF BEING HERE SINCE I STILL LIVE THERE"

of my difficult conditions. We Kurds face fierce oppression, and nobody knows how long it will last.

Our body is here, but our heart, mind, and soul in Kurdistan!
—Cengo—Germany

We continue to have uninterrupted contact with our homeland and are involved in interactions with our people. Our body is here, but our heart, mind, and soul are in Kurdistan. When we decided to leave our homeland and escape to Germany, it was not our voluntary intention or choice. We were forced to come over here because we were forced to leave our homeland. There was a war and chaos that caused our dispersion. We did not prepare for our escape from our homeland towards exile; everything happened suddenly. Therefore, we became dispersed and left our mother in the homeland and our father in another country. This situation was very painful and continues to affect our interactions in Germany. Life in Kurdistan is very hard now. After this long-term war, there is nothing left—neither doctors nor nurses. There is no medication anymore. It is very difficult to survive. We make efforts to help each other. The conditions in some areas of Kurdistan might be difficult and unmanageable. For example, the conditions in Afrin are not like those in Qamishli. However, we continue to feel the pain of our homeland on a daily basis. We are not separated from our homeland.

Loving and caring for the homeland comes from faith!
—Shoresh—France

Loving and caring for the homeland comes from faith. Even when our prophet Muhammed prayed in Medina, he had to face in the direction of Jerusalem, which was the qibla of Muslims, but he always had Mecca in mind because he was born and raised there and spent his childhood there. There was a mosque in Medina that had two qiblas. When the prophet faced in the direction of Jerusalem, God sent him a message to turn his face towards Kaaba. Therefore, wherever we live and whatever we do, we are spiritually connected with our people in the homeland, and our ears are always there. In the last three years, what our compatriots in the homeland have organized and established in terms of our imams and religious intellectuals, the Turkish state has destroyed and dispersed. The Turkish

220   V. DAG

authorities have arrested some of them, killed others, or forced them into exile. In every Kurdish city, our people established hundreds of mosques and madrasas where people visited and had religious entertainment with our religious intellectuals. Unfortunately, the Turkish state has obliterated all these places and arrested individuals. In this sense, Kurdistan's Islamic Society is always networked and connected with the four parts of Kurdistan. We bring up Kurdistan in all our conferences and meetings. Many Kurdish refugees tell me that they have clothes, blankets, and other stuff they want to donate, but we cannot transport them because of the borders. Since our hearts are broken, we collect donations and aid to send to Kurdistan but fail to take these over due to border restrictions. There was recently a flood in East Kurdistan, and we wanted to supply the aid we collected in France through the donations of our Kurdish community, but we could not take it over because of the borders controlled by ruling states.

COMMITTED MOBILIZATION

Each of us here has a commitment to various individuals… in the homeland!
    —Gulan—Austria

It was very difficult for me to establish my life in Austria, as I am in a remote place far from my homeland, my family, my mother and father, and my language. Austria is not my homeland, and our language is not spoken here. I grew up in the homeland where I went to school, to which I was used. I was among my people, living with my mother and father. I escaped from my homeland because I did not have another choice. Rights and justice for us were abdicated and abolished. We were not allowed to live in peace with our community, and our lives were threatened. Therefore, I was forced to abandon my mother and father and my homeland. My escape was not voluntary, but very painful. However, my heart is with my fellow Kurds and my homeland, where I opened my eyes, grew up, went to school, and could work. All of these are gone; what can we do? We must settle here, as our homeland is a battlefield and faces destruction. We cannot return anymore. These homeland events affect my life in Austria, as my mind and attention are always in Rojava, where everything is banned, violent conflicts are ongoing, people are being killed, and security is absent. Our relatives do not have water, electricity, or the medication on which my mother and father rely. There is also an economic crisis, famine, and food shortages. The prices for food have skyrocketed. Therefore, the whole time, we are thinking about our homeland and worrying about our people. We help send clothes, medication, and money to my family members, orphans, and poor people according to my possibilities. We collect money here among ourselves and send it to them. My sister lost her husband and left many children behind. I keep supporting them too.

Each of us here has a commitment to various individuals, such as siblings, aunts, uncles, and neighbors in the homeland. My relatives tell me and my friends that they urgently need more support. Based on their information, we send them everything according to our opportunities. Moreover, we support each other to overcome our boredom here and there. My family members there advise me to avoid getting upset and that I must feel thankful that I am not in the homeland, facing violent conflict everywhere, daily. They tell us that all the schools and universities are closed, and teenagers aged between 14 and 15 are forcefully taken to the battlefield, which tears their parents' hearts out. They regret that they did not leave too. It is our destiny that we are refugees and miss our sweet homeland. We can never forget it because we grew up and spent our childhood there and could speak our language there. It is about our emotions, which we developed in the homeland. Otherwise, I am ok with being in Austria too. I have all the material resources, but I have to cope with the language, education, and employment. I will not be lacking anything when I have overcome these challenges. I am hopeful that my children can go to school, have their education, advance themselves, and build a safe future.

...all us Kurds are committed and tied to Kurdistan!
—Dewran—Germany (2)

The colonization of our homeland renders our political orientation immediately apparent. These colonizers have made efforts to wipe out our language, assimilate us, and eradicate our culture. As a result, each and every one of us Kurds has a strong sense of devotion and commitment to Kurdistan. The politics and events that take place in Kurdistan have an immediate bearing on our situation. Our fates in other countries are intertwined with those of our countrymen back in the homeland. Every single Kurd long for the day when Kurdistan, the Kurdish people, and our language are all liberated. We engage in all legitimate and democratic events and actions in order to achieve this goal, and we regard our role as one of responsibility for the Kurdish struggle. We have no desire to eradicate or

222   V. DAG

subjugate other people's ways of life, nor do we have any animosity towards their countries or languages. The liberation of both our native country and our language is the one and only objective that drives our actions. We want to be able to live freely on our land just like every other human being, replete with the freedom to preserve our language, culture, and nation. To this end, we are accountable for utilizing democratic and legal means and participating in political, cultural, societal, and economic undertakings. No matter how overwhelming, we will never shirk our responsibilities. We engage in initiatives that collect donations and resources, such as money, clothes, medication, etc., and deliver them to our population in Kurdistan. We manage the distribution of aid to those in Kurdistan based on our capabilities.

We were on the streets day and night to show our solidarity!
   —Helimo—France

Events in Kurdistan have had an immense impact on our lives in France. During the Turkish attacks, we were on the streets day and night to show our solidarity. I frequently skipped work as I was with other Kurdish refugees, raising our voices for and participating in the resistance. We went before the European Parliament, the Foreign Ministry, and other ministers, and occupied airports. We launched various forms of protest actions against IS, which was a project of the Turkish state and other countries. They wanted to eliminate the Kurds and remove them from the Middle East. They started with Yezidis, but they were not the only target; all Kurds were under attack. The aim was to commit genocide against the Kurds, and many states were involved in this genocidal crime, but they did not succeed as the Kurds were united and strongly resisted these attacks. The Kurds have agendas and perspectives that encourage their resistance. Events in Kurdistan occupy our lives here, and many Kurdish refugee families are highly traumatized as they have lost half of their families in Kurdistan. They experienced their second trauma during their journey of escape, as they lost another half of their families. They arrived here with either one or two family members or on their own, as they lost the rest of their family members. You cannot expect a lot from these people, as they are suffering from serious psychological distress. This causes traumatic situations.

7 EXILE: "I HAVE NOT DREAMED OF BEING HERE SINCE I STILL LIVE THERE"   223

We escaped to Europe not for fun or to enjoy its comfortable life but for our homeland's struggle.
    —Cihan—Italy

My commitment is connected to the loss of my brother, which caused severe pain in our lives. We will not be able to forget when the Turkish government murdered him, and this wound will never heal. Moreover, we were forced to escape because the Turkish state did not allow us to live in our homeland in freedom and peace, enjoying our rights with our people, and speaking our Kurdish language. The Turkish state left us stateless to live like nomads. So, we are permanently refugees: squeezed, tyrannized, stifled, brutally oppressed, and banned from raising our voices. Being a refugee means that we do not have an identity, language, or rights. These normally exist but do not apply to us as the Turkish state denies our existence, although we exist. When we were in the village, our home was always raided, and everything was destroyed. We cannot forget this brutality. My brother composed a song about our village and our homeland. When I listen to this song, I have to cry. He emphasizes that if our state exists, our homeland, language, and identity also exist. However, people without a state are not accepted in the world. My homeland is my existence and life. It belongs to us, as we exist thanks to God and the leader who introduced us to the world, but it is divided and colonized. Subsequently, we have to organize activities everywhere for the benefit of the homeland's struggle for liberation. We should never leave the streets and cease to launch our activities. We escaped to Europe not for fun or to enjoy its comfortable life but for our homeland's struggle. Being engaged for the homeland is therefore our overall responsibility. We follow on the news each day how our people are on the streets and in public places, launching demonstrations and rallies, and raising their voices to call for solidarity. We also escape from this oppression in our homeland and come abroad to raise our voice and join them. I think there is no difference between the homeland and Europe as far as the struggle for liberation is concerned. We are in Europe and have to be the voice of our people.

    ...I use my music to bring out the pain and grief of my Kurdish....
    —Merwan—Austria

Through music, I reveal our Kurdish pain and communicate it with artists and people in Austria who pay attention to my stories and become sad when they hear our grief and predicament. They develop an interest and ask me for Kurdish music and singers, whose names I share with them to look up on YouTube. When they see what kind of instruments we play and how we sing, they admire us. This is very important for me: to introduce people to Kurdish culture and raise awareness of the Kurdish cause. Moreover, I gain access to them through my music, and when they listen to it, they understand me and are nice to me. When I tell them about my situation in Syria and why I came here as an asylum seeker, they help me and encourage me to advance myself. Thus, music is a crucial instrument for me to forget my pain and trauma, but at the same time, I use my music to bring out the pain and grief of my Kurdish people and explain it to Austrians. For these reasons, I feel very relieved through my music. Music was a crucial instrument for making friendships with them. When the Austrian citizens heard my songs of pain, they asked me to be honest and explain this pain to them. They communicate this among each other and collect donations for our people. This donation takes place through churches. Music is an instrument for solidarity with my people through raising awareness and donation collection.

> ...*whatever happens in the four parts of Kurdistan, these events have a direct impact on our activities and constituencies....*
> —Avesta—Sweden

Our focal point is political activities in Kurdistan, which dominate our lives in Stockholm. Homeland politics have a direct impact on our situation and our way of life in this country. We do not have time to breathe and hear about the issues, wishes, questions, and demands of the Kurdish community in Stockholm from our associations and assemblies. Since our opportunities and capacity are limited, we neglect our community in Stockholm. For example, we are now on hunger strike in solidarity with our compatriots. In the past, we organized activities for Kobanî and Afrin. So, whatever happens in the four parts of Kurdistan, these events have a direct impact on our activities and constituencies in Stockholm, who are from all four parts. When we have a conflict in Kobanî, we cannot focus on our lives in Stockholm or launch cultural and integration-related activities because our members expect us to deal with and focus on events in Kurdistan, so we must meet their expectations. They keep asking us what we have undertaken for Rojava. Accordingly, our activities in Stockholm consist of diplomatic events, demonstrations, and rallies in solidarity with the Kurdish people embedded in violent conflicts that are waged against the Kurds. In this way, we try to raise greater awareness among the global public that a war is going on in Kurdistan and that Kurdish people are being killed as a consequence.

The Kurds are forced to leave their homeland and become refugees, but we do not want them to leave the homeland in Rojava and become refugees in Europe, dispersed and assimilated. Our activities in Stockholm have a political, psychological, and social impact on our compatriots. Therefore, we cannot just focus on cultural and language matters and the integration of Kurdish refugees in Swedish society. We believe these are not our priorities but rather homeland politics aspiring to the liberation of Kurdistan, where we will return. I have been living in this country for many years and do not want to live here anymore, as I do not feel that I am part of this society. Rather, I feel Kurdish and Kurdistani. Therefore, I want to go back to Kurdistan and live there. I did not escape to Sweden voluntarily but was forced to seek asylum to live as a refugee in Sweden. If I had my own country where I could feel free, I would not have stayed even for a minute or two in Sweden. Most Kurdish refugees are assimilated into the Swedish system because life is comfortable. They survived a war in Kurdistan but might fail to survive assimilation in Sweden as a result of relaxed and less difficult conditions. This capitalist system absorbs these Kurdish refugees and assimilates them. This also affects the new generation. However, our organizations and compatriots actively resist the assimilation of Kurdish refugees within the system and try to protect our community from the implications of the system. This capitalist system does not appreciate human beings and destroys the nature of humanity.

Reference

McDowall, D. 2005. *A Modern History of the Kurds*. 3rd ed. London and New York: I.B. Tauris & Co Ltd.

CHAPTER 8

Conclusion

This book is an unconventional academic and collaborative work that presents alternative and reflective perspectives of refugees to understand various themes shaping their lives. It serves as an autonomous space for Kurdish-Yezidi refugees from the Kurdish regions of Turkey, Iraq, Syria, and Iran to tell their descriptive and analytical stories about tragic events and lived experiences accumulated throughout their journeys. These include political persecution, displacement, interaction with smuggler networks, asylum procedures, and refugeehood, as well as barriers in settlement and integration processes, the formation of diasporic communities and structures, political activism, the dilemma of exile, and the prospect of return. The book also constitutes a vast reservoir of first-hand and original knowledge about Kurdish-Yezidi refugees in Germany, France, Sweden, Austria, Italy, and Denmark. It offers a fresh perspective on refugee reality as well as alternative approaches in academic domains and policy-making processes. The refugees in question not only present their testimonies but also embody the anthropological, political, and sociological realities of their counterparts in their home countries. They discuss their intra-community relationships and their historical and contemporary ties to mainstream societies in the original and receiving countries, as well as bureaucratic and structural obstacles in the receiving countries.

Kurdish-Yezidi refugees act as co-authors of this book at all stages of their trajectories of refugeehood and describe their actions, experiences, and emotions of suffering and hope for a new life, struggles for survival,

© The Author(s), under exclusive license to Springer Nature   227
Switzerland AG 2024
V. Dag, *Voices of the Disenfranchized*, Mobility & Politics,
https://doi.org/10.1007/978-3-031-46809-4_8

228   V. DAG

and against ostracism and everyday discrimination, as well as responsibility for their homeland affairs. By performing as the storytellers of their personal tales about their ideas, emotions, and experiences, they make detailed and analytical assumptions about themes surrounding their realities and use their lived experiences as evidence for their arguments and claims. This allows them to develop theories that contribute to the foundation for knowledge production. In other words, they are the primary interpreters and theorizers of their own stories. They reflect on their lives by telling, remembering, and experiencing past and present events that shape their future. Thus, refugees refuse to fall back on the representation of their epistemological stance by colonial scholarship that attempts to exploit their narratives for entrepreneurial interests and the continuation of the refugee plight by minimizing their transition into emancipated human beings. Refugees underscore that they are also epistemic subjects who are arguing against colonial and state-centric knowledge production. They are not just victimized "survivors" who are seeking humanitarian protection, ignoring their political struggle and stateless agency to challenge state dominance, but they also transcend their objectification of integration through state-centric agendas and regulations. By telling their stories in their own words, Kurdish-Yezidi refugees offer political and academic stakeholders, as well as grassroots advocacy groups and civil society actors, immediate and intimate insights into their past and present social worlds.

As a former refugee and non-career researcher who followed an unconventional path in the academia, I initiate to produce this book to render refugee testimonies visible and enable them to recover their suppressed voices. However, I did not attempt to theorize the narratives of refugees or construct hypotheses in accordance with Western academic standards. With restricted access to resources, I performed as a gatekeeper, enabling refugees to make claims based on their unique experiences and recollections as well as encouraging them to generate their own theories. My role boiled down to the discussion and presentation of the historical, political, and social context of the Kurdish-Yezidi refugees, as well as the structuring of sections and chapters. Nonetheless, while listening to them, recording, translating, and transcribing their stories, I felt overwhelmed with intense feelings. I reflected on my lived experience of torture, imprisonment, escape in Turkey, and discriminatory, exclusive, and racist behaviors of individuals in my integration and settlement process in Europe, as well as the ignorant and othered approach I continue to endure in the fields of academia. I additionally played a vital role in translating the Kurdish-Yezidi refugees' languages and, more importantly, their emotions. The Kurdish-Yezidi refugees frequently lacked adequate terms to describe their ongoing predicament, which could not be translated into existing theoretical and methodological concepts applied by Western-centric and state-centric studies. Therefore, they commonly employed alternative languages to express their emotions, which were overwhelmed with uncontrollable and unshed tears, agonizing recollections, and sorrowful moments, but certainly assertive claims. They commonly exhibited wistful facial expressions and cried during interviews when recounting their prior experiences or those of their deceased or imprisoned family members. I promptly discontinued recording as I was already familiar with their emotions, which reminded me of my earlier tragedy. It is crucial that the refugees' languages of emotion receive attention in the academic, political, and public spheres. It untangles the intricate relationship between refugees and their producers, who still control their home countries, the representation of their experiences, and the realities that underlie their refugeehood. In an interactive endeavor with refugees, the book concludes with an analysis of key aspects pertaining to the origins, causes, and consequences of Kurdish-Yezidi refugeehood, as well as coping strategies and practical suggestions for future collaborative studies.

Refugee Production

Each section and chapter of this book is comprised of multiple descriptive and analytic underlying ideas that the Kurdish refugees constructed from their lived experiences, which serve as evidence of their truth. Kurdish-Yezidi refugees cited various policies and conditions as the fundamental sources of their refugeehood, along with associated treatments in receiving nations. They pointed to statelessness as the underlying cause of their ongoing political persecution and subjugation at the hands of the Turkish, Iranian, and Arab governments, as well as the primary culprits behind their displacement and refugeehood. They equated their statelessness with persistent and everyday humiliation, inferiority, and worthlessness. Since the division of the traditional Kurdish-Yezidi homeland, the Kurdish-Yezidi population has been subjected to a miserable existence characterized by denial, oppression, and resistance. This triadic relationship has persisted to the present day and continues to influence the present and uncertain future of the Kurdish-Yezidi population and refugees. Serkeft, an asylum seeker from Turkey, described his past and current experiences in the following words:

> In our homeland, we are essentially stateless and endure repressive and inhumane conditions. We flee permanent oppression that causes our suffering. When we would have had our own state, Kurdistan, we would not have voluntarily fled to Europe. We do not escape for money! In our homeland, we could fill a bottle with water streaming from the Kurdish mountains throughout Kurdistan to sell it and easily fund our education and become physicians, academics, and professionals. It is not by choice that we make the effort to come here and perform the filthy and low-level works of these European societies. Not only do I and my peers face this fate, but as a population, we have been suffering for hundreds of years from vicious assaults and are unable to regain our senses due to the non-stop oppression with which we are confronted. I can see great Kurdistan when I look at photographs of Kobanî. Through a savage strategy, Kobanî has been completely destroyed. For generations, Kurdistan has been devastated too, and the Kurdish people have been subjected to similar tyranny as the inhabitants of Kobanî.
> —Serkeft—France

This perpetual plight is not unique to Kurdish-Yezidi refugees from Turkey. Their Syrian counterparts do not have it easy either. They share a common fate in Syria at the hands of the ruling Arab regimes and Islamic Sunni and Shia mercenaries affiliated with Turkey, Iran, or other Arab states in the Middle East. While a large number of Kurdish-Yezidi segments were stripped of their de-jura citizenship by the pan-Arab regime in the 1960s, living as de-jura stateless communities (Tejel 2009), they have been subjected to "ethnic cleansing" and subsequent displacement by Turkish forces and their Islamic jihadists from Afrin, Serê Kaniyê (Ras-Al-Ayn), and neighboring villages. Sergewaz referred to his calamitous family events:

> In April of 2013, my brother was murdered in Syria by a jet fighter aircraft of the Bashar regime. The majority of my family members thereafter began to depart from Syria. Some of them fled to the Kurdistan region of Iraq, while others made their way to Beirut or Turkey. We were inevitably devastated and scattered. However, I felt obligated to look after my brother's family and elderly parents. I therefore moved to the Kurdistan region of Iraq to work as well. I spent approximately six to seven months there before returning to Qamisli, Syria. I lingered in Qamishli for two or three months,

but I was unable to survive there as a destitute person as a result of conflict conditions. I returned to Kurdistan again. After being in Kurdistan for two months, I learned that Syrians were offered the opportunity to escape to Europe. I decided to join the caravan of refugees too.

—Sergewaz—Denmark

The Kurdish-Yezidi population endured one of the worst catastrophes in Iraq by DAES (Arabic acronym for IS). The Kurdish segments with Yezidi faith were the main target of radical Islamic jihadists. This catastrophe, recognized as "genocide" at the international level and 74 Ferman (pogrom) among Kurdish-Yezidi population, is insightful in the words of Xeyal from Shengal:

> We walked for many days without food, drink, or clothes to escape IS' genocidal acts against us Yezidis in 2014...We have managed to flee but could not take our children, who live currently in abandoned Shengal (Sinjar)... Our houses were grazed to the ground and plundered. The Arabs cut off the heads of our people. They abducted our 9 years old girls and took many hostages... If Shengal would not have been destroyed, I would have lived there with my children now, but we cannot return to Iraq. We have gathered many severe experiences and lost everything.
>
> —Xeyal—Germany (2)

The Kurdish-Yezidi population dispersed in states ruling their traditional homeland is ascribed a status of de facto stateless people that lack protection and are exposed to permanent oppressive policies by state-linked and non-stated forces in association of economic underdevelopment and absence of democratic orders which drive them to seek asylum and shelter abroad. The anecdotes and evaluations of Kurdish-Yezidi refugees suggest that their forced refugee status is not a temporary trend. It will continue at various paces. This fact necessitates the development of a sustainable strategy to address their dilemma in the Middle East and their difficulties throughout Europe. To express it more precisely, the refugee issue is multidimensional and multilocal. The refugee waves cannot be stopped unless the sources of refugee production are eradicated through the acknowledgment of voices raised by concerned refugee communities. Nonetheless, Europe lacks this strategy and is unable to provide refugees with a sense of belonging and a stable home. They continue to experience disappointment and statelessness due to the lack of cultural, political, and social recognition.

Europe in Refugees' Viewpoint

Europe does not necessarily provide Kurdish-Yezidi refugees with a comfortable and hospitable home or shield them from traumatic experiences. Kurdish-Yezidi refugees continue to face new bureaucratic, social, and structural obstacles despite the democratic and lawful orders and multicultural social environments in European countries that are absent in their countries of origin. Additionally, they frequently suffer from social isolation and cultural alienation and lead monotonous lives. Servan recounted his past encounters in Turkey and contrasted them with his current living circumstances in France.

> Due to the repressive policy of the Turkish state, we fled our homeland for these European countries to begin new lives, but we face a variety of challenges, including being separated from our homeland, our souls, relatives, families, fathers, mothers, culture, and everything else, and becoming refugees in a foreign country where we neither know anyone nor their ways of life nor their language. We must put forth an enormous amount of effort to merely resolve our own individual issues. The system prevents us from thinking about anything besides surviving by working from sunrise to sunset.
> —Servan—France

The experiences of Kurdish-Yezidi refugees also illustrate the contradictions and repercussions of the diverse asylum, reception, and integration policies of European states, where they are culturally and socially equivalent to non-beings, resulting in perpetual suffering. While inconsistent reception, asylum, and integration policies abandon refugees and result in human tragedy, these policies not only limit but also assault refugee autonomy to prevent them from directing and determining their way of life. Their freedom of movement and organizations are the target of policy-makers determined to eradicate any chance and collective will of refugees to accomplish their integration process from below (Lentin 2012). Reber is mindful of his experience.

> When I was granted refugee status, the authorities instructed me to leave Italy and seek employment elsewhere. I set out for Germany, Sweden, and Norway, but all three nations detained me and sent me back to Italy. When I arrived in Rome as a result of my deportation, Italian police officers escorted me off the aircraft with chained hands and dumped me in a salvage yard. They do not care that we, as refugees, are perishing on the streets. We

refugees are continually insulted and disrespected by the government. Italy is not a country that respects or upholds human rights. We are all unemployed, destitute, homeless, despised, disrespected, and ill.
—Reber—Italy (2)

European policies degrade refugees to a dehumanized standard, which has catastrophic consequences for the subjects in question. Refugees are left with no choice but to struggle for their settlement and adaptation processes, which are associated with significant local, national, and transnational dimensions. It entails insurmountable obstacles and a constant struggle on the part of the refugees to overcome its traumatizing implications, as will be discussed below.

Refugees' Constraints and Agency in the Integration Process

Integration of Kurdish-Yezidi refugees is multidimensional and multilevel. It is comprised of diverse actors, policies, implementation practices, and sites involving multiple receiving and sending countries, lived experiences, and the capacity of subjects. Asylum procedures and resident permits are the central elements and linchpins of the integration and settlement processes. It provides refugees with a sense of certainty and stability that serves as the foundation for other pertinent structural requirements, such as learning the language of receiving societies, education, employment, housing, and other aspects of psychological and social well-being. Shiyar's remark concerning the integration approach is insightful:

> Every day, this government makes a new decision regarding our resident permits, causing uncertainty that has detrimental effects on our lives. It prevents us from establishing a secure life and planning for the future. As a result, we feel threatened with deportation and fail to continue our education to acquire a certificate for our qualification. I spoke with a student advisor about the resident permit and eligibility to study in Denmark. He stated that my refugee status permits me to study, but he could not guarantee that I could continue undertaking a study next year. He stated that it's conceivable that the government might alter the law and ask me to leave. However, the certainty could contribute to my stable life, with implications for my mental health and well-being, and help me develop long-term, healthy, and social relationships here.
> —Shiyar—Denmark

In addition, the integration process is contingent on the approach of the stakeholders and authorities who determine and implement integration requirements. These actors frequently lack comprehension and recognition of the lived experiences, associated effects, educational levels, and capacity of a variety of refugees to meet these requirements. As a consequence, a great number of refugees are confronted with an impasse, resulting in their disappointment, frustration, and failure. Munzir talked about his experiences throughout the integration process, which had a detrimental impact on his life:

> Since my arrival in 2014 from Rojava, it has become more difficult for me. This difficulty affects my ability to adjust to these new living conditions, speak German, and deal with bureaucratic paperwork. I receive numerous letters daily, but I am unable to understand their contents. Four years after my arrival, I am still overwhelmed with letters and demands. This is not my country, and the government does not permit me to breathe. They disregard the fact that I am a refugee who escaped to their country from a region where I endured several terrible conflicts and hardships. They lack tolerance and patience while disregarding my experience with discrimination. It is emotionally impossible for me to stand out, but I understand that I must comply with their demands because I live in their country.
> —Munzir—Austria

Nonetheless, some refugees may count on their peers in the integration and settlement processes, and they are encouraged to strive for their integration regardless of bureaucratic, psychological, social, and structural ramifications. The Kurdish-Yezidi immigrants stressed the necessity of their own individual efforts in overcoming their memories of their mistreatment and displacement as well as the present cultural and structural barriers to integration in unfamiliar social environments. Multiple generations of Kurdish-Yezidi refugees claim the relevance of intra-community and intercultural integration within their recipient societies. The long-term Kurdish-Yezidi refugees or their offspring recognize the context of their peers in their home countries and their circumstances in receiving countries. Therefore, they provide a forum via cultural production to engage with them and encourage their integration in the new social surroundings (Dag 2022). Havin, the daughter of a Kurdish-Yezidi refugee, referred to how they adapted a strategy to help her newly arrived refugees in their search for societal incorporation through the production of culture.

8 CONCLUSION   235

I was born in Sweden and have been active in Kurdish organizations for fifteen or sixteen years. I have begun to offer circle dance lessons... We organize primarily cultural activities such as dancing, language, and music events to facilitate the integration of Kurdish refugees into Swedish society and their acquisition of the Swedish language. After our activities, we all hang out together to get to know each other better in person. We interact with others and develop deep friendships... Some refugees do not know their birthdays, but we remind them and take them out for drinks. Simply put, we give them the impression that they are a part of us. We also assist them with orientation to the Swedish educational system. Therefore, we encourage them to move on by emphasizing their positive and successful experiences and plans.
—Havin—Sweden (2)

Self-integration of refugees with and for refugees through a cultural production strategy is an effective pattern, yet economic independence is vital for a successful settlement and integration process. This, however, necessitates the empowerment of refugees by the authorities, which entails the recognition of their contexts, an understanding of their lived experiences of political persecution and social discrimination, as well as their needs, self-will, and agency to navigate through their difficulties in receiving states from the past. Shemal serves as an intriguing example:

I work as a hairdresser at a salon that I co-own with a partner. I have always worked tirelessly throughout my entire life. The difficult work is a part of our everyday lives. Previously, I spent two years working in a storage facility where the temperature was consistently minus 15 degrees Celsius. I feel like a robot working here forever, from dawn to evening. I do all this work not only for myself or my homeland, but I also pay the government half of my earnings in taxes. I do not want the Austrians to get the impression that I am a refugee and only receive welfare benefits.
—Shemal—Austria

The empowerment of refugees might also result in the formation of self-established diaspora communities and structures that play a vital role in the lives of refugees. These diasporic institutions are cognizant of the struggles and experiences of refugees and have the necessary linguistic proficiency as well as awareness of cultural, political, and social norms and values. Despite the positive impact of these diaspora structures, some of these organizations may exclude and discriminate against certain refugee

236   V. DAG

segments based on political and social differences anchored in the social structures of the Kurdish-Yezidi population. Nonetheless, the organizational structures of the diaspora serve as gatekeepers and guides for traumatized and disoriented Kurdish-Yezidi asylum seekers and refugees. They assist refugees in a variety of new situations by providing information services, acclimating them to the local bureaucracy and culture, and navigating them through this process. The recently arrived asylum seekers underlined how these self-created organizational structures had served as their compass. What Lolan encountered in France is striking:

> When I first arrived in France, I had nowhere to go and was forced to sleep on the streets. I was instructed to submit an asylum application at the airport, but when I asked the police for the address, they were unable to provide it. However, I visited numerous restaurants and kebab shops with Turkish names, but when I entered, the entire staff was Kurdish. I described my circumstances to them. The Kurdish kebab shop owners recommended that I visit the Kurdish home (Kurdish associations refugees called it as their home). I went there and told my companions at the Kurdish home about my predicament. They assisted me with each of my concerns. I was able to submit my asylum application. The Kurdish home offered me material and spiritual assistance that contributed to my well-being.
> —Lolan—France

In response to the unwillingness of governments in countries with underdeveloped welfare systems and integration policies to meet the fundamental requirements of refugees, the function of these structures is of critical importance. These community structures emerge to provide refugees with fundamental material and non-material resources, such as food, housing possibilities, and a social space, as well as vital information about illicit activities to deter refugees from engaging in criminal and drug-related behaviors. Merivan pointed out how these organizational structures of the Kurdish-Yezidi diasporas assisted him and catered to his needs:

> The authorities neglected to provide us with life's necessities upon our arrival. We requested employment from the authorities, but they informed us that the Italian populace is unemployed, so they are unable to assist us in finding employment for refugees. We were forced to sleep on the streets and in parks throughout our asylum process. For sustenance, we were directed to churches and charitable organizations where we were able to eat for free. We were stuck in an extremely difficult circumstance and barely managed to

survive until we learned about the Kurdish organization. When we visited the organization, our peers offered us food and a secure place to sleep. They also dissuaded us from engaging in certain types of criminal activities.
—Merivan—Italy

The function of these organizations is not confined to their special skills to serve as distinctive, competent guiding actors in the process of overcoming the bureaucratic and structural impediments; rather, it also includes the manner in which they nurture a sense of belonging and sentiments of home among Kurdish-Yezidi refugees. Many refugees view Kurdish associations as a place where they can feel at home due to the intra-community interaction, symbols, and images within them, as well as the spoken Kurdish language. These characteristics of Kurdish-Yezidi associations generate a mental, social, and physical homeland, promote intra-community solidarity, and enhance the overall well-being of these refugees. Harun in Sweden noted favorable characteristics of these organizational structures:

I perceive the Kurdish home (diaspora association) as a space of solidarity for us Kurdish refugees, since it helps us preserve our common values and handle our issues. I have a sense of being sheltered and supported there. Kurdish refugees organize themselves there, speak their native language, and learn about their culture. The Kurdish home facilitates a social environment and encourages us to demonstrate solidarity with our people in need and promote community cohesion in European countries as a whole.
—Harun—France

However, the favorable aspects generated by organizational Kurdish-Yezidi structures among refugees might sometimes vary according to the ideological and political approaches adopted by each organization in the same or different receiving countries. Politically radical networks operating in accordance with political parties in Kurdish regions form some diaspora associations. Since they serve as the extended limbs of political compatriots and their agendas come from various regions in their home countries, their attitudes toward the political positions of Kurdish-Yezidi refugees might change. While some of these organizations support refugees who are loyal to their common ideologies and politics, they neglect other Kurdish-Yezidi refugees who fail to pledge allegiance to their political agendas. Their ideological and political allegiances are conveyed

238   V. DAG

through the donations and participation of refugees in the activities of these diaspora structures. Cewdet addressed his experience of neglect as a result of his non-political position and lack of commitment to any political networks operating as a transnational segment:

> On my arrival, I visited Kurdish associations, known as the House of the Kurds, and repeatedly requested assistance with regard to my settlement and adaptation. However, they were unable to provide me with a permanent address and sent me from one person to another without success. Yet, the leaders of these organizations urge me every month to make a donation or to travel to France to participate in their political activities, such as demonstrations. I attended these organizations because I wanted to speak and hear Kurdish to feel at home in my hometown. Nonetheless, everyone spoke Turkish and asked, Nasilsin? (How are you?)
> —Cewdet—Austria

The diaspora organizations play a crucial role in a variety of subject areas, including intra-community relationships, functioning as intermediaries between refugees and recipient societies, and transnational ties to the homeland. The inclusive or restrictive approach of authorities in each European nation could affect the dynamic policies and impact of these self-constructed diaspora structures. The oral accounts of the refugees are enlightening and unquestionably merit a greater degree of recognition. Regardless of these self-established organizational structures and successful adaptation into new environments, the Kurdish-Yezidi refugees endure an exile dilemma. Uprootedness, loss, social isolation, and persistent uncertainty are all circumstances that prevent refugees from living in a secure space that can be perceived as their home.

CONTRADICTION OF EXILE

Exile is a contractionary situation among Kurdish-Yezidi refugees characterized by forced migration, rupture with social and physical environments rooted in home countries, and discontinuity of living experiences and social order as a result of their stagnation in the past and isolation and uncertainty in the present, as well as continuous commitments to their homeland as burdens in their daily lives. Dominated by the past, Kurdish-Yezidi refugees often fail to complete their transition into the present in receiving environments and suffer as a result of a lack of longing for

8 CONCLUSION 239

belonging. Merdan depicted his predicament in terms of his hometowns, loss in social surroundings, and stagnation in the past:

> Being refugees entails challenging circumstances because we are not with our people and away from our homeland, where we can experience our culture, whereas exile involves solitude and suffering... Our bodies are in Europe, but our spirits are in Kurdistan. While there are many Kurds in Italy, we do not interact, even when we see each other. Kurdish communities in Europe no longer have social and community lives, and they neglect one another, although this does not exist in our homeland... Even if someone were to perish here, nobody would feel compassion for him.
> —Merdan—Italy

Some Kurdish-Yezidi refugees become sensitive in exile but seek to overcome their sense of incompleteness and lack of belonging through connectedness, which is based on objective elements such as language and traditions as well as subjective attributes such as cultural sentiments and values, resulting in collective undertakings that remind them of their past lives in their homeland and give rise to their momentous well-being. Mehdi presented his approach for dealing with the exilic situation:

> We usually miss our Kurdish sentiments when we are in a foreign country amid people who speak various languages and have distinct traditions. If we are going down the street and hear a Kurdish voice—the language of our nation and people—we turn our heads without considering whether the person speaking Kurdish is good or evil or what types of sentiments, they are expressing. We want to greet them and speak with them. It means a lot to us to eat something together or have a cup of tea. It regenerates us all when we remain connected.
> —Mehdi—Sweden

The exile of Kurdish-Yezidi refugees is a situation that encompasses refugees' lived experiences in their traditional homeland in the past as well as negative sentiments about it in receiving nations now. The ancestral homeland is fundamental to the daily lives of Kurdish-Yezidi refugees. It is transmitted via communication and information networks into their lives and requires the commitment of refugees. Despite tangible separation from the physical homeland, cultural, political, and spiritual elements associated with the homeland persist, albeit at a reduced pace. Similarly,

240   V. DAG

the negative influence stemming from distressing events in the homeland has also become prevalent.

Homeland Dilemma

The homeland has played an important role in the lives of refugees in exile since it continues to be the target of tragic incidents manifested as persecution, oppression, violence, and displacement that the Kurdish-Yezidi population endures. To put it another way, the homeland is the cause of the most severe concerns for Kurdish-Yezidi refugees. They were subjected to a process of forced migration in which they either left or lost members of their families. Their families have been separated, and their whereabouts are unknown. Thus, the refugees are concerned about their homeland and family members, who lead futureless lives. In addition, Kurdish refugees witness the plight of their homeland and brethren through a variety of remote communication and information means, which exacerbates their suffering and diminishes the likelihood of their reunion or return, as Memu described.

> The events in Kurdistan have had a profound effect on us in Germany. Every day, I watch Kurdish TV networks to keep up with current events. We are completely focused on Kurdistan in Syria, where we have our houses, lands, siblings, relatives, and friends. They are not safe, and their lives are always under threat. The assaults on Afrin were brutal, and we Kurdish refugees grieved many times a day. Every day, we see our people being displaced, detained, and abducted. They have been threatened with death if they do not pay the extortion money. I sometimes see elderly people's backs that have changed color as a result of being battered by Turks and Islamists. I switch off the TV to avoid it inflicting suffering on us. This is a tragedy. This circumstance and these occurrences have a significant influence on us here and divert our attention away from our responsibilities in Germany.
> —Memu—Germany (2)

While the homeland creates a dire and dramatic climate for the lives of refugees, it additionally pushes them to give voice to its concerns. Therefore, as a byproduct of their traditional homeland, many Kurdish-Yezidi refugees are actively organizing to represent their compatriots back home. The homeland acts as a two-edged sword for Kurdish-Yezidi refugee populations in Europe. While it remains an integral part of their sense of belonging and identity, it is also a factor that demands refugees' mobilization and acts as a concerning element due to familial and spatial links, as well as oppressive and violent occurrences that threaten their brethren on a daily basis. Serdar underlined how their mobilization potential depends on certain events caused by political conflicts or natural disasters in their homeland:

> In response to discriminatory and repressive events in Kurdistan, we mobilize for the sake of our homeland. We are committed to taking to the streets and demonstrating to express our rejection of oppression against our people. This is our power: to condemn the tyrannical policies of the governments that rule our homeland. If oppressive regimes did not discriminate against our relatives and people in Kurdistan, we would not need to organize protests and rallies. We could then concentrate on our lives in Germany, acquire the language skills, and conduct our usual businesses. This expectation is also our obligation in the joint struggle for our homeland. We are committed to supporting politics at home.
> —Serdar—Germany

The homeland is frequently perceived as a real place among Kurdish-Yezidi refugee and diaspora groups, although returning to it is rarely desired by newer generations. However, the homeland is perpetually ingrained in the lives of Kurdish-Yezidi refugees, a place they have not mentally abandoned and where their immediate and extended relatives live in insecure and unprotected conditions molded by oppression and violent events. These refugee stories expose their convoluted situations and hidden truths, which persist in their countries of origin and follow them to their new homes. They give accounts of their transnational connections to compatriots from their home countries and cast light on how events and affairs from their home countries have affected their lives in new environments. Most accounts of Kurdish-Yezidi refugees who were forcibly displaced highlight the fact that many aspects of their homeland (its history, culture, psychology, pain, and geography) remain indispensable to them despite the distance between them and the rest of their compatriots and the homeland. This can be evident in narratives, conversations, jokes, and dreams. Their lives abroad are inextricably entangled with the events and situations of their compatriots in their own homeland. They stressed how they feel the pain and happiness of their homeland peers on a daily basis. They also suffer from a politics of denial regarding their Kurdish identity, a suffering that is reproduced abroad when the

242   V. DAG

governments of receiving states associate them with oppressive regimes. Overall, these extensive accounts represent organic knowledge production and are situated at the intersection of living cultural, historical, political, and social processes and contexts, which appear disconnected in uncritical and unreflective studies. Thus, the refugees' self-narration, self-interpretation, and self-presentation of their narratives about their lived experiences constitute powerful voices for social justice, equality, and dignity that must be felt, embodied, and acted upon.

FINAL WORDS

This book is guided by the refugee-centric episteme of Kurdish-Yezidi refugees, with and about themselves, through oral testimonies about their lived experiences and contextual circumstances from their countries of origin and countries of settlement in a collaborative knowledge production process. The book encouraged refugees to talk about their stories in autonomous space with a researcher who shared a common refugee background, not only to break silence but also to restore their realities, community spirit, and lives, as well as to preserve their fundamental values, traditions, identities, and sense of dignity. The other goal of the book is to give marginalized and disenfranchised Kurdish-Yezidi refugees the power to speak out in the process of knowledge production, not as ill-equipped people who are at the mercy of politically and subjectively constructed scholarship from the epistemological perspectives of humanitarianism, methodological nationalism, and colonialism, but as collaborative and collective participants who can contribute to critical, emancipatory, and self-reflective scholarship. In this context, it aimed at empowering refugees with equal and collective participation in the construction of this book with immediate and intimate insights into their historical and social connections, experiences of refugeehood, collective actions, emotions, and lives abroad. By emphasizing the Kurdish-Yezidi refugees' unique role and epistemological agency, this book appears as an uninterpreted organic work for political and academic stakeholders to reflect on refugees' narratives and perspectives, which are frequently pushed to the margins of mainstream societies and academic and political environments. Thus, refugee-centric production of knowledge plays an essential role in confronting constructed scholarship that identifies Kurdish-Yezidi refugees as objects of humanitarian intervention, reliant on the aid of government agencies from the point of view of methodological nationalism. Thus, the refugees in question argue against being subjected to "coloniality of power," "coloniality of knowledge," and "coloniality of being" (Maldonado-Torres 2007). They urge political and academic actors to recognize, comprehend, and scrutinize their cultural, political, and social settings and realities, as well as their practical challenges within this framework, in their own languages and voices.

This book entertains the hope that its reflective contribution will initiate a paradigm shift in refugee and migration studies, moving beyond the instrumentalization of refugees as objects of mainstream theories and concepts. Instead, it promotes a collaborative process in which refugees, as equal and active research participants, find their representational positions in the production of knowledge via data presentation, interpretation, and analysis for reflective and critical approaches and thoughts. In concrete terms, refugees' participation in producing knowledge entails that they represent themselves in mainstream conferences, publications, and policy-making settings. Finally, the book advocates an inclusive and democratic approach to the process of knowledge production by decentralizing the power of interpretation and analysis from privileged Western-centric research bodies to sharing it with underprivileged refugees. This is the key to preventing the misrepresentation of refugee realities and their exploitation as experimental and statistical data sources, as well as promoting their role as co-producers of knowledge through their accounts of lived and ongoing experiences and adaptation to new social environments.

REFERENCES

Dag, V. 2022. The Politics of Cultural Production: Exile, Integration and Homeland in Europe's Kurdish Diaspora. *Diaspora Studies* 15: 1–26.

Lentin, R. 2012. Conclusion: Integration from Below? In *Migrant Activism and Integration from Below in Ireland*, ed. R. Lentin and E. Moreo, 182–200. Hampshire and New York: Palgrave Macmillan.

Maldonado-Torres, N. 2007. On the Coloniality of Being: Contributions to the Development of a Concept. *Cultural Studies* 21 (2–3): 240–270.

Tejel, J. 2009. *Syria's Kurds: History, Politics and Society.* Oxon and New York: Routledge.

APPENDIX A: INTERVIEW QUESTIONS

PERSONAL PROFILE

The following personal profile will need to be filled by interviewees:

1. Name: _____
2. Gender: _____
3. Age: _____
4. Birthplace: (Region) _____ (City) _____ Country: _____
5. Date of Departure: _____ and Arrival: _____
6. Status of residence permit: _____
7. Profession/Occupation: _____
8. Position in the Organization: _____
9. Education Background:
□ University
□ High School
□ Primary School
□ Illiterate □ Others: _____
10. Your contact information: _____

(A) Questions for Leaders and Representatives of Diaspora Organizations

---

© The Author(s), under exclusive license to Springer Nature Switzerland AG 2024
V. Dag, *Voices of the Disenfranchized*, Mobility & Politics, https://doi.org/10.1007/978-3-031-46809-4

246   APPENDIX A: INTERVIEW QUESTIONS

1. Would you kindly provide us with a short description of your organization? When did your organization start operating? What kind of activities does your organization engage in? Has your organization participated in any of these specific initiatives or programs pertaining to the orientation and integration of refugees and asylum seekers? If so, how would you characterize the objectives of these projects?

2. Do you hold elections to determine your organization's representation? If so, who chose these officials, and how do they represent the Kurdish population in this city?

3. How do newly arrived refugees learn about your organization, its offerings, and its activities? How often do people visit your organization for advice? What specific problems or difficulties do the refugees want you to help with?

4. How efficiently do you handle their issues? How? Are the refugees eager to participate in the events your organization organizes? If so, how do you draw them in?

5. How many people make up your organization's membership? Do Kurdish refugees have to meet any requirements to join your organization? Has the number of visitors to your organization increased since the 2015 refugee crisis?

6. Do you collaborate with the city's government officials? Do they assist you in your efforts to provide certain services? In both cases, why and how? How would you characterize the overall circumstances and connection between your organization and national and local government institutions? What opportunities or limits do you see in the government's policy regarding the organization you run? Do they have an impact on your organization's operations? How? What do you believe the key issues facing your organization are? Can you explain these difficulties? What steps may be taken to alter these partnerships' dynamics? Do there need to be any improvements to anything?

7. Do you collaborate with Kurdish diaspora organizations in your country or in other European cities? What kind of organizations are they, and what activities do you collaborate on? What does your collaboration accomplish?

8. What is the stance of your organization in relation to the politics of the country? How would you politically characterize your organization's interaction with domestic politics? Is your organization engaged in these activities in the home country or in this host city that deal with home politics? How? And what motivates your organization's participation in initiatives related to your country?

APPENDIX A: INTERVIEW QUESTIONS   247

(B) Questions for Organizations Serving Refugees in the Diaspora in Cities

1. Would you kindly identify yourself? Can you tell us how and when you were able to get here, as well as how you managed to settle? Do any of your relatives live here? Are there any other Kurdish refugees, or are there any organizations in this region that can help you settle?
2. What kind of residency permit do you have? What does your residency permit entail for you in terms of having access to the public services, job market, and educational institutions in the host state? Do you believe you must undergo structural, organizational, social, cultural, economic, and political adaptation processes (in terms of employment, education services, language abilities, union membership, and political party membership)? How?
3. Can you describe your familiarity with Kurdish associations and institutions, as well as their activities in this city? How? What does the Kurdish diaspora organization mean to you? How do you feel while visiting Kurdish organizational centers? Do you believe that the diaspora organizations represent you and provide you with the necessary assistance to reside in this city?
4. Are these organizations' meetings open to the public? How often did you take advantage of opportunities to attend their meetings, if the answer is yes? What's the purpose of these meetings?
5. What do you discuss when you attend these meetings, and what motivates you to participate?
6. Do these organizations offer you support in the form of language courses, employment and accommodation seminars, and information about your new life that enables you to address your social, economic, and cultural concerns? If so, how successful are they? Do you feel like these organizations provide you with a place where you can feel at home? Why? How then?
7. How often do you use one or more of these support services? Do they assist you in running your life around here? How? Do you believe that these activities hinder or facilitate your integration into the social, political, cultural, and institutional structures of this host society? Do you believe that these actions have affected your connections with other Kurdish refugees in this city or with people in this society?

248   APPENDIX A: INTERVIEW QUESTIONS

8. How frequently do you receive assistance from local and national authorities in your host country? Are you pleased or dissatisfied with local and national government services? Do you believe that Kurdish organizations initiate programs or services that are neglected by government institutions? And if so, which of these? How do these Kurdish organization activities assist you in orienting yourself and managing your life in this city?

9. If you inquire, do Kurdish diaspora organizations provide you with connections to Kurds from the homeland and other European countries? How does it impact you when Kurdish organizations help you communicate with Kurdish refugees outside of your communities and in your native country? Do you take part in events that involve your homeland? Why?

(C) Issues Concerning Refugees in Border Cities

1. How and when did you manage to escape here? Do any of your relatives exist here? Are there any other Kurdish refugees here? Are there any organizations in this place that can help you settle in?

2. What is your residency status? What does your residency permit entail for you in terms of having access to the public services, job market, and educational institutions in the host state?

3. Do you believe you must undergo structural, organizational, social, cultural, economic, and political adaptation processes (in terms of employment, education services, language abilities, union membership, and political party membership)? How?

4. What difficulties do you encounter when you need any form of assistance? Where and how can you receive assistance or acquire information to address legal, bureaucratic, and social challenges? Are there members of your native country assisting you? If not, how difficult is it for you to organize and manage your life, acquire the language, interact with people, and find a job or an apartment on your own? Do you believe that you need any type of assistance?

5. Do you maintain contact with other Kurdish refugees in other American or European cities? Do you prefer to reside in one of their cities or another to be closer to them? Is there any news concerning your homeland?

APPENDIX A: INTERVIEW QUESTIONS   249

(D) Group Questions for Diaspora Organizations

1. How would you characterize your interactions with one another as representatives of this organization and refugees? What do you think about how this organization helps refugees integrate into society? Do you believe that it provides you with a sense of empowerment, safety, respect, and recognition? Do these activities make you feel least satisfied?

2. How would you characterize the function of Kurdish diaspora organizations and their initiatives to assist refugees in adjusting to new environments? In your opinion, how capable and effective are diaspora organizations at addressing the needs of refugees in the integration process in terms of educational opportunities, housing, and employment opportunities, as well as language classes? How much do these diaspora groups encourage your social, cultural, political, and institutional participation in the city's life? How do you weigh the benefits and drawbacks of these organizations for your integration efforts or your home country's causes?

3. Could you share with me your view on the specific concerns that have become more or less significant for you and your organizations since the pre-refugee crisis in 2015? What do you think—could you accommodate demands from refugees, assisting them in resolving their specific problems, and otherwise improve their situation?

4. How are you and your organizations affected by the integration policy and the government's stance? Can you discuss its advantages or disadvantages?

5. Do Kurdish diaspora organizations launch political campaigns for homeland affairs? What are these activities, if any? What are your thoughts on their involvement in homeland politics?

LIST OF INTERVIEWED PARTICIPANTS

© The Author(s), under exclusive license to Springer Nature
Switzerland AG 2024
V. Dag, *Voices of the Disenfranchized*, Mobility & Politics,
https://doi.org/10.1007/978-3-031-46809-4

No.	Name	Host country	Country of origin	Reason for immigration	Date of arrival	Legal status	Nationality	Gender	Age	Occupation	Employment
1	Merdem (2)	France	Turkey	Political	2009	Refugee	Turkish	Male	49	Plumber	Employed
2	Mir	Italy	Turkey	Civil war	2017	Asylum seeker	Turkish	male	21	Painter	Unemployed
3	Mervan	France	Turkey	Political	2018	Refugee	Turkish	Male	56	Self-employed	Employed
4	Serdest (2)	Sweden	Turkey	Political	2017	Asylum seeker	Turkish	Male	33	Musician	Unemployed
5	Serger	Italy	Iraq	Civil war	2011	refugee	Iraqi	Male	44	Peshmerga	Unemployed
6	Ihsan (2)	Italy	Turkey	Political	2019	Asylum seeker	Turkish	Male	49	Activist	Unemployed
7	Serbaz	Italy	Iraq	Political	2018	Refugee	Stateless	Male	39	Teacher	Unemployed
8	Xeyal	Germany	Iraq	Civil war	2015	Asylum seeker	Iraqi	Female	43	Housewife	Unemployed
9	Erdehan	Denmark	Syria	Civil war	2016	Refugee	Syria	Male	53	Construction worker	Employed
10	Oramar	Austria	Turkey	Economic	2001	Citizen	Austrian	Male	42	Translator	Employed
11	Serhat	Italy	Turkey	Political	1999	Migrant	Turkish	Male	38	Self-employed	Unemployed
12	Kerwan	France	Turkey	Political	2006	Asylum seekers	Turkish	Male	47	Construction worker	Unemployed
13	Ardan (2)	Italy	Turkey	Political	1998	Refugee	Turkish	Male	56	Self-employed	Employed
14	Aynur	France	Turkey	Political	2015	Refugee	Turkish	Female	27	Student	Employed
15	Mavan	France	Turkey	Political	2017	Refugee	Turkish	Male	45	Self-employed	Unemployed
16	Saman (2)	Italy	Turkey	Political	2016	Asylum seeker	Turkish	Male	41	Shepherd	Unemployed
17	Afran	Germany	Syria	Civil War	2018	Refugee	Syrian	Male	44	Self-employed	Unemployed
18	Yekdan	Italy	Turkey	Political	2003	Citizen	Italian	Male	52	Self-employed	Employed
19	Sherzad	Italy	Iraq	Civil war	2009	Refugee	Iraqi	Male	28	Waiter	Unemployed
20	Mako	Italy	Turkey	Political	2013	Refugee	Turkish	Male	46	Self-employed	Unemployed

No.	Name										
21	Serwer	Germany	Syria	Civil war	2016	Refugee	Syrian	Male	35	Self-employed	Unemployed
22	Amed	Austria	Turkey	Political	2015	Asylum seeker	Turkish	Male	38	Shepherd	Unemployed
23	Cotkar	France	Turkey	Political	2019	Asylum seeker	Turkish	Male	42	Self-employed	Unemployed
24	Arshin	Italy	Turkey	Political	2012	Refugee	Turkish	Female	44	None	Unemployed
25	Bawer	France	Turkey	Political	2016	Refugee	Turkish	Male	24	Student	Employed
26	Ozcan	Sweden	Turkey	Political	2018	Asylum seeker	Turkish	Male	26	Student	Study
27	Mergewer	France	Turkey	Political	2003	Refugee	Turkish	Male	51	Construction worker	Employed
28	Serbilind	Austria	Turkey	Political	2017	Asylum seeker	Turkish	Male	29	University Student	Unemployed
29	Sinem	Germany	Turkey	Political	2018	Refugee	Syrian	Female	36	Housewife	Unemployed
30	Dengdar (2)	Germany	Syria	Civil war	2015	Refugee	Syrian	Male	58	Self-employed	Unemployed
31	Merdo	Italy	Turkey	Political	2017	Refugee	Turkish	Male	47	Self-employed	Unemployed
32	Kawa	Sweden	Iran	Political	2011	Asylum seeker	Iranian	Male	40	None	Unemployed
33	Ceger	Austria	Turkey	Political	2017	Asylum seeker	Turkish	Male	21	Student	Unemployed
34	Agir	France	Turkey	Political	2016	Asylum seeker	Turkish	Male	26	None	Unemployed
35	Ajar	Italy	Turkey	Political	1996	Refugee	Turkish	Male	54	Translator	Unemployed
46	Pesheng	France	Turkey	Civil war	2006	Refugee	Iraqi	Male	47	Carpenter	Unemployed
37	Yado	Italy	Turkey	Political	2012	Refugee	Turkish	Male	29	Construction worker	Employment
38	Rezan	Sweden	Turkey	Political	2016	Asylum seeker	Turkish	Male	41	Activist	Unemployed
39	Bekes	France	Turkey	Civil war	2003	Refugee	Turkish	Male	43	None	Unemployed

(continued)

(continued)

No.	Name	Host country	Country of origin	Reason for immigration	Date of arrival	Legal status	Nationality	Gender	Age	Occupation	Employment
40	Merxas	Austria	Turkey	Political	2014	Asylum seeker	Turkish	Male	44	Peasant	Unemployed
41	Kani	Sweden	Turkey	Political	2002	Asylum seeker	Turkish	Male	67	Journalist	Unemployed
42	Deza	France	Turkey	Political	2008	Asylum seeker	Turkish	Male	55	Construction worker	Unemployed
43	Shehriban	Sweden	Turkey	Political	2012	Asylum seeker	Turkish	Female	56	None	Unemployed
44	Argesh	Germany	Iraq	Civil war	2017	Asylum seeker	Iraqi	Male	44	None	Unemployed
45	Alan	Sweden	Turkey	Political	2016	Asylum seeker	Turkish	Male	32	Shop owner	Unemployed
46	Dana	Italy	Iraq	Civil war	2011	Refugee	Iraqi	Male	29	Waiter	Unemployed
47	Kosret	Denmark	Syria	Civil war	2016	Refugee	Syrian	Male	27	Student	Employed
48	Kendal	Sweden	Turkey	Political	1990	Citizen	Swedish	Male	69	Shop owner	Employed
49	Erdelan	Italy	Turkey	Political	2013	Refugee	Iraqi	Male	36	none	Unemployed
50	Rodan	Austria	Syria	Civil war	2016	Refugee	Syrian	Male	43	Hairdresser	Employed
51	Alwan	Germany	Syria	Civil war	2015	Refugee	Syrian	Male	22	Student	Employed
52	Kuvan	Sweden	Syria	Civil war	2016	Refugee	Syrian	Male	33	Van driver	Employed
53	Osman (2)	France	Turkey	Political	2017	Refugee	Turkish	Male	52	Construction worker	Employed
54	Dadyar	Sweden	Turkey	Political	2018	Refugee	Turkish	Male	31	Shop keeper	Unemployed
55	Jiwan	Germany	Syria	Civil war	2017	Refugee	Syrian	Male	27	Factory worker	Employed
56	Shevger	Austria	Syria	Civil war	2016	Refugee	Syrian	Male	29	Freight carrier	Employed
57	Bermal	Denmark	Syria	Civil war	2016	Refugee	Syrian	Female	27	Educator	Employed
58	Delal	Austria	Syria	Civil war	2015	Refugee	Syrian	Female	26	Housewife	Unemployed
59	Dara	Denmark	Syria	Civil war	2017	Refugee	Syrian	Male	23	Waiter	Employed

60	Mirza	Italy	Turkey	Civil war	2014	Refugee	Turkish	Male	28	Agriculture worker	Employed
61	Dewran (2)	Germany	Turkey	Political	2015	Refugee	Turkish	Male	52	Imam	Unemployed
62	Reber (2)	Italy	Turkey	Political	2012	Refugee	Turkish	Male	56	None	Unemployed
63	Evraz	Germany	Syria	Civil war	2007	Refugee	Syrian	Male	52	Construction worker	Unemployed
64	Ferman	Germany	Syria	Civil war	2014	Refugee	Syrian	Male	28	None	Unemployed
65	Gulaw	Germany	Turkey	Political	1996	Citizen	German	Female	46	Teacher	Employed
66	Birusk	Austria	Syria	Civil war	2013	Refugee	Syrian	Male	42	Musician	Employed
67	Nimet	Austria	Syria	Civil war	2017	Refugee	Syrian	Male	33	Housewife	Unemployed
68	Ferze	France	Turkey	Political	1999	Refugee	Turkish	Male	56	Self-employed	Unemployed
69	Mezdar (2)	Germany	Iraq	Political	2002	Citizen	Iraqi	Male	58	Shop keeper	Employed
70	Ruken	Austria	Turkey	Economic	1989	Citizen	Austrian	Female	55	Educator	Employed
71	Elwand	Germany	Turkey	Political	2006	Refugee	Turkish	Male	41	Construction worker	Employed
72	Yawer	Germany	Turkey	Political	2003	Citizen	German	Male	54	Self-employed	Employed
73	Ferda	Germany	Turkey	Political	2011	Refugee	Turkish	Male	38	Advisor	Employed
74	Mirhat	Sweden	Syria	Civil war	2014	Refugee	Syrian	Male	46	Factory worker	Employed
75	Sipan	Germany	Iraq	Civil war	2015	Refugee	Iraqi	Male	24	Student	-
76	Serhildan	France	Turkey	Political	2018	Asylum seeker	Turkish	Male	33	Journalist	Unemployed
77	Ako	Sweden	Syria	Civil war	2016	Refugee	Syrian	Male	43	None	Unemployed
78	Memu	Germany	Syria	Political	2015	Refugee	Syrian	Male	56	Shop keeper	Employed
79	Ibrahim	Italy	Turkey	Political	2009	Refugee	Turkish	Male	50	Agriculture worker	Employed
80	Zehra	Austria	Syria	Civil war	2013	Refugee	Syrian	Female	21	Student	-
81	Serbest	Sweden	Syria	Political	2014	Refugee	Syrian	Male	39	None	Unemployed
82	Awaz	France	Turkey	Political	2010	Refugee	Turkish	Male	45	Construction worker	Employed
83	Udan	Sweden	Turkey	Political	2006	Refugee	Turkish	Female	46	Nurse	Employed

(*continued*)

(continued)

No.	Name	Host country	Country of origin	Reason for immigration	Date of arrival	Legal status	Nationality	Gender	Age	Occupation	Employment
84	Sertan	Italy	Turkey	Political	2000	Refugee	Turkish	Male	26	Waiter	Employed
85	Filya	France	Turkey	Political	2007	Refugee	Turkish	Female	42	Restaurant owner	Employed
86	Felemez	Austria	Syria	Civil war	2015	Refugee	Syrian	Male	62	Teacher	Unemployed
87	Kardux	Germany	Syria	Political	1996	Citizen	German	Male	64	Shop keeper	Employed
88	Xezal	France	Turkey	Political	2001	Refugee	Turkish	Female	43	Housewife	Unemployed
89	Demhat	France	Turkey	Political	1988	Refugee	Turkish	Male	68	Construction worker	Retired
90	Keyo	Italy	Turkey	Political	2017	Refugee	Turkish	Male	33	None	Unemployed
91	Havin (2)	Sweden	Turkey	-	Born	Citizen	Swedish	Female	21	Student	-
92	Berxwedan	France	Turkey	Political	2016	Asylum seeker	Turkish	Male	23	Construction worker	Employed
93	Mertal	Italy	Turkey	Political	2004	Refugee	Turkish	Male	42	Waiter	Unemployed
94	Mazin	Sweden	Syria	Civil war	2015	Refugee	Syrian	Male	47	Driver	Employed
95	Armanc	Austria	Syria	Civil war	2013	Refugee	Syrian	Male	37	Educator	Employed
96	Xebat	Germany	Syria	Civil war	2015	Refugee	Syrian	Male	25	Hairdresser	Employed
97	Serpehat	France	Turkey	Political	2018	Asylum seeker	Turkish	Male	47	None	Unemployed
98	Felat	Austria	Syria	Civil war	2016	Refugee	Syrian	Male	46	Self-employed	Employed
99	Alin	Austria	Syria	Political	2009	Refugee	Syrian	Female	45	None	Unemployed
100	Hisyar	Sweden	Syria	Civil war	2016	Refugee	Syrian	Male	56	Teacher	Unemployed
101	Mendal	Austria	Syria	Civil war	2017	Refugee	Syrian	Male	49	Self-employed	Unemployed
102	Arya	France	Turkey	Political	2016	Refugee	Turkish	Female	46	Educator	Employed
103	Sedan	Italy	Turkey	Political	2009	Refugee	Turkish	Male	33	Activist	Unemployed
104	Ilhan	Italy	Turkey	Political	2003	Refugee	Turkish	Male	56	Agriculture worker	Employed
105	Koban	Austria	Syria	Civil war	2016	Refugee	Syrian	Male	25	Waiter	Employed
106	Zerdest	Italy	Turkey	Political	2017	Refugee	Turkish	Male	48	Self-employed	Unemployed
107	Xece	Austria	Syria	Civil war	2016	Refugee	Syrian	Female	66	Housewife	Unemployed

No.	Name	Country of residence	Country of origin	Reason	Year	Legal status	Nationality	Gender	Age	Occupation	Employment status
108	Herdem	Sweden	Syria	Civil war	2014	Refugee	Syrian	Male	47	Self-employed	Unemployed
109	Alaz	Germany	Syria	Civil war	2015	Refugee	Syrian	Male	25	Student	
110	Cekdar	France	Turkey	Political	2016	Refugee	Turkish	Male	33	Construction worker	Employed
111	Cengo	Germany	Syria	Civil war	2015	Refugee	Syrian	Male	27	Self-employed	Employed
112	Shoresh	France	Turkey	Political	1994	Citizen	French	Male	65	Imam	Employed
113	Gulan	Austria	Syria	Civil war	2017	Refugee	Syrian	Female	36	Housewife	Unemployed
114	Helimo	France	Turkey	Political	2010	Asylum seeker	Turkish	Male	44	None	Unemployed
115	Cihan	Italy	Turkey	Political	2013	Refugee	Turkish	Female	41	Activist	Employed
115	Merwan	Austria	Syria	Civil war	2012	Refugee	Syrian	Male	42	Musician	Employed
116	Avesta	Sweden	Turkey	Political	1992	Citizen	Swedish	Female	38	Teacher	Employed
117	Sergewaz	Denmark	Syria	Civil war	2014	Refugee	Syrian	Male	49	Restaurant owner	Employed
118	Servan	France	Turkey	Political	2016	Asylum seeker	Turkish	Male	23	Construction worker	Employed
119	Shiyar	Denmark	Syria	Civil war	2015	Refugee	Syrian	Male	27	Student	Employed
120	Munzir	Austria	Syria	Civil war	2014	Refugee	Syrian	Male	47	Athlete	Unemployed
121	Shemal	Austria	Syria	Civil war	2015	Refugee	Syrian	Male	44	Hairdresser	Employed
122	Lolan	France	Turkey	Political	2019	Asylum seeker	Turkish	Male	22	Student	Unemployed
123	Merivan	Italy	Turkey	Political	2012	Refugee	Turkish	Male	49	None	Unemployed
124	Harun	France	Turkey	Political	2017	Asylum seeker	Turkish	Male	45	Construction worker	Employed
125	Cewdet	Austria	Syria	Civil war	2015	Refugee	Syrian	Male	42	Waiter	Employed
126	Mehdi	Sweden	Turkey	Political	1986	Refugee	Turkish	Male	77	Retired Journalist	Unemployed
127	Serdar	Germany	Syria	Pollical	1998	Refugee	Syrian	Male	57	None	Unemployed
128	Serkeft	France	Turkey	Political	2009	Refugee	Turkish	Male	36	Construction worker	Employed
129	Merdan	Italy	Turkey	Civil war	2007	Refugee	Iraqi	Male	32	Waiter	Unemployed

REFERENCES

Abdelhady, D. 2008. Representing The Homeland Lebanese: Diasporic Notions of Home and Return in a Global Context. *Cultural Dynamics* 20 (1): 53–72.

Abrams, L. 2010. *Oral History Theory*. London and New York: Routledge.

Aksoy, O.E. 2013. Music and Reconciliation in Turkey. In *The Kurdish Question in Turkey: New Perspectives on Violence, Representation and Reconciliation*, ed. C. Gunes and W. Zeydanlioglu, 225–244. Oxon and New York: Routledge.

Ali, M.H. 2021. Historical and Political Dimensions of Yezidi Identity before and after the Ferman (Genocide) of August 2, 2014. In *Kurds and Yezidis in the Middle East: Shifting Identities, Borders, and the Experience of Minority Communities*, ed. G.M. Tezcür, 43–58. London and New York: I.B. Tauris Bloomsbury Publishing Plc.

Allison, A. 2001. *The Yezidi Oral Tradition in Iraqi Kurdistan*. Surrey: Curzon Press.

Ammann, B. 2000. *Kurden in Europa: Ethnizität und Diaspora*. Münster: Lit Verlag.

Angrosino, M.V. 2005. *Projects in Ethnographic Research*. Long Grove: Waveland Press, Inc.

Baser, B., M. Toivanen, B. Zorlu, and Y. Duman, eds. 2019. *Methodological Approaches in Kurdish Studies: Theoretical and Practical Insights from the Field*. Lanham, Boulder, New York and London: Lexington Books.

Bengio, O. 2012. *The Kurds of Iraq: Building a State within a State*. Boulder and London: Lynne Rienner Publishers.

Benton, A. 2016. Risky Business: Race, Nonequivalence and the Humanitarian Politics of Life. *Visual Anthropology* 29 (2): 187–203.

© The Author(s), under exclusive license to Springer Nature Switzerland AG 2024
V. Dag, *Voices of the Disenfranchized*, Mobility & Politics,
https://doi.org/10.1007/978-3-031-46809-4

260 REFERENCES

Bishop, A.R. 1995. Collaborative Research Stories: Whakawhanaungatanga. PhD Thesis, Presented to the University of Otago, Dunedin.

Bulhan, A.H. 1985. *Frantz Fanon and the Psychology of Oppression.* New York: Plenum Press.

Christou, A., and R. King. 2014. *Counter-diaspora: The Greek Second Generation Returns 'home'.* Cambridge, MA: Harvard University Press.

Çiçek, C. 2017. *The Kurds of Turkey: National, Religious and Economic Identities.* London and New York: I.B. Tauris.

Ciofalo, N. 2019. The Ecological Context and the Methods of Inquiry and Praxes. In *Indigenous Psychologies in an Era of Decolonization,* ed. N. Ciofalo, 39–80. West Hills: Springer.

Dag, V. 2017. Stateless Transnational Diaspora Activism and Homeland Politics: Motivations, Opportunities and Challenges A Comparative Case Study on the Mobilisation of Stateless Kurdish Diaspora Activists in Berlin, Stockholm and London. PhD Thesis, Submitted to the Free University of Berlin.

———. 2020. Decolonising Kurdish Refugee Studies: The Need for a Critical, Reflective and Emancipatory Approach. Refugee Research Online. Available at: https://refugeeresearchonline.org/decolonising-kurdish-refugee-studies-the-need-for-a-critical-reflective-and-emancipatory-approach/ (Accessed 8 April 2023).

———. 2022. The Politics of Cultural Production: Exile, Integration and Homeland in Europe's Kurdish Diaspora. *Diaspora Studies* 15: 1–26.

———. 2023. The Implications of Turkish Interventions in Rojava for US and EU Foreign Policies. *The Commentaries* 3 (1): 51–69.

Dag, V., C. Craven, and F.B. Adamson. 2021. Mapping the Kurdish Refugee Community and Diaspora in Europe: Case Study. *Report Deliverable* 5.2, EU H2020 Grant 822806.

Darder, A., ed. 2019. *Decolonizing Interpretive Research: A Subaltern Methodology for social Change.* London and New York: Routledge.

Edmonds, C.J. 1971. Kurdish Nationalism. *Journal of Contemporary History* 6 (1): 87–106.

Eliassi, B. 2021. *Narratives of Statelessness and Political Otherness: Kurdish and Palestinian Experiences.* Cham: Palgrave Macmillan.

Entessar, N. 1992. *The Kurdish Ethnonationalism.* Boulder and London: Lynne Rienner Pub.

Fanon, F. 1963. *The Wretched of the Earth.* New York: Grove Press.

———. 1968. *Black Skin White Masks.* London: Pluto Press.

Fisher, T., N. Zagros, and M. Mustafa. 2020. Palliative Prophecy: Yezidi Perspectives on Their Suffering under Islamic State and on Their Future. In *Refuge in a Moving World: Tracing Refugee and Migrant Journeys across Disciplines,* ed. E. Fiddian-Qasmiyeh, 249–272. London: UCL Press.

REFERENCES 261

Fleischmann, L. 2019. Making Volunteering with Refugees Governable: The Contested Role of 'Civil Society' in the German Welcome Culture. *Social Inclusion* 7 (2): 64–73.

Fontana, B. 1993. *Hegemony and Power: On the Relation between Gramsci and Machiavelli*. Minneapolis and London: University of Minnesota Press.

Fuccaro, N. 1999. *The Other Kurds: Yazidis in Colonial Iraq*. London and New York: I.B. Tauris Publishers.

Gatzhammer, S., J. Hafner, and D. Khatari, eds. 2021. *Ferman 74: Der Genozid an den jesiden 2014/15- Analysen- Interviews- Dokumentatonen*. Baden-Baden: Ergon Verlag.

Gourlay, W. 2020. *The Kurds in Erdogan's Turkey: Balancing Identity, Resistance and Citizenship*. Edinburg: Edinburg University Press Ltd.

Griffiths, J.D. 2002. *Somali and Kurdish Refugees in London: New Identities in the Diaspora*. Aldershot: Ashgate.

Gündoğan, N.Ö. 2023. Kurdish Studies Journal: The Homeless Journal of an Orphan Field. (online). Available at: https://www.jadaliyya.com/ Details/44879 (Accessed 23 August 2023).

Gunes, C. 2012. *The Kurdish National Movement in Turkey: From Protest to Resistance*. London and New York: Routledge.

———. 2019. *The Kurds in a New Middle East: The Changing Geopolitics of a Regional Conflict*. Cham: Palgrave Macmillan.

Gurses, M., D. Romano, and M.M. Gunter, eds. 2020. *The Kurds in the Middle East: Enduring Problems and New Dynamics*. Lanham, Boulder, New York and London: Lexington Books.

Halliday, Fred. 2006. Can We Write a Modernist History of Kurdish Nationalism? In *The Kurds: Nationalism and Politics*, ed. Faleh A. Jabar and Hosham Dawod, 11–20. London, San Francisco and Beirut: Saqi.

Hamelink, W. 2016. *The Sung Home Narrative, Morality, and the Kurdish Nation*. Leiden and Boston: Brill.

Haraway, D. 1988. Situated Knowledges: The Science Question in Feminism and the Privilege of Partial Perspective. *Feminist Studies* 14 (3): 575–599.

Hassanpour, A. 1992. *Nationalism and Language in Kurdistan, 1918–1985*. San Francisco: Mellen Research University Press.

———. 1994. The Kurdish Experience. *Middle East Report* 189 (24). Available at: http://www.merip.org/mer/mer189/kurdish-experience (Last accessed on 26 August 2023).

Hassanpour, A., and S. Mojab. 2005. Kurdish Diaspora. In *Encyclopaedia of Diasporas Immigrant and Refugee Cultures Around the World, Volume I Overviews and Topics*, ed. M. Ember, C.R. Ember, and I. Skoggard, 214–224. New York: Springer.

Hassouneh, N., and E. Pascucci. 2022. Nursing Trauma, Harvesting Data: Refugee Knowledge and Refugee Labor in the International Humanitarian

262 REFERENCES

Regime. In *Refugees and Knowledge Production: Europe's Past and Present*, ed. M. Kmak and H. Björklund, 199–2014. London and New York: Routledge.

Hosseini, S.B. 2020. *Trauma and the Rehabilitation of Trafficked Women The Experiences of Yazidi Survivors*. London and New York: Routledge.

Izady, M.R. 1992. *The Kurds: A Concise Handbook*. Washington, Philadelphia and London: Crane Russak.

Jackson, R. 2012. Unknown Knowns: The Subjugated Knowledge of Terrorism Studies. *Critical Studies on Terrorism* 5 (1): 11–29.

Janesick, V.J. 2020. *Oral History for the Qualitative Researcher: Choreographing the Story*. New York and London: The Guilford Press.

Jwaideh, W. 2006. *The Kurdish National Movement: Its Origins and Development*. New York: Syracuse University Press.

Kartal, C. 2002. *Kurdistan und der Grundsatz der Selbstbestimmung: Der Rechtstatus der Kurden im Osmanischen Reich und in der modernen Türkei*. Hamburg: Kovak.

Kelly, M.J. 2008. *Ghosts of Halabja: Saddam Hussein and the Kurdish Genocide: Saddam Hussein and the Kurdish Genocide*. Westport, Connecticut and London: Praeger Security International.

Khatari, D. 2021. Die Massenvernichtung der Jesiden in Sintschar, Baschiqa und Bahzani. In *2021. Ferman 74: Der Genozid an den jesiden 2014/15- Analysen-Interviews- Dokumentatonen*, ed. S. Gatzhammer, J. Hafner, and D. Khatari, 117–136. Baden-Baden: Ergon Verlag.

King, R., and K. Kuschminder, eds. 2022. *Handbook of Return Migration*. Cheltenham and Northhampton: Edward Elgar Publishing.

Knapp, M., A. Flach, and E. Ayboga. 2016. *Revolution in Rojava Democratic Autonomy and Women's Liberation in Syrian Kurdistan*. London: Pluto Press.

Knights, M., and W. van-Wilgenburg. 2021. *Accidental Allies: The U.S.–Syrian Democratic Forces Partnership Against the Islamic State*. London, New York, Oxford, New Delhi and Sydney: I.B. Tauris.

Kreyenbroek, P.G., and K. Omerkhali. 2021. Kurdish' Religious Minorities in the Modern World. In *the Cambridge History of the Kurds*, ed. H. Bozarslan, S. Gunes, and C. Yadirgi, 533–549. Cambridge, New York, Melbourne and New Delhi: Cambridge University Press.

Kreyenbroek, P.G., and Khalil J. Rashow. 2005. *God and Sheikh Adi are Perfect: Sacred Poems and Religious Narratives from the Yezidi Tradition*. Wiesbaden: Harrassowitz Verlag.

Lentin, R. 2012. Conclusion: Integration from Below? In *Migrant Activism and Integration from Below in Ireland*, ed. R. Lentin and E. Moreo, 182–200. Hampshire and New York: Palgrave Macmillan.

Magalhães, P.T., and L. Sumari. 2022. Methodological Nationalism and Migration Studies: Historical and Contemporary Perspectives. In *Refugees and Knowledge Production*, ed. M. Kmak and H. Björklund, 19–37. London and New York: Routledge.

REFERENCES 263

Mahmud, B. 2022. *Emotions and Belonging in Forced Migration: Syrian Refugees and Asylum Seekers*. Oxon and New York: Routledge.

Maldonado-Torres, N. 2007. On the Coloniality of Being: Contributions to the Development of a Concept. *Cultural Studies* 21 (2–3): 240–270.

Malone, K. 1999. Reclaiming Silenced Voices Through Practices of Education and Environmental Popular Knowledge Production. *Canadian Journal of Environmental Education* 4: 231–243.

Mayblin, L., and J. Turner. 2021. *Migration Studies and Colonialism*. Cambridge: Polity Press.

McDowall, D. 2005. *A Modern History of the Kurds*. 3rd ed. London and New York: I.B. Tauris & Co Ltd.

Medya News. 2022. Kurdish Teacher in Iran Jailed for Teaching Kurdish to Kurds. (online), Available at: https://medyanews.net/kurdish-teacher-in-iran-jailed-for-teaching-kurdish-to-kurds/ (Last accessed 10 May 2023).

Meho, L.I. 1997. *The Kurds and Kurdistan: A Selective and Annotated Bibliography, Bibliographies and Indexes in World History*. Westport, Connecticut and London: Greenwood Press.

Memmi, A. 1974. *The Coloniser and the Colonised*. London: Earthscan Publications Ltd.

Minahan, B.J. 2016. *Encyclopedia of the Stateless Nations: Ethnic and National Groups Around the World*. 2nd ed. Santa Barbara, Denver and Colorado: Greenwood Press.

Minoo, A. 2004. Space of Diasporas, Kurdish Identities, Experiences of Otherness and Politics of Belonging. *Göteborg Studies in Sociology No. 22*, PhD Thesis Presented at Department of Sociology Göteborg University, Goteborg.

Miserez, D. 2020. *Trauma and Uprooting*. Leicestershire: Matador.

Mouffe, C., ed. 1979. *Gramsci and Marxist Theory*. London, Boston and Henley: Routledge and Kegan Paul.

Muñoz, M. (Xicana Tejana). 2019. River as Lifeblood, River as Border: The Irreconcilable Discrepancies of Colonial Occupation From/With/On/ Of the Frontera. In *Indigenous and Decolonizing Studies in Education: Mapping the Long View*, ed. L.T. Smith, E. Tuck, and W.K. Yang, 62–81. New York and London: Routledge.

Mustafa, M.S. 2021. *Nationalism and Islamism in the Kurdistan Region of Iraq: The Emergence of the Kurdistan Islamic Union*. London and New York: Routledge.

Nisan, M. 2002. *Minorities in the Middle East: A History of Struggle and Self-Expression*. 2nd ed. Jefferson, North Carolina and London: McFarland & Company, Inc. Publishers.

Olivius, E. 2016. Constructing Humanitarian Selves and Refugee Others. *International Feminist Journal of Politics* 18 (2): 270–290.

Omarkhali, K., ed. 2014. *Religious Minorities in Kurdistan: Beyond the Mainstream*. Wiesbaden: Harrassowitz Verlag.

264   REFERENCES

———. 2017. *The Yezidi Religious Textual Tradition: From Oral to Written: Categories, Transmission, Scripturalisation and Canonisation of the Yezidi Oral Religious Texts*, 1–19. Wiesbaden; London and New York: I.B. Tauris Bloomsbury Publishing Plc.; Harrassowitz Verlag.

Phillips, D.L. 2019. *The Great Betrayal: How America Abandoned the Kurds and Lost the Middle East*. London and New York: I.B. Tauris.

Jadaliyya Reports. 2021. Open Letter to the Public: About the Article 'Beyond Feminism? Jineolojî and the Kurdish Women's Freedom Movement. In *Jineolojî*. Available at: https://www.jadaliyya.com/Details/42819 (Accessed on 24 July 2021).

Ritchie, D.A. 2015. *Doing Oral History*. Oxford and New York: Oxford University Press.

Romano, D. 2006. *The Kurdish Nationalist Movement: Opportunity, Mobilization and Identity*. Cambridge, New York, Melbourne, Madrid, Cape Town, Singapore and Sao Paulo: Cambridge University Press.

Romano, D., and M. Gurses, eds. 2014. *Conflict, Democratization and the Kurds in the Middle East: Turkey, Iran, Iraq and Syria*. New York: Palgrave Macmillan.

Said, W.E. 2003. *Orientalism*. London: Penguin Books.

Scalbert-Yücel, C., and M.L. Ray. 2006. Knowledge, Ideology and Power. Deconstructing Kurdish Studies. *European Journal of Turkish Studies* 5 (5). https://journals.openedition.org/ejts/777 (Accessed 5 February 2022).

Skubsch, S. 2000. Kurdische Migrantinnen und Migranten im Einwanderungsland Deutschland: Wie werden sie von der Pädagogik und Bildungspolitik wahrgenommen? PhD Thesis Presented at the Universität—Gesamthochschule-Essen.

Smith, L.T. 1999. *Decolonizing Methodologies: Research and Indigenous Peoples*. London, New York and Dunedin: Zed Books Ltd. and University of Otago Press.

Smith, L.T., E. Tuck, and K.W. Yang, eds. 2019. *Indigenous and Decolonizing Studies in Education: Mapping the Long View*. New York and London: Routledge.

Spolsky, B. 2016. *The Languages of Diaspora and Return*. Leiden and Boston: Brill.

Tamadonfar, M., and R. Lewis. 2023. *Kurds and their Struggle for Autonomy: Enduring Identity and Clientelism*. London: Lexington Books.

Tas, L. 2023. *Authoritarianism and Kurdish Alternative Politics: Governmentality, Gender and Justice*. Edinburg: Edinburg University Press.

Taylor, S.J., and R. Bogdan in Berg L. Bruce. 2001. *Qualitative Research Methods for the Social Sciences*, 4th ed. Needham Heights: Allyn & Bacon.

Tejel, J. 2009. *Syria's Kurds: History, Politics and Society*. Oxon and New York: Routledge.

Tezcür, G.M. 2021. Introduction: Toward a Cross-Fertilization between Kurdish and Yezidi Studies. In *Kurds and Yezidis in the Middle East: Shifting Identities*,

REFERENCES 265

Borders, and the Experience of Minority Communities, ed. G.M. Tezcür, 1–19. London and New York: I.B. Tauris Bloomsbury Publishing Plc.

Tezcür, G.M., Z.N. Kaya, and B.M. Sevdeen. 2021. *Survival, Coexistence, and Autonomy: Yezidi Political Identity after Genocide.* In *Kurds and Yezidis in the Middle East: Shifting Identities, Borders, and the Experience of Minority Communities*, ed. G.M. Tezcür, 77–99. London and New York: I.B. Tauris Bloomsbury Publishing Plc.

Timar, F. 1998. Die Wahrnehmung der Kurdischen MigrantInnen in Deutschland— durch die Brille der Türkischen Politik?. *Kurdische Migranten in Deutschland: Problemfelder Hintergründe Perspektiven und die Rolle der Nichtregierungsorganisationen*, ed. Navend—Kurdisches Informations and Dokumentationszentrum e. V., 33–46. Bonn: As-Druck.

Tölölyan, K. 2010. Beyond the Homeland: From Exilic Nationalism to Diasporic Transnationalism. In *The Call of the Homeland: Diaspora Nationalisms, Past and Present*, ed. A. Gal, A.S. Leoussi, and A.D. Smith, 27–46. Leiden and Boston: Brill.

Tsuda, T. 2009. *Diasporic Homecomings: Ethnic Return Migration in Comparative Perspective.* Stanford: Stanford University Press.

Tucker, M. 2006. *Hell Is Over: Voices of the Kurds After Saddam.* Guilford and Conn: Lyons Press.

Unluer, S. 2012. Being an Insider Researcher While Conducting Case Study Research. *The Qualitative Report* 17 (58): 1–14.

Vali, A. 2003. Genealogies of the Kurds: Constructions of Nation and National Identity in Kurdish Historical Writing. In *Essays on the Origins of Kurdish Nationalism*. Costa Mesa: Mazda Publishers, Inc.

Voller, Y. 2014. *The Kurdish Liberation Movement in Iraq.* London and New York: Routledge.

Wahlbeck, Ö. 1999. *Kurdish Diaspora: A Comparative Study of Kurdish Refugee Communities.* Hampshire and London: Macmillan Press Ltd.

Wane, N.N. 2014. *Indigenous African Knowledge Production.* Toronto: University of Toronto Press.

Wane, N.N., M.S. Todorova, and K.L. Todd, eds. 2019. *Decolonizing the Spirit in Education and Beyond: Resistance and Solidarity.* Cham: Palgrave Macmillan.

Wimmer, A. 2002. From Subject to Object of History: The Kurdish Movement in Northern Iraq since 1991. *Kurdische Studie* 2 (1): 115–130.

Wimmer, A., and N.G. Schiller. 2002. Methodological Nationalism and Beyond: Nation State Building, Migration and the Social Sciences. *Global Networks* 2 (4): 301–334.

Yeğen, M. 2006. Turkish Nationalism and the Kurdish Question. *Ethnic and Racial Studies* 30 (1): 119–151.

Zinn-Baca, M. 2001. Insider Field Research in Minority Communities. In *Contemporary Field Research: Perspectives and Formulations*, ed. R.M. Emerson, 159–166. Long Grove, IL: Waveland Press.

INDEX[1]

A
Adamson, Fiona, xiv
Afghani human smuggler, 54
Afghanistan, 62, 96, 117, 131, 133
Afran, 252
African countries, 62
Agir, 105, 253
Ajar, 107, 253
Ako, 255
Alaz, 217, 257
Albania, 72, 73
  Albanian, 72
Alin, 196, 256
Alwan, 134, 254
Amed, 83, 91, 253
Amînî, Jîna, 45
Anatolia, 205
Anthropology, 34
  anthropological, 3, 227
Arab, xx, 7, 11–13, 18, 19, 22, 44–47,
    54, 62, 112, 230
  Arabic, 13, 20, 61, 107, 136, 142,
    149, 163, 172, 200, 231

Arabs, 11–13, 47, 53, 54, 58, 62,
    79, 87, 150, 156, 162, 210,
    214, 231
  Arab settlers, 11
  pan-Arabists, 11
Ardan, 252
Armanc, 191, 256
Armenia
  Armenians, 7, 8, 10, 12, 14
Arshin, 253
Arya, 208, 256
Australia, vii
Austria, xiii, 5, 28, 34, 59–61,
    82, 83, 93, 94, 96, 103,
    113, 115–117, 126, 134,
    141–144, 152, 153, 157,
    174, 181, 191, 192, 194,
    196, 201, 211–213, 220,
    221, 223, 227, 234, 235,
    238, 252–257
  Salzburg, 28
  Vienna, 14, 28, 143, 157, 158,
    181, 194

---

[1] Note: Page numbers followed by 'n' refer to notes.

© The Author(s), under exclusive license to Springer Nature
Switzerland AG 2024
V. Dag, *Voices of the Disenfranchized*, Mobility & Politics,
https://doi.org/10.1007/978-3-031-46809-4

267

268 INDEX

Avesta, 224, 257
Awaz, 175, 255
Aynur, 64, 252
Azeris, 156

B

Bangladeshis, 54
Barzani, Mustafa, 14
Battle of Jalawla, 11
Bedir Khan Beg, 12
Bekes, 253
Belgium, 178
Berlusconi, Silvio, 132
Bermal, 142, 254
Berxwedan, 256
Birusk, 152, 255
Boochani, Behrouz, vii–viii
Bosnia and Herzegovina, 73, 74
Botan, 88, 90, 194, 209

C

Ceger, 103, 253
Cekdar, 218, 257
Celebi, Evlîya, 12
Cengo, 219, 257
Cewdet, 238, 257
Christian, 8, 169
Christianity
  Christians, 11
Cihan, 223, 257
Colonialism, viii, 16, 22, 120, 242
  colonial, viii, 2, 4, 16, 17,
      19–23, 25, 37, 44, 60,
      64, 189, 228
  colonization, vii, viii, 24, 26, 48,
      50, 64, 221
Cotkar, 84, 253
Craven, Catherine, xiv
Croatia, 73, 82
Croatian, 8

D

Dadyar, 138, 254
DAES, 59, 231
Dana, 128, 254
Dara, 144, 254
Delal, 143, 254
Demhat, 256
Dengdar, 253
Denmark, xiii, 5, 28, 34, 58, 59, 89,
      126, 129, 130, 142, 144, 227,
      231, 233, 252, 254, 257
  Bornholm, 28, 126
  Copenhagen, 190
  Danish, 129, 130, 144
Dersim, 11, 44
Dewran, 146, 221, 255
Deza, 254
DFG (Deutsche
      Forschungsgemeinschaft), xiv
DITIB, 146
Dublin Treaty, 81, 111, 132

E

Egypt, 96
Elwand, 158, 255
English, 28, 32, 62, 69, 73, 76, 111
Erdehan, 252
Erdelan, 131, 254
Europe, vii, 1, 10, 12–14, 16, 23, 26,
      33, 34, 49, 54, 57, 59, 61, 65,
      70, 71, 75, 76, 80, 82, 84–86,
      89, 93, 96, 99, 107, 110,
      113–115, 121, 128, 130, 132,
      133, 140, 147, 161, 162, 165,
      167, 169, 174, 183, 191, 196,
      199, 202, 206, 209, 211, 212,
      216, 223, 225, 228, 230–233,
      239, 240
European cultures, 22
European nations, 5, 13–15, 47, 88,
      89, 93, 94, 112, 130, 206

INDEX   269

European Parliament, the Foreign
Ministry, 222
European states, 5, 13, 14, 43, 45,
85, 86, 94, 129, 156, 162,
165, 196, 232
European Union (EU), 111
Euros, 54
Indo-European languages, 6
North, xix, 1, 26
South, 1, 54, 75, 76, 78, 93, 94,
102, 133, 180, 183, 201, 215
West, viii, 1, 26, 45, 71, 85,
94, 114
Western academics, 11
Evraz, 148, 255

F
Facebook, 87
Fascism, 132
Felat, 194, 256
Felemez, 256
Ferda, 162, 255
Ferman, 149, 231, 255
Ferze, 154, 255
Filya, 179, 256
Finland, 129, 189
France, xi, xiii, 5, 8, 15, 28, 34, 36,
47, 63–66, 71, 76, 84, 86, 88,
90, 91, 93, 94, 105–108, 113,
119, 120, 125, 137, 138, 154,
162, 169, 175, 177, 179, 183,
184, 187, 188, 193, 194, 206,
208, 214, 218–220, 222, 227,
232, 236–238, 252–257
AME (state medical aid), 120
Antipas, 28
Cannes, 28
French, xix, 7, 8, 44, 52, 65, 90,
108, 113, 114, 120, 137, 155,
156, 170, 184, 194, 257
Nice, 28

OFPRA (Protection of Refugees and
Stateless Persons), 52
Paris, 28, 88, 119, 179, 182,
183, 209

G
Georgia, 10, 12, 14
Germany, xi–xiii, 5, 10, 12, 14, 28,
32, 34, 58, 76, 77, 79, 81, 82,
86, 88–90, 93, 94, 97, 98, 118,
121, 126, 129, 132, 134, 135,
139–141, 144, 146, 148–150,
156–158, 160, 162, 163, 168,
169, 173, 182, 183, 186, 187,
192, 199, 206, 211, 216, 217,
219, 221, 227, 231, 232, 240,
241, 252–257
Berlin, xiv, 14, 28, 82, 121, 140,
141, 146, 149–151, 157, 159,
161, 163, 168, 182, 186, 192,
193, 199, 218
German, xix, 28, 32, 58, 79, 81, 89,
99, 117, 118, 121, 122, 132,
134, 135, 141, 142, 146–149,
151–153, 156, 158–163, 193,
195, 200, 207, 211, 214, 216,
234, 255, 256
Landshut, 28, 171
Munich, 28
Ghandism, 161
Gnosticism, 11
Google, 117
Gramsci, 4
Great Britain
British, 7, 8, 44, 170
United Kingdom, 14, 32, 90, 93, 162
Greece
Flako Refugee Camp, 87
Greek police, 86, 87
Greeks, 8, 26, 72, 76, 77, 79, 82,
86–89, 93, 94, 97, 98, 111

270 INDEX

Guavaraism, 161
Gulan, 220, 257
Gulaw, 150, 255
Gutis, 6

H
Haraway, Donna, 24
Harun, 237, 257
Havin, 234, 235, 256
Helimo, 222, 257
Herdem, 216, 257
Hisyar, 197, 256
Humanitarianism, 16, 17, 23, 33, 242
  humanitarian, 2, 16–18, 25, 37, 90,
    101, 166, 180, 228, 242
Hussein, Qusay, 54
Hussein, Saddam, 46, 54
Hussein, Uday, 54

I
Ibrahim, 21, 172, 255
Ihsan, 75, 252
Ilhan, 210, 256
Independent Social Research
  Foundation (ISRF), xiv
International Red Cross, 88
Iran, xix, 6, 8, 10, 11, 13, 14, 26, 28,
    34, 35, 44, 45, 54, 70, 71, 76,
    96, 97, 101, 206, 207, 227,
    230, 253
  Baluchistan, 45
  Gilan, 45
  Hashd al-Sha'bi Iranian militias, 47
  Iranian, 6–8, 10, 14, 18, 19, 22, 44,
    45, 47, 70, 76, 101, 102,
    200, 253
  Isfahan, 45
  Jin Jîyan, Azadî (Woman, Life, and
    Freedom), 10
  Mashhad, 45

monarchy, 14
morality police, 45
Mullah regime, 14, 45
Pahlavi regime, 7
Persian, 6–8, 12, 20, 44
Qazwin, 45
Sefavid Empire, 7
Tehran, 45
West Azerbaijan, 45
Iraq, xix, 1, 2, 6–8, 10, 13, 14, 26, 28,
    34, 35, 43, 44, 46, 47, 52, 54,
    57, 59, 70, 71, 76, 78, 94, 118,
    121, 126, 128, 131, 180, 206,
    207, 210, 227, 230, 231, 252,
    254, 255
  Anfal, 14, 44, 46
  Anfal campaign, 14
  Ba'ath regime, 11, 44, 46
  Baghdad, 57, 58
  Duhok, 187
  Iraqi regime, 6, 10
  Kerkuk, 7
  Kirkuk, 59
  Mosul, 7
  PMF (Popular Mobilization
    Units), 54
  Saddam regime, 14, 54
IS, xix, 2, 10, 15, 46, 47, 52, 57, 131,
    170, 207, 212, 222, 231
Islam, 11, 146
  Muslim, 8, 10–12, 47, 169
  non-Muslims, 7
  Sheikh Adi, 11
Italy, x, xiii, 5, 8, 26, 28, 34, 36, 49,
    53, 54, 61, 62, 72, 74–81, 85,
    90, 93, 94, 99, 100, 104, 105,
    107–109, 113, 125, 128,
    131–133, 145, 147, 172, 178,
    179, 185, 188, 209–213, 223,
    227, 232, 233, 237,
    239, 252–257
  Bari, 28

INDEX 271

Grosseto, 28, 133
Napoli, 109, 132
Questura, 62
Rome, 28, 75, 81, 101, 108, 112,
133, 189, 210, 232
Ufficio Immigrazione, 62
Ventimiglia, 28

J
Japan, 8
Jerusalem, xiv, 219
Jiwan, 139, 254
Johannesburg, 76

K
Kani, 117, 254
Kardux, 182, 256
Kawa, 101, 253
Kemal, Mustafa, 205
Kendal, 130, 254
Kerwan, 63, 252
Keyo, 185, 256
Kosret, 129, 254
Kurdî, Alan, xiv
Kurds, vii, 5–11, 13, 14, 22, 36,
43–47, 49, 51–54, 59, 61–65, 72,
76, 79, 80, 86, 87, 91, 101, 102,
104–106, 112, 129, 136–138,
147–151, 154, 156–159, 161,
162, 168–171, 174, 177–184,
186, 187, 189, 190, 194–199,
205, 209, 214, 215, 217,
219–222, 225, 238, 239, 248
Alevi, 6, 14, 34, 44
Barzani, 46, 54, 168
Bawer, 60, 86, 253
Dimili/Zaza, 6
Hewrami/Goran, 6
Jewish, 6, 169
Journal of Kurdish Studies, 21

Komalah, 45
KRI (Kurdistan Region of Iraq), 47
Kurdish, vii, viii, x–xiv, xix, 1–37,
1n1, 43–54, 58–65, 69–71,
75–79, 81, 84–91, 93–95, 97,
99–107, 109, 112–114,
120–122, 125–127, 129, 131,
133, 137–140, 143–163,
165–203, 205–207, 209–211,
213, 214, 216, 217, 220–225,
227–242, 246–249
Kurdish studies, viii, 20
Kurdish Women's Freedom
Movement, 21
Kurdish-Yezidi people, 2, 6, 44,
126, 165, 166
Kurdish-Yezidi refugees, x–xiii, 1–5,
1n1, 12, 13, 15–23, 26–30,
32–37, 43, 47, 70, 71, 93,
125–127, 165–167, 205–207,
227–234, 237–242
Kurdistan, vii, viii, xix, xx, 6–9, 11,
20, 31, 35, 45–49, 52–54,
57–59, 61, 63, 64, 70, 75, 76,
78, 81, 85, 88, 90, 91,
101–105, 113, 115–120, 122,
133, 136, 144, 150–155,
157–162, 166, 168–171,
177–183, 186, 187, 190, 191,
193, 196, 197, 199–202, 206,
207, 209–213, 215–222, 224,
225, 230, 231, 239–241
Kurdistan's Islamic Society, 220
Kurmancî, 6, 10, 28, 151
Mem û Zîn, 7
Newroz, 53, 144, 148, 150, 154,
192, 217
Palewani, 6
PDK, xix, 11, 14, 44, 45, 47,
55–57
PDK-Iran, xix, 14
PJAK, xx, 45

272 INDEX

Kurds (*cont.*)
  PKK, xx, 2, 11, 15, 43, 44, 47, 50,
    54, 87, 122, 123, 150, 155,
    157, 158, 160–163, 198, 210
  PUK, xx, 11
  Rojava, 75, 88, 102, 134, 149, 151,
    157, 177, 181, 187, 191, 197,
    201, 202, 215, 217, 220, 224,
    225, 234
  Sorani, 6, 28, 34, 151
  Talabani, 46, 54
  Welat, xx, 60, 69
  Xanî, Ehmedî, 7
Kuvan, 136, 254

L
Lausanne, 8, 170
League of Nations, 7
Lebanon, 76
  Beirut, 230
Libya, 96
Lolan, 236, 257

M
MAGYC (Migration Governance and
  Asylum Crises), xiv
Mako, 80, 252
Manichaeism, 11
Mavan, 66, 252
Mazin, 190, 256
McDowall, David, 7
Mecca, 61, 219
Medes, 6
Medina, 219
Medrese, 61
Memu, 240, 255
Merdan, 239, 257
Merdem, 47, 71, 252
Merdo, 99, 253
Mergewer, 90, 253
Merivan, 236, 237, 257

Mertal, 256
Mervan, 252
Merwan, 223, 257
Merxas, 115, 254
Mesopotamia, 6, 11
Methodological nationalism, 242
Mezdar, 156, 199, 255
Middle East, 5–7, 9, 10, 20, 22, 43,
    75, 162, 165, 170, 222, 230, 231
  Middle Eastern, xix, 16, 17, 22,
    23, 34, 165
Mir, 12, 49, 252
Mirhat, 167, 255
Mir Muhammad of Rawanduz, 12
Mohammadi, Zahra, 45
Montenegro, 72, 73
Muhammed, 219
Munzir, 234, 257

N
Nationalism, 7, 9, 16, 18, 23, 242
NATO, xix, 157, 162, 207
Neoliberal, 2, 17
Netherlands, 88, 89, 93
New Zealand, vii
Nigeria, 109
Nimet, 153, 255
Norway, 79, 82, 93, 94, 129, 232

O
Öcalan, Abdullah, 50
Oral history, 25, 26, 28
Oramar, 59, 252
Osman, 137, 214, 254
Ozcan, 88, 253

P
Palgrave Macmillan, xiv
Pan-Arab regime, 45, 230
Patriotism, 180, 184, 196

Penaber, 69, 70, 208
Pesheng, 107, 253

Q
Qadi Muhamed uprising, 44
Qibla, 219

R
Racism, 3, 23, 28, 29, 32, 133
   racist, 109, 168, 185, 228
Reber, 147, 232, 233, 255
Refugee, viii, ix, xiii, 1n1, 2, 4, 13–18,
   20, 23–25, 27, 28, 30–32, 34,
   36, 37, 47, 48, 52, 58, 59, 62,
   65, 70, 73–75, 77, 81–88, 90,
   91, 93–98, 100, 104, 108–111,
   114, 117, 119, 120, 125–128,
   130–134, 138, 141, 146,
   149–153, 155, 162, 165, 166,
   168–170, 172, 181–183, 187,
   188, 190, 194, 198, 207–211,
   214, 222, 223, 225, 227, 228,
   231–235, 240–243, 246,
   249, 252
Rezan, 110, 253
Rodan, 134, 254
Roman Mithraist religion, 11
Romania, 8
Rote Hilfe, 160
Ruken, 157, 255
Russians, 8

S
Said, Edward, 22
Said Riza uprising, 44
Salvini, 109, 132, 133
Saman, 72, 104, 252
Self-governance, 44, 46, 165,
   166, 179
Serbest, 175, 255

Serbian, 8
Serbilind, 253
Serdan, 209
Serdar, 241, 257
Serdest, 52, 252
Serger, 53, 252
Sergewaz, 230, 231, 257
Serhat, 61, 90, 252
Serhildan, 169, 255
Serkeft, 229, 230, 257
Serpehat, 193, 256
Servan, 232, 257
Serwer, 82, 253
Shabaks, 11
Sheikh Said rebellion, 44
Shemal, 235, 257
Sherzat, 78
Shevger, 141, 254
Shoresh, 219, 257
Simko Shikaki rebellion, 44
Sinem, 97, 253
Sipan, 168, 255
Sirkeci, Ibrahim, 21
Slovenia, 73
Slovenian, 8
Snowball sampling, 28
SOAS, xiv
Social constructivism, 15
Spain, 76
State-centric, 2, 4, 16, 18, 22, 23, 25,
   37, 228, 229
Sweden, xii, xiii, 5, 15, 28, 34, 53, 88,
   89, 93, 94, 101, 102, 108, 110,
   111, 117, 118, 120, 122, 123,
   126, 129–131, 136, 138, 139,
   167, 170, 171, 175, 177, 178,
   186, 187, 190, 197, 206, 207,
   216, 224, 225, 227, 232, 235,
   237, 239, 252–257
   Lund, 28, 170, 171
   Malmo, 28, 190
   Stockholm, 28, 120, 138, 197,
      224, 225

274 INDEX

Sweden (*cont.*)
Swedish, 79, 90, 101, 102, 108,
111, 112, 117, 118, 122, 123,
130, 131, 136, 138, 139, 167,
168, 175, 178, 186, 207, 217,
225, 235, 254, 256, 257
Swedish krona, 102, 139
Switzerland, 8, 76, 87, 88, 90, 188
Swiss francs, 188
Syria, xix, 1, 2, 6–8, 10, 13, 15, 26,
28, 34, 35, 43–45, 47, 58, 59,
70, 71, 76, 98, 99, 126, 128,
131, 134, 141, 149, 153, 186,
205–207, 215, 216, 224, 227,
230, 240, 252–257
Afrin, 58, 59, 177, 181, 187, 201,
202, 219, 224, 230, 240
Al-Darbasiyah, 181
Aleppo, 58
Amude, 44, 181
Bashar al-Assad, 46
Free Syrian Army, 58
Kobanî, 82, 158, 177, 181, 187,
202, 211, 212, 224, 230
Qamishli, 76, 181, 219, 230
Serê Kaniyê (Ras-Al-Ayn), 230
Syrian regimes, 6, 44
Taqa, near Raqqa, 58

T
Tamils, 6, 92
Tigran, Aram, 69
Treaty of Lausanne, 8
Treaty of Sévr, 7, 8
Turkey, 1, 2, 6, 8, 10, 13, 14, 19, 26,
28, 34, 35, 44–46, 49, 51–54,
59, 60, 62–65, 70–72, 74–77, 80,
82–84, 86, 88, 94, 97, 99, 100,
103–105, 107, 109, 113,
115–117, 119, 120, 122, 123,
130, 131, 133, 136, 139, 156,

157, 168, 178, 179, 184, 194,
202, 205, 207–209, 212, 218,
227, 228, 230, 232, 252–257
AKP (Justice and Development
Party), 45
Antalya, 50
Bingol, 185
DBP (Democratic Regions Party), 51
Erdogan regime, 53
Gaziantep, 50
HDP (Peoples' Democratic
Party), 45
Istanbul, 14, 47–50, 52, 53, 61,
82, 86, 208
Izmir, 49, 82
Kemalist, 14
Mardin, 50–53, 170
MHP (Nationalist Movement
Party), 45
Ottoman Empire, 7, 12, 14, 87
Ottoman Millet System, 43
Return to Village and Rehabilitation
Project, 50
Rize, 50
TOKI (Mass Housing Development
Administration), 51
Turkish, 2, 6–9, 12–15, 17–22, 28,
32, 43–45, 47–54, 59–62, 70,
71, 74, 75, 82, 83, 95, 96, 98,
100, 103, 104, 112–114, 116,
117, 119, 120, 122, 123, 130,
133, 136, 142, 146, 148,
156–160, 162, 163, 168, 170,
184, 185, 187–189, 192,
194–197, 201, 202, 205,
209–212, 219, 220, 222, 223,
230, 232, 236, 238, 252–257
Turkish armed forces, 2
Turkish Black Sea Region, 50
Turkish embassy, 116
Turkish Law Code, 49
Turkish military, 2, 15, 51

INDEX 275

Turkish state, 2, 9, 19, 20, 43, 45, 49–52, 54, 60, 103, 104, 122, 123, 158, 159, 162, 170, 189, 205, 210, 219, 220, 222, 223, 232
Turkish War of Independence, 8
Turks, 7, 8, 12, 13, 49, 53, 54, 58, 59, 61, 63, 64, 72, 79, 91, 103, 162, 168, 184, 185, 189, 209, 210, 215, 218, 240
Urfa, 185
Young Turks, 7
Turkmens, 156

U
Udan, 177, 255
Umayyad caliph, 11
Umayyad Caliph Merwan, 11
UN, xx
UNCHR, 171
United States (US), 16, 46, 170
American, 14, 207, 248

V
Vali, Abbas, 9

W
Western-centric, 4, 16, 229, 243
Western colonial powers, 22
Western Union, 74
Wilson, Woodrow, 7
Wilson's Fourteen Points, 7
The World War I, 9, 162

X
Xebat, 192, 256
Xece, 213, 256
Xeyal, 57, 231, 252
Xezal, 182, 256

Y
Yado, 108, 253
Yarsans, 11
Yawer, 160, 255
Yekdan, 77, 252
Yezid Ibn Mu'awiyya, 11
Yezidis, x, 1n1, 2, 5, 10, 15, 45, 47, 57, 169, 222, 231
Ezdîtiyatî, 11
Mirids, 11
Pirs, 11
Serfedîn, 11
Sheikh Adi, 11
Sheikhs, 11
Shengal, 47, 57, 58, 169, 202, 231
Yezidi, vii, viii, x–xiii, 1–37, 1n1, 43–47, 70, 71, 93–95, 125–127, 163, 165–169, 205–207, 227–234, 236–242
Yezidism, 11

Z
Zagreb, 73
Zehra, 174, 255
Zerdest, 212, 256
Zoroastrianism, 11
Zuhab Treaty (Treaty of Qasr-e Shirin), 6

Printed in the United States
by Baker & Taylor Publisher Services